First published 1969
by Routledge & Kegan Paul Limited
Broadway House, 68–74, Carter Lane
London, E.C.4
Printed in Great Britain
by C. Tinling & Co. Ltd
Liverpool, London and Prescot

SBN 7100 6623 6

Moral judgement from childhood to adolescence

Norman J. Bull MA PhD
St Luke's College Exeter

Routledge & Kegan Paul
London

Moral judgement

Contents

Preface

This book is an account of a research project, the aim of which was to seek empirical evidence of the development of moral judgement in the child and adolescent: and thereby to seek a pattern for moral education in schools.

The original suggestion to undertake such a project came from Dr. R. J. Goldman, formerly of Reading University, who also acted as supervisor; and the consideration of Reading University made it possible.

It was a particular pleasure to have the keen and generous co-operation, throughout this research, of two of my former students, R. J. Ferris and A. R. Gregg.

I am also indebted to my colleague, J. G. Priestley, of St. Luke's College, and P. Biven of the Exeter College of Art. Mr. P. Atherton, of Exeter College of Art, gave generous help in the planning of visual tests, and Mr. S. Thompson designed them. Mr. J. R. Ruck, Librarian of the Institute of Education of the University of Exeter, was indefatigable in securing research papers and books, and Mrs. W. Molland, Librarian of St. Luke's College, gave similar generous help.

For assistance with statistics I am indebted to Mr. D. J. Holding and Mr. D. A. Hobbs, both formerly of Exeter School, Mr. M. G. Farringdon, formerly of St. Luke's College, and Mr. C. A. Robertson of the Department of Mathematics of Exeter University. Mr. W. R. G. Wood gave invaluable secretarial help throughout. Miss P. Boines, Mrs. A. Frazer, Miss S. Rockey and Miss M. White made patient and frequent revision of testing materials. Mr. D. J. Rutter designed charts and histograms.

This research would have been impossible without the generous co-operation of the County Education Officers, head teachers, staffs and, above all, pupils of the schools involved in it.

Finally, I am indebted to Dr. Lewis Couper for help and encouragement throughout this project; and to my wife for laborious secretarial help throughout the three years of research.

St. Luke's College of Education
Exeter

NORMAN J. BULL

Illustrative material

Visual tests

Chapter 1
The study of moral judgement

The contemporary scene

We are witnessing today a dramatic growth of interest in the processes of giving moral education in our schools. It is seen in official reports on education, in the setting up of research groups, and, not least, in local experiments within schools to meet the moral needs of young people in a changing and morally permissive society. Such concern is indicative in itself that traditional assumptions as to the roots of morality are no longer tenable, that the traditional modes of moral education are no longer reliable, and that therefore new approaches must be sought to foster the moral development of the young through moral education.

Complaints as to the moral decadence of the young are, of course, as old as history. From Egypt, and from 1,000 B.C., for example, comes the lament: 'Young people are not what they were: they no longer obey their parents.' The Westminster Assembly of Puritan divines, meeting in 1649, was at least more constructive in ascribing the production of 'badde children and badde servants' to the influence of 'badde parents and badde masters'. Such complaints could be quoted from most centuries, and the adult predilection for lamenting the morals of the young is today as common as ever.

The fact remains, however, that the young must mirror adult society, and not least in the moral sphere. We shall find ample evidence that moral development is shaped and patterned by society – that the adult influences bearing upon the child are the determinants of his moral outlook. If, therefore, the young seem morally confused, and lacking in assured standards, they must in a real sense reflect their 'elders and betters'.

Our contemporary society, a Welfare State, is founded upon laudable principles of social justice and of equity, deriving from high-minded men and women inspired by religious idealism and social concern. It has, however, become the ground floor of an affluent society that finds its goal in hedonism, is dedicated to the accumulation of material possessions, offers life on easy terms, and tolerates the steady erosion of social morality by commercial interests and pressures. The traditional Puritan values – with their typical attitudes to work, sex, money, thrift, and the stewardship of time – are in steady retreat before the advancing forces of permissiveness. The young have a surfeit of money, of leisure, and of energy; they have a deficiency of agreed and accepted moral norms.

Such is the backcloth of the contemporary moral scene, against which the drama of moral development is enacted. The theme of its plot is the gap between the generations. This has always been a reality, however dominated by the demand for strict obedience, and however disguised by the symbolic dressing of children as miniature adults. Potentially, this can be a gap of creative tension. In practice, it can be accentuated into a well-nigh unbridgeable chasm by a variety of factors. Parents have traditionally fulfilled duties on behalf of society, above all of serving as moral guardians and guides. But the latch-key child is a symbol of abdication, neglect or incapacity to fulfil this duty; and, where this is the case, the home may be well provided with material things, but lack the effective presence of its foundation-stone, a mother. Moreover, changes in family life, not least the rise of the nuclear family, deprive the child of the support of a tight-knit community of relatives.

Other factors in children themselves contribute to this gap between the generations. Earlier physical maturation is not only a biological factor; it is also associated with psychological development in both thought and emotion. Relevant, too, is the far greater economic independence of the young which, whatever its merits, cuts at both unity and parental authority in the home. So does the comparatively better education of children, and the wider knowledge that comes to them through the mass media. Above all, there is the teenage cult, avidly promoted by commercial interests, that elevates a transient and unstable in-between stage of development into an artificial culture in its own right, a 'society' that seeks to evolve its own values.

A changing society

Deeper factors in the social background lie at the root of moral confusion in the contemporary society. We use the term 'moral' in two distinct senses. One is the pursuit of the good life. The other is conformity to the prevailing moral code of society, and this is the more common meaning. Genuine morality can only stem from free and convinced moral judgement that is the expression of internal values controlling conduct. The question is whether mere conformity to the prevailing code is any longer adequate. Democratic society must, by its very nature, be morally tolerant, save of such creeds as would destroy democracy itself. Hence the conflicts and dichotomies within society that express themselves, not only in distinct sub-cultures, but also in conflicting moral codes. Hence, too, the weakening of traditional values. It might be held that the child's experience of diverse and conflicting moral codes would develop subtlety and fluency in moral judgement, as distinct from blind and narrow rigidity. There is increasing evidence that such experience breeds uncertainty and moral confusion.

There is stark contrast between the transmission of moral values in primitive societies and the situation in a modern democratic society. In a tight-knit and narrow community, all the influences bearing upon the individual were united in their pressure towards social conformity. While such a system ruled out moral development, it had the supreme merit of ensuring social unity and moral conformity. Here is an extreme contrast with the morally foot-loose teenager of our increasingly urbanised and industrialised society. Many, of course, find their moral code within a sub-culture grouping, and follow it with blind rigidity. Many are confused by the claims of confusing codes, and muddle through as best they can. Some, personally unloved and socially unaccepted, turn against their society to delinquent modes of behaviour. Some achieve genuine moral attitudes that are both rational and altruistic, thus attaining moral maturity.

The old signposts are not clearly visible for those who grope their way through this fog of moral confusion. Indeed, their very existence is challenged by those who deduce, from their experience of conflicting codes, that morality is a purely social or personal construct. The *mores* of society are viewed simply as man-made conventions. In short, one moral system is as good as another; nothing is absolute in the moral field; relativism is all. Nothing, therefore, can be held to have claims upon the individual unless he chooses to accept it. Such a view totally ignores the characteristic propensity of man to evaluate, and thereby to form schemata of values. It ignores the subconscious processes at work in the child that shape him into a moral being – imitation, suggestion, identification, and thus the formation of an ego-ideal. It is such processes, biologically inborn, that give man his characteristic moral self-consciousness, and his universal sense of moral obligation. The content of any moral system must be relative, given all the limitations that impinge upon man. But underlying all such relative systems is the moral absolute, the imperative that he must obey to be true to himself. This is the very hallmark of man as distinct from the animal. To lose sight of it is a tragedy indeed.

The impact of new knowledge

The modern explosion of knowledge – about man, his world, and his universe – has similar profound bearings upon the contemporary moral scene.

An outstanding, if obvious, example is increased knowledge of contraception. Groucho Marx suggested, if facetiously, that the invention of the motor-car had revolutionised sexual morality in the United States; and there is some evidence that the coming of the scooter is doing something of the same today in Latin countries. But these are of minimal influence compared with the increasing perfection of modes of contraception, stemming, of course, from increased knowledge of human biology. A revolution in sexual morality is here, however concealed or ignored. A new pattern of marriage may emerge, as new patterning of pre-marital and of extra-marital relations are emerging. On a wider scale, the world population explosion, with consequent food-shortages, makes contraception more than a matter of personal convenience. Traditional preconceptions about sexual morality are, to say the least, challenged by such new knowledge.

More subtle is the influence of modern psychology upon the moral field. New understanding of the development and working of the human personality digs away at the roots of traditional moral assumptions. Thus, belief that conscience was an innate faculty, allied with the dogma of original sin, meant that the child's misbehaviour was deliberate evil-doing – and not, as we now realise, the natural and inevitable expression of his innate immaturity and egocentricity. Hence the enormities of cruelty that have been perpetrated upon children in the history of education. Hence too the adult's deliberate effort to break the child's will – to prevent him, that is, as we now realise, from developing into a unique personality in his own right.

The insights of developing sociology, as a social science, add to the impact of new knowledge upon the moral scene. We can no longer ascribe delinquency and crime to sheer wilful malevolence, to be punished objectively with the full severity of the law. Just as psychology shows the causes at work within the individual, so does sociology evidence the enormous power of the environment.

The old authoritarianism may seek to stem the tide of new knowledge. Thus, for example, the Roman Catholic Church has recently reaffirmed the prohibition of all forms of artificial contraception to its members. Their growing revolt, reasoned and conscientious, is ample evidence of the impact of new knowledge. Again, there are those who vociferously demand the reintroduction of flogging and judicial execution as the sovereign remedies for delinquency and crime. The reform of the penal system, a relatively modern development, made in the light of new understanding of environmental and psychological factors in human motivation, has gone too far for society to go back to the dark ages of man's inhumanity to man.

Religion and morality

In this confused and permissive society, the organised Churches are the only social agencies explicitly dedicated, *inter alia*, to the transmission of moral values. They, however, find active support from a decreasing proportion of the population. The growing sociology of religion shows not only that participation in religious activities has diminished during this century, but also that it diminishes through the life of the individual. Hence a decline in the moral influence of the Churches. Such a decline, coupled with specialist new knowledge, means that ecclesiastical pronouncements no longer carry the authority they once had in the moral sphere; and that scriptural quotations are no longer acceptable as adequate answers to the complex moral problems of society.

Far more serious is the situation arising from the traditional assumption that morality is wedded to religion, and that both its content and its authority derive from religion. For some decades, thinkers have realised the danger inherent in such an assumption – that, should religious faith diminish, so would the authority of the morality wedded to it. This, surely, is what we are witnessing. Rejection of traditional religion is accompanied by rejection of the morality tied to it. The tragedy of such rejection is that much of the morality thus discarded did not derive from religion; it had become entangled with it. It is almost impossible, for example, to disentangle the Hebraic and the classical strands in the traditional body of Christian morality in the West. Much of it derives from man's hard-earned moral experience, accumulated over the centuries – not from religious revelation as such. Thus a body of precious 'natural law', rooted in human wisdom, experience and reason is tossed aside with the religion to which it had become attached.

Coupled with this rejection is the conviction, growing throughout this century, that morals are a private concern. The occasional public scandal does provoke a rare outburst of public moral controversy, itself revealing the confusion and divisions within society. Otherwise, there is a progressive lowering of the moral demands made by religion and, in particular, by social sanctions that were buttressed by religious convictions. Thus, for example, divorce and illegitimacy, both formerly public scandals, are increasingly neutral in their moral significance.

This, however, is not the complete picture. It is becoming a truism to say that there was never a time when so much interest is shown in religion, and so little in the organised Churches. One reputable survey after another shows, not only a majority of the population professing belief in God, but also desiring the continuance of religious education in schools. A substantial proportion of adults, as well as of young people, see a relationship between religion and morality, and also see a link, however vague, between religion and the good life. Many young people seek after meaning and purpose in life, and not least in their personal relationships, with integrity and sincerity. Yet such searching interest largely bypasses the Churches. All such facets of the contemporary situation cannot but further circumscribe the influence of the organised Churches, and so further weaken their moral authority.

Assessing moral development

Even so sketchy a picture of the contemporary moral scene gives ample justification for concern, and for the growing interest in moral education in schools. Such education bristles with difficulties. It must clearly be educationally sound, broad-based, and rooted in reason, not in any form of authoritarianism. Above all, it must be closely geared to the moral development of the child. It must therefore be based upon solid, empirical evidence of the stages through which the child passes in his moral growth, and of the key factors that influence and shape it. The fact is, however, that the moral field is one of the most neglected areas in the study of child development.

Reasons for the lack of research into moral development are not hard to find. The very nature of the study has its own inherent difficulties. Not least is the problem of securing data that is objective, rather than subjective; factual, rather than inferential; scientific, rather than evaluative. An area so full of problems, and so unproductive of concrete results, is scarcely inviting.

A more serious difficulty is that of securing evidence of moral development. There are two broad approaches that might be used, the theoretical and the practical. The more theoretical approach seeks the child's judgements upon hypothetical, if realistic, moral situations. It is open to the obvious criticism that a child's cognitive judgements upon theoretical situations may bear little or no relation to his actual conduct. The more practical approach observes the child's actual behaviour in concrete, if fabricated, moral situations. It is open to the obvious criticism that the child cannot but be aware of what is happening, and that therefore his conduct may not be genuine. Both approaches have been used, as we shall see; both have their defects.

A third difficulty is that of having a yardstick by which to assess moral development. The paucity of research in this field is due above all to such a lack of norms; and, of course, it does little to fill the gap. Can we find stages through which a child passes in his moral growth? If so, how can those stages be distinguished? And what variable factors shape the child's development through such stages? It is these three questions that will be our concern.

The origin of conscience

But no such study is possible unless we can first assume that there is such a process as moral development. The traditional assumption has been that conscience is an innate and unique faculty in the child. It found familiar expression in the concept of conscience as 'the voice of God within'. The child was thus held to know from the outset the difference between right and wrong. This assumption, combined with the dogma of original sin, meant that child misbehaviour was deliberate malevolence. It meant, too, that there could be no study of moral growth in the child.

Such an assumption is no longer tenable. We know of no such independent organ or faculty in man as an inborn conscience. Nor, of course, would a static conscience be of help in coping with the variegated moral situations met in daily life, least of all in our complex modern world. The older moralists treated the individual in isolation, neglecting his social environment. Hence their hypothesis that the child is endowed with an inborn moral consciousness. Such a developed faculty would be totally at variance with every other aspect of the child's being. We would naturally expect a process of moral development, as of physical and mental development.

The normal child is certainly born with a moral potential. Indeed, even if he were given no direct moral education whatsoever, he would still become in some sense a moral being through the subconscious biological processes we have already noted – imitation, suggestion, identification and the construction of an ego-ideal. It is, therefore, society that shapes and patterns his conscience.

We have solid evidence for this truth. Attested cases of feral children, exposed or lost in infancy and reared by animals, give poignant significance to Aristotle's dictum that 'man is a social animal'. As contrasted with Rousseau's romantic myth of 'natural man', the stark reality is far closer to Hobbes' definition of the life of man, in isolation from human society, as 'solitary, poor, nasty, brutish and short'. Feral children are wholly bestialised. Unable to recognise and to pattern themselves in converse with other human beings, they never develop their human potential. Without human society, the individual personality cannot develop; nor can moral potential become actuality. The feral child remains an animal.

Further sorry evidence is provided by the psychopathic personality. This is a type of personality, so that cases of it may be placed along a continuum according to degree. The complete psychopath is a moral imbecile, lacking any form of interiorised moral attitudes. Lacking any moral controls, he is at the mercy of impulse, totally amoral. Psychopathy may be due to a deficiency in the central nervous system that prevents any form of conditioning. Recent research suggests evidence of genetic abnormality in the psychopath; and hence a deficiency in moral responsibility that must be reflected ultimately in law.

Both the feral child and the psychopath provide ample evidence that conscience is not a unique, inborn faculty. The infant is neither moral nor immoral, but, in fact, amoral. Through his moral potential, shaped by his environment, the normal child develops into a moral being. Clearly, then, the nature of his morality will be dependent upon his society.

Both heredity and environment are thus involved in the process of moral development; both nature and nurture play their part. In any study of moral growth, therefore, we are concerned with both psychology and sociology.

The relevance of psychology

It seems almost incredible that some psychologists should have proclaimed neutrality in their attitude to human values. It is tempting to see indifference to values and obsession with facts as themselves deriving from desire to achieve respectability for psychology as a 'pure' science. Such an attitude has been reflected in blindness to values even in areas of psychological investigation where they are central factors – for example, personality and character. Nor are they any the less involved in psychotherapy, with its basic premise that mental health is 'good' and mental ill-health is 'bad'. The formation of schemata of values is a supremely characteristic activity of the human personality. But even the concept of the ego was itself long discarded in the attempt to build up a pure social science, and to construct unitary psychological theories.

Relevant to our study is the broad distinction between the two main traditions in psychology, stemming respectively from Locke and Leibnitz. Locke's notorious *tabula rasa* concept of the mind has taken root in the psychology of Britain and America. The individual is reactive, the mind passive, and causation is from without. Hence the massive stress upon conditioning. The learning process is wholly one of Stimulus and Response; the individual, it has been aptly said, is the hyphen between the S and the R. Typical of such an outlook is the concept of conscience as a conditioned reflex. Such a unitary theory ignores all the other influences and processes that shape moral growth. To put it another way, conditioning becomes so much a blanket term that it ceases to have precise meaning. Conditioning is certainly a factor in moral development; but it is by no means the only one.

For Leibnitz, on the other hand, the individual is self-directed, the mind active, and causation is from within; and such activity implies purpose. Here is the root of the typically Continental tradition, so clearly seen in the genetic, developmental psychology of Jean Piaget. Hence the significant fact that support for Piaget's thesis on the development of moral judgement is strongest in Europe and weakest in America. His massive stress is upon internal maturation, rather than upon external influences.

Thus the one tradition over-emphasises nurture, and the other nature. But both are involved in moral development; and hence our concern with both sociology and psychology. An understanding of the process of moral growth is no more likely to be achieved by myopic stress upon one approach than by insistence that either social science is not concerned with values.

Values are simply facts of the activity of the personality. Applied psychology cannot even begin its work without the inescapable assumption of values – for example, that the delinquent should be helped to achieve a desirable moral outlook, and therefore socially acceptable behaviour. Nor can a rigid distinction be maintained between means and ends so that psychology can claim to be concerned only with describing the means, and not with constructing ends. The distinction is relative, not absolute; values form a hierarchy, so that a value can itself be a means to achieving the one above it. Only at the apex of the pyramid can there be such absolute values as beauty, truth, goodness. It therefore becomes impossible to state a fixed point at which psychology ceases to be concerned. Indeed, as we have observed, psychology has already profoundly affected moral attitudes.

To deny psychology's concern with moral values is, then, to deny three inescapable truths – that evaluation is a supreme characteristic of the activity of human personality; that inherent in all applied psychology is the assumption of values; and that psychological insights have already had great influence upon moral values.

The relevance of sociology

It seems no less incredible that some sociologists similarly insist upon neutrality in their attitude to human values. Here, too, we might see the subconscious desire to achieve scientific respectability. Moreover, the insights of depth psychology might conceivably find the idealisation of neutrality as itself rooted in unconscious prejudice. To hold that sociology is a descriptive science, concerned with means and not with ends, is, again, to confuse the relative with the absolute.

Life in society, essential to both the development and the happiness of the human personality, is made up of interpersonal relationships. These must be woven out of recognised principles of interaction; they demand at least the recognition of the other and of his inherent, reciprocal rights. Hence the evolution of rules – that is, of morality. While society alone develops individual personality, it no less patterns and shapes personality within the confines of its moral tradition. The social and the moral are therefore inextricably bound up together. Any society must have institutions and forms of control; both are regulative, both therefore involve the moral. Morality is, then, the heart of social living.

It would be folly indeed to hold that sociology, or psychology – or, indeed, any other science – can or should seek to solve moral problems. But it is no less fallacious to hold that they have no concern with moral values. Both are involved; the insights of both are needed in studying moral development. Neither the individual nor society can be fully understood in isolation.

Early studies

The traditional concept of conscience as an innate faculty, the assumption that psychology and, latterly, sociology had no concern with moral values – these were further obstacles to a reasoned study of the moral development of the child. It is not, therefore, surprising that such a study has but a short history of some seventy years; and that, even within that time, there should have been periods of stagnation.

The earliest empirical studies recorded arose from interest in the moral concepts of children at Stanford University, about the turn of the century. The themes, and, indeed, the conclusions, of these early studies foreshadowed later work. Thus, a study of child attitudes to punishments revealed that they were generally accepted as just, coming from adult authority; that punishments were held to expiate offences; and that this expiatory concept of punishment decreased with age. Similarly, the punitive emphasis decreased with age, being replaced by recommendations of restitution and of reasoning with the offender. Moreover, while younger children judged actions by their consequences, older children judged them by their motives. The climacteric change in moral judgement came at about 12 years of age.

Some thirty years were to elapse before Piaget's pioneering work in this field. Yet here in embryo were some of his key themes.

The work of Piaget

Piaget was indebted to Kant for his two key terms – *heteronomy* and *autonomy*. Kant introduced these Greek terms to make a clear-cut distinction between two types of morality. Heteronomy, rule imposed by others, is the moral constraint of external authority laid upon the individual, whether with physical or social sanctions. Such imposed morality may be legal, but it is not moral. The only true morality is autonomy, self-rule, the action of an individual guided by internal controls. Its essential characteristic is free choice; imposed morality can never be genuine morality.

Other Continentals also followed Kant's terms. Thus Hessen sought to pattern moral growth in three stages – early childhood, the stage of anomy, absence of rule; the school period, the stage of heteronomy; and the period of higher education, the stage of maturing autonomy. Above all, he followed Kant in his realisation that heteronomy is an essential stage if the child is to achieve autonomy. For Kant, it was the child's long apprenticeship of moral discipline and training that could alone produce the moral master-craftsman. Thus Hessen reconciled freedom and discipline. Discipline is the essential training for freedom, although discipline imposed as an end in itself produces only a moral automaton, indoctrinated into drilled behaviour. Thus heteronomy and autonomy are inseparable.

Piaget rejected this crucial insight, not least through his attachment to the theories of Durkheim. Durkheim's purpose was to construct a secular morality whose authority would be Society, almost personified as a divinity, and not the God of traditional religious morality. His new morality had three elements – discipline, attachment to social goals, and the autonomy of self-responsibility. But such autonomy was social, not personal; morality was held to be socially determined throughout. Hence the thesis of Piaget – that since the child experiences two types of social relationships, first with adults and then progressively with his peers, he develops two types of morality. The first is the morality of heteronomy, of unilateral respect for adult constraint. The second is the morality of autonomy, born of the mutual respect with his peers. Both moralities are social, but they derive from different authorities. Heteronomy is totally harmful in its results. It is only as the child is released from his strait jacket that he is free to develop, in mutual relationships with peers, towards the genuine morality of autonomy.

But while thus stressing the influence of social environment, Piaget is typically Continental in interpreting child behaviour on a genetic basis. Development is from within; adult constraint merely retards it. It reinforces the child's egocentricity, while the co-operation developed in peer-group relations is only made possible by inner growth away from egocentricity. The process is essentially one of maturation; it is characterised by sequential stages; the stages are defined in terms of age changes. Here is the typically developmental tradition, defined in terms of ontogenetic changes. In his overwhelming emphasis upon age changes, Piaget ignores those variable factors in the individual that may advance or retard them. Subsequent studies have clearly demonstrated the grave weakness in this obsessive, one-sided approach.

Piaget's overriding concern is also with intelligence – with moral judgement, rather than behaviour. Here is the theoretical approach to the study of moral development in the child. His interviews with children were certainly based upon moral situations relevant to their lives; but his characteristic question, what 'ought' the child in the story to do, rather than what 'would' he do, reinforces this theoretical type of investigation. Piaget's interest was in securing insights into the mental activity of the child, and in elucidating the moral concepts they revealed. His investigation of the moral judgements of the child thus dove-tails neatly into his whole massive, systematic analysis of the child's world revealed through his brilliant studies of other areas.

The morality of constraint

Piaget finds the first of the child's two moralities, the heteronomy of adult constraint, to be dominant in the child until the age of 7 or 8 years. It is a morality of authority and of duty; to be good is to be obedient. It forms in the child a 'moral realism', akin to the 'intellectual realism' that Piaget deduced from studies in other fields. Adult commands become sacred absolutes; for the child 'reifies' them through his innate egocentricity, with its inability to distinguish between subjective and objective, reinforced by adult constraint. Duty becomes an independent reality; the circumstances of the individual have nothing to do with it. Thus, in his investigation of children's consciousness of rules in their games Piaget found that, after the early stage of purely personal play with no awareness of obligatory rules, there followed a second stage in which rules were sacred, immutable and eternal. Any alteration would be a shocking transgression.

If the first characteristic of moral realism is that goodness lies in obedience, the second is that the letter, not the spirit, of the law is to be obeyed. Hence the stress upon punishment, in the young child, and in particular upon expiatory punishment which demands that the offender should suffer for his misdeed, and so expiate it. Such punishment is arbitrary; and, since rewards and punishments have no intrinsic place in the concepts of right and wrong, the idea of expiation must be born of adult constraint. For, given an external rule imposed from above, only the pain of punishment can bring the offender back to dutiful obedience, and expiate his offence. Collective punishment is similarly characteristic of the younger child; justice can only be satisfied if everyone is punished. A fascinating by-product of such ideas is the concept of immanent justice – that punishment is immanent in nature, so that nature is in league with adults, and a natural calamity simply an extension of universal expiatory punishment. Whatever is commanded is just; disobedience must be punished, whether by man or by nature. Punishment is the criterion of wrongdoing.

A third characteristic of moral realism is that responsibility is objective, not subjective – actions are to be judged, not by their motives, but by their exact correspondence to adult commands. Hence a preoccupation with the material results of actions, overriding any concern with obeying or disobeying rules. It is far worse to break twenty cups, through accident, than to break one in the course of deliberate wrongdoing; motives have nothing to do with the matter.

Such, for Piaget, are the limitations of the morality of adult constraint. The child, embedded in it, is totally incapable of truly moral actions, whether in terms of inner motivation or of their social significance. It is an unstable equilibrium, in that the natural growth of personality is hindered and thwarted. True equilibrium can only be achieved through free co-operation, reciprocal relations and mutual respect among peers.

Heteronomy is, therefore, wholly bad. In cavalier fashion, Piaget rejects as 'adult sermons' those responses of his subjects that interfere with his thesis, seeking to delve below them to genuine concepts. He thus fails to see the roots of moral concepts in adult precepts, rejects heteronomy, and throws out the baby with the bath-water.

The morality of co-operation

The typical age for these hallmarks of the morality of constraint was found to be 7 to 8 years. Towards the age of 10 years, Piaget found the development of his second morality of the child. Progressively released from his internal egocentricity, and from external constraint, the child co-operates with his peers in free association as an equal, sharing with them common perspectives. Now there develops the morality of co-operation. Its hallmark is reciprocity; to be good is to be strictly fair.

Rules of the game are no longer sacred absolutes, no longer rooted in authority. Their basis is mutual consent, so that, while they may now be changed by agreement, they must none the less be scrupulously observed thereafter. Co-operation thus breeds reciprocity. Rules are now internal, rather than external; reason and democracy replace the traditions of the elders and adult constraint; progress to autonomy now becomes not only possible, but also, for Piaget, an almost automatic process.

Objective responsibility is now replaced by subjective responsibility, with its increasing concern for motives and intentions; and such a development itself presupposes co-operation and mutual respect. Lying, for example, is no longer so objective an offence that even a mistake could come under the category of a lie, as with younger children. Lying is now seen as deliberate, motivated deceit. The crude concept of expiatory punishment is now replaced by reciprocal punishment, directly and logically related to the offence. The sole concern is to 'make the punishment fit the crime' by putting things right, making the offender suffer the consequences of his offence in terms of reciprocal action. Such a concept, too, could only come from co-operation and equality between peers; for the growing child, bound to his equals solely by freely accepted rules, realises that deception simply destroys mutual trust and offence harms co-operation. The breach of solidarity is quite adequately put right by reciprocal punishment, making the offender aware of the significance of what he has done. Such punishment, far from being arbitrary, is motivated, and both related to and proportionate to the offence.

Growth in moral judgement is revealed above all in concepts of justice – an area to which Piaget devotes his main attention. Up to 7 or 8 years, justice is dominated and determined by adult authority. Between 8 and 11 years there develops a progressive concept of strict equality, when fairness is all. From 11 to 12 years such rabid equalitarianism is tempered by equity – by considerations of motives, circumstances and relationships; and concern for such considerations, far from weakening equality, make it far more effectual.

Such developments confirm Piaget's thesis of a strict dichotomy between the two moralities of constraint and co-operation. Since they presuppose free and mutual consent among equals, there can be no genuine moral development until the child is freed from the shackles of adult constraint.

Critique of Piaget

Such a brilliant analysis of development in the moral concepts of the child made Piaget the outstanding pioneer in this field. All subsequent studies must be indebted to him in some sense. Indeed, many have been inspired by his work. His insights were profound. It is his interpretation of them that is so open to criticism.

We have already noted Piaget's total rejection of heteronomy in constructing his thesis. No less questionable is his theory as to the development of autonomy. For him, autonomy is born of mutual co-operation with peers. Such reciprocity, he holds, contains within itself the seeds of autonomy. It 'tends of itself' towards the highest morality of 'forgiveness and understanding', as the child comes to realise that there can be reciprocity only in benevolence to others. The process is, then, automatic. It is the simple practice of reciprocity that changes behaviour from within, both shaping and developing it. Thus the crude concept of stark and rigid equality merges of itself into the practice of the Golden Rule; reciprocity matures into a universal morality of love and forgiveness.

Such a thesis is an article of faith, rather than a sober conclusion from empirical research. Piaget offers no evidence for such massive optimism. Indeed, we observe that Piaget ended his interviews with children at about the age of 12 years. Since the classic period of reciprocity we find to be from 9 to 11 years, and since climacteric development towards autonomy comes at about 12 years, Piaget has assumed, on the principle of *post hoc propter hoc*, that autonomy is born of reciprocity. Had he continued interviewing into adolescence, he must undoubtedly have found strict tit-for-tat reciprocity still strongly in evidence – as, of course, it is in many adults.

We shall find overwhelming evidence that autonomy is, in fact, born of heteronomy. Here, too, Piaget's cavalier rejection of heteronomy as an obstruction to moral development is a serious defect. We can certainly sympathise with his views on the discipline imposed by so many adults upon children – physical rather than psychological, erratic rather than consistent, impulsive rather than thoughtful. Yet, on Piaget's own thesis, the child cannot treat all that he learns from social relations other than the way he does. He *must* learn social behaviour from adults; he *must* interpret what he learns within his own narrow conceptual limits. It would not seem an adequate answer to reply that the adult-child relationship should be more democratic. Much has to be learned that is alien and antipathetic; much has to be learned that cannot be reasoned. Hence the necessity for constraint. Its true end is not moral imprisonment, but moral freedom – the freely exerted self-discipline that can only originate from the external discipline of heteronomy.

We can fully agree that mutual co-operation with peers is the second great social influence upon the moral development of the child. The relationship is one of free association, reinforced by natural sympathy. Its intertwining roots are a common relationship to authority, a common outlook, and a common sympathy; and it is in such commonalty that the sense and practice of reciprocity develop. Here is a moral education, learnt from free experience and not from forced instruction, that heteronomy cannot give. But we find the moral concepts developed and practised in reciprocity to have a prior origin in heteronomy. Therefore, while such reciprocity may potentially develop towards autonomy, it does not follow that it is the source of autonomy, nor that the process is in any way automatic.

Piaget, in fact, fails to show the learning processes involved in the development of moral judgement. He assumes a stimulus-response process, the stimulus being the two types of social pressure – that of adults, and that of peers. He gives no evidence of the complexity of relationships between children and adults; indeed, it is difficult, on his thesis, to understand how relationships between children and parents can deepen, rather than wither, over the years. Nor do we become aware of the subtlety of relationships among children themselves; Piaget never seems to have encountered the classic phrase, 'it all depends', in his analysis of the behaviour of children towards each other. Above all, his theory fails to explain either the anti-social child or the child who rises morally above the level of his peers. Both have been through the same mechanical sausage-machine learning process of the two moralities. Why, then, do they deviate?

Obviously other factors are involved; and it is these individual variables that are ignored by Piaget. While there is some evidence that Piaget is aware of them, his theoretical blinkers blind him to them. Thus, socio-economic background has been found to be a powerful influence upon moral growth. Yet Piaget built his theory upon investigation of children from one ethnic group and, in particular, from one social class. Even more striking is his blindness to the sex factor. The majority of his subjects were boys, chosen on the ground that they have a more developed legal sense than girls. He thus remains unaware of the striking sex differences that we find to be evident in almost all areas of moral judgement. Such blindness is the more understandable if we take into account Piaget's overriding concern with the cognitive. But even here, paradoxically enough, he fails to take intelligence into account as at least a potentially vital factor in the development of moral judgement.

Clearly, cognition must play a vital part in all moral judgements. But moral judgement is by no means a purely mental activity. It has a strong affective content, and we find moral concepts to be powerfully emotionally toned. It is, no doubt, legitimate for purposes of study to differentiate between the cognitive and the orectic aspects of moral judgement. Piaget's supreme interest in the former patterns his approach, asking what 'ought' to be done; and thereby he ignores the non-cognitive, orectic elements. Yet not only is this 'emotional variable' a vital factor in moral judgement itself. It is also the key to motivation; and hence the frequent lack of clear association between moral knowledge and moral behaviour.

Stages of development

Such deficiencies in Piaget's work have paradoxically become apparent in studies inspired by it. They make it impossible for us to accept his monolithic theory. Yet he remains the outstanding pioneer in the study of the child's moral growth; and both the breadth and the depth of his analysis make his work of immense value, even if the theories built upon it must be rejected.

In particular, Piaget has made it possible to think of the child's moral development in terms of stages. Each such stage may be distinguished by its differentiation from the content of judgements before it and after it. But we must be very clear as to exactly what the term 'stage' means in this context; and no less clear as to the factors involved in such sequential development. Both will be our later concern.

We have at least come far enough to distinguish four main stages in moral growth. The first is anomy, absence of rule, a stage in which Piaget has no interest at all. The second is heteronomy, rule imposed by others, so castigated by Piaget. The third is the stage of social relations which he defines broadly as reciprocity. But since, as we shall see, reciprocity covers so vast an area as to become no more than a blanket definition, we prefer the term socionomy, which is also in keeping with our nomenclature. Finally, we have the highest stage of autonomy, self-rule. Piaget, being more interested in the journey than in its goal, nowhere fully defines autonomy. His whole concern is with the second and third of these four stages.

The Character Education Enquiry

Before we turn to examine this stage process of development, we must first take note of other studies bearing directly upon it. Not the least of these is the massive Character Education Enquiry, initiated at Columbia University, which produced the startling conclusion that there is no such thing as consistent character, and thereby stultified the study of moral development for a decade. For, if moral behaviour is no more than 'a series of specific responses to specific situations', as the Enquiry claimed and seemed to prove, it follows that there can be no process of moral development and no such thing as moral character.

Piaget represents the theoretical, cognitive approach to the study of child morality. The Character Education Enquiry used the empirical approach, making ample redress for Piaget's one-sidedness in a monumental research that filled three volumes (Hartshorne & May, 1928, 1929, 1930). It was, moreover, behaviourist in its approach. Ingenious tests were devised to measure actual moral conduct in concrete situations, unbeknown to the subjects. Some 170,000 tests were administered to over 8,000 public school pupils, and nearly 3,000 pupils in private schools, between the ages of 11 and 16 years. The tests included measures of moral knowledge and foresight, as well as of actual conduct. Character data were used to establish the validity of the tests. Reputation, carefully assessed, was found to be an almost complete index of character. Character portraits completed the statistical analysis.

The main, stunning conclusion of the work was that there is no such thing as generality in moral behaviour. Little evidence was found of unified character traits, such as honesty, and much evidence of conduct that was specific to the situation. There was, therefore, no such thing as individual character structured of virtues and vices. The child could only learn specific habits, in specific situations, one at a time. Indeed, habit was the highest activity of the human personality. Such a mechanistic view of personality had obvious attractions for behaviourists, and no less for sociologists laying massive stress upon the situation.

Rome seemed to have spoken, and the issue thereby settled, once and for all. But sober analysis of the findings of the Enquiry brought searching questions. Why was there positive, if small, correlation between consistency in test performance and honest conduct? Why, given the reality of temptation and of varying degrees of moral significance attaching to different situations, should complete generality in moral behaviour be demanded? Do we really expect individuals to be either perfect saints or totally imperfect criminals? Why did one of the associates in the Enquiry deduce from the same data a consistent element of character running through all conduct?

Defects could be found both in the Enquiry itself, and in the conclusions drawn from it. It was based upon the conduct values of society, not upon natural qualities; and since such values are acquired and not innate, socialisation is a long process. Low correlations would, therefore, be expected in immature subjects, so that the 'doctrine of specificity' naturally finds its strongest support from psychologically weak individuals. This was indeed confirmed by evidence of growing consistency with age in positive moral virtues, but not in vices; so that specificity also finds its strongest support from wrongdoing, not from good conduct.

Such critical analysis of the Enquiry leads to a far more sober conclusion than the exuberant doctrine of specificity. There is consistency in moral behaviour; but there is also inconsistency. In practice, there is both specificity and generality in normal human conduct; behaviour is never wholly and infallibly predictable. We cannot, on the one hand, live together in society without assuming some consistent pattern in the moral behaviour of an individual. Without it, character could never be defined, let alone described; no 'character reference' could ever be given. Reputation, which the Enquiry itself found to be a strongly valid criterion of character, would be a meaningless term. But, on the other hand, no such definition or reference is wholly infallible – 'I would never have expected it of him', we say.

Neither extreme doctrine, whether of generality or of specificity, is therefore valid. It is clearly a matter of degree. The stronger the character, the more will general attitudes be evidenced. The weaker and the less mature the character, the greater will be the influence of the situation and of such habits as have been acquired.

University of Chicago Studies of Values

Can we, finally, make a more precise definition of what we mean by 'character'? Can we, in fact, produce a typology of character? The attempt was made at the University of Chicago, and it produced valuable results. It used 'Prairie City', a mid-West town of 6,000 people, for a number of studies.

One, a study of character and of its development, is reported by Havighurst and Taba (1949). It was concerned with character as defined by grouped moral traits, and it analysed five – honesty, responsibility, loyalty, moral courage, and friendliness. The subjects were the boys and girls of the city who became 16 years of age in the calendar year of 1942. Doubting the value of artificial test situations, however ingenious, the research took reputation as a more realistic index of character. Reputation ratings were derived from peers, day-school teachers, Sunday-school teachers, youth leaders, and employers.

The main influences on character were found to be the home, the community code, religion, and the influence of peers. The concepts derived from them tended to be stereotyped, and so to produce rigidity in moral outlook. Types of character were delineated. Subjects with high reputations were divided into self-directive, adaptive, and submissive characters. Those with low reputations made two groups, the defiant and the unadjusted, the latter being potentially in the higher category, but confused over moral values. Sex differences were not statistically significant. The self-directive group – the largest, forming 21% of the sample – was closely linked with high social status.

A further study was based upon the population of 'Prairie City' born in 1933, much evidence having been gathered about it during an intense longitudinal study, and new projective and sociometric testing instruments suggesting a new type of research. Tests were augmented by character ratings, and an intensive investigation made of a cross-section of each sex, over the years from 10 to 17. Taking intention as the universally defined essence of all genuine morality, the study was based upon a motivational definition of character.

While motivation was not consistently unitary, four character types were found, representing sequential stages in psycho-social development. The amoral type was characteristic of infancy; the expedient of early childhood; the conforming, and the irrational-conscientious, of later childhood; and the rational-altruistic of adolescence and adulthood.

Both the breadth and the depth of this study make it a striking contrast to the studies of Piaget and of the Character Education Enquiry. It differed from both in being longitudinal. It differed from Piaget in its concern with motivation, and not with cognition; and thus took the orectic aspects of moral concepts into full account. It differed from the Enquiry in using tests that were concerned with inner attitudes and motivations, not practical tests of actual conduct in fabricated situations. In short, it sought to plumb the meaning of behaviour, not its purely mental content, nor its outward expression.

In the event, this study produced striking evidence for generality, rather than for specificity, in moral behaviour. Individual character was clearly evident. Inconsistency was to be found in every subject; but, most striking of all, even individual inconsistency had its own consistent pattern, differentiating it from that of other individuals. Moreover, consistency was maintained throughout the process of maturation. Thus character, defined as a composite of strong, emotionally-toned attitudes and motives forming habitual patterns of moral behaviour, was found to be a reality that persisted over the years. (Peck & Havighurst 1960).

The psychoanalytic approach

Given the key role of motivation in all genuine moral judgement and action, an approach from the psychoanalytic viewpoint could make its own contribution. Its predominant concern would naturally be with the processes of interiorisation. Mackinnon, pioneered this approach in the 1930s. While repudiating the theory of specificity, he used the methodology of the Character Education Enquiry. After interviewing his adult subjects, in order to predict their likely behaviour, he observed it in a situation that offered the opportunity of apparently unseen cheating. Consistency was apparent in both honest and dishonest subjects, and a general trait of honesty was evidenced. Dynamic processes at work were characterised in the broad distinction between physical and psychological discipline. Experience of psychological discipline, and of remorseful feelings of guilt after yielding to temptation, were typical of honest subjects. Subsequent studies confirmed this suggested relationship between parental discipline and internalisation. (Bronfenbrenner 1962).

Hoffman (1962) drew three conclusions from such psychoanalytic studies. First, the child's identification with the parent was promoted by display of parental affection, if also by punitiveness in some cases; and hence the influence of withdrawal of affection in promoting internalisation. The process was found to be facilitated, secondly, by psychological discipline which involved the child's deepest needs; while physical discipline tended towards an external morality dependent upon fear of detection and punishment. Thirdly, studies suggested that the quality of the internalised morality might be influenced by the specific need – whether of love, of self-regard, of concern for others – to which the type of psychological discipline appealed.

Such a developing distinction, between two broad types of parental discipline and the types of morality they engender, has strong bearings upon the moral education of the child.

Moral values

Any moral education that aims to instil specific rules for conduct could never be adequate, however internalised they might become; for they could not possibly cover all the ramifications of subtly different moral situations. Only general rules – that is, broad moral principles – could be adequate to making genuine moral judgements in daily life; and, in their higher insights, they might well conflict with conventional rules. Kohlberg (1963, 1964) investigated specifically moral values through Piagetian-type stories which, however, deliberately involved conflict between conventional rules and human needs. They went much further, too, in their concern with general moral principles, to be applied to the situation, rather than with the simple vices and virtues with which Piaget was concerned. Kohlberg was concerned with moral evaluations, not with moral judgements of pure cognition.

His subjects consisted of boys only – about 100 in all, between 7 and 17 years of age, representative of all social classes, including social isolates and delinquents. Records of the lengthy individual interviews were exhaustively analysed. They yielded 30 aspects of morality, and 6 developmental stages allotted to three moral levels. The first, pre-moral level consisted of the first two stages which, in their concern with punishment and reward, parallel Piaget's heteronomy. The second level, comprising stages three and four, was that of conventional conformity and concern to avoid adult condemnation with subsequent feelings of guilt. The third level consisted of stage five, the morality of mutual contract: and of the final stage six in which the controls were internal standards of conduct, that is, autonomous conscience.

Kohlberg found no evidence to support Piaget's thesis that heteronomy derives from unilateral respect for the adult, or autonomy from mutual respect. He rejects, too, Piaget's simple dichotomy between heteronomy and autonomy as a total account of moral development, seeing it, rather, as a long-term and complex process that proceeds from the re-patterning of experience. Hence a series of stages, in moral growth, so that it cannot be wholly accounted for in terms of internalisation of external values; and a process of development that culminates in personal autonomy.

Moral education

All such studies of the moral growth of the child, finally, must have bearings upon moral education in its widest sense. It includes vast areas of indirect moral influence, as well as of direct guidance, absorbed in home, school and church. There is growing interest in processes of moral learning in schools. Among the many factors contributing to this felt need is the moral confusion of the young arising, not least, from the rejection of authoritarian codes and of conventional, often hypocritical, adult standards. Behind it all is the chaotic tangle of religion and morality, made increasingly apparent by the decay of transcendental religious faith. For the traditional binding of morality to religion has a fatal defect – that religious decline must lead to moral rejection. Hence today the rejection of a vast store of hard-earned moral wisdom, traditionally bound up with religion, but not integral to it.

In such a chaotic situation we need to go back to first principles – to define, that is, what are the constituents of morality, and so to find a genuine basis for moral education. The Farmington Trust has established a ten year research project on moral education that seeks to meet this need. Its first production (Wilson et. al. 1967a) is a theoretical, as distinct from an empirical, work that sets about clearing the contemporary jungle of confusion. It approaches morality from the philosophical, psychological and sociological viewpoints. Each, in clearing and defining the ground, makes positive proposals for both practical application and for further investigation.

The main approach is philosophical. It is specifically concerned, not with the content of morality, even less with any search for an ideal moral code, but with the pre-conditions of morality. It seeks, that is, a set of principles which will make it possible to judge between rival leaders and codes. Such a unitary body of principles would have the authority of reason behind them. The approach is, therefore, rational, liberal, and neutral as between partisan convictions. The goal of moral education is the personal autonomy of the adult, free from irrationality and expediency.

The concept of morality is broken down into six component parts, each named from classical Greek words.

PHIL defines the degree of ability to identify with others, to accept them, that is, as equals.

EMP describes insight into the feelings of oneself, or self-awareness, termed AUTEMP: and awareness of the feelings of others, termed ALLEMP. There is a psychological link between these first two components.

GIG refers to necessary knowledge, above all, for example, of the likely consequences of actions.

DIK defines the moral rules or principles, formulated rationally by the individual through the first three components, to which he commits himself. They define for him what is good and right in his relations with others.

PHRON describes the same process of formulating moral rules or principles relating to self and self-interests.

KRAT describes the ability to put accepted moral principles into action.

Given a method of assessing and scoring these component qualities, an average of the resulting scores would give a general rating of moral education, termed ARI.

Such a rational and liberal approach is not to replace irrational authoritarianism with the new authority of reason (Wilson 1967b); for it is not a true parallel. It is, rather, to be reasonable in morality, facing facts, being sensible, being honest. Nor is it opposed to imagination and emotion; for to be reasonable is to judge and to control emotion in the light of the principles held. The aim of moral education, therefore, is not to teach values but to develop these defined moral skills.

The same criteria apply to religious education (Wilson 1967c). Its justification is the abiding human concern, even in a largely secular society, with ultimate metaphysical questions of meaning and purpose. Religious education, too, should be rational, neutral, non-partisan; education, that is, in the sphere of religion, rather than the process of seeking to sell, even less to impose by essentially irrational indoctrination, a particular religious outlook. Its core is not the traditional teaching about religion as a phenomenon. Its essential concern is with the forms of thought, with the purpose, of religion; and hence with the child's 'emotional world-picture', with his attitude to life.

Religion may therefore assist morality in providing motivation, in developing skills and attitudes, in promoting ideals. But morality is a separate field of discourse, with its own criteria. It is the sphere of personal relationships; its essence is, therefore, care and concern for other persons.

Our survey of such studies has opened up the field from various approaches and helped to clear the ground. We are now free to seek a pathway through it in tracing a sequential pattern of development in the child from research evidence.

Chapter 2
The pattern of development

Stages of development

Any morality is made up of a body of laws which become rules or principles of conduct. The Greek term *nomos*, meaning 'law', therefore serves admirably as the basis of our terminology. We can use it to define the four broad stages through which the child passes in his moral development.

He begins in a state of anomy – that is, lawlessness – in the true sense of the word. Being without rules governing behaviour, he is at the mercy of instinct and impulse.

Hence, secondly, the need of heteronomy, that is, rules imposed by others. The child comes under the sway of such heteronomy from the very beginning. The rules are external to him, and he inevitably interprets them within the narrow limits of his egocentric immaturity. Their purpose is the increasing control of impulse, and their sanctions are rewards and punishments. Without such heteronomy the child could not develop an inner morality of his own.

Towards the age of 8 years we begin to observe an inner moral awareness. The child, in developing relationships with his peers, becomes conscious of the give and take between them. Hence the development of the sense of reciprocity, for which the classic age is 9 to 11 years. Such strict reciprocity is typically expressed in the parrot cry, 'It isn't fair.' From the Latin word *socius*, meaning 'comrade' or 'friend' – and hence our word 'society' – we can define this as the stage of socionomy. This term is broad enough to include, not only the sense and activity of reciprocity, but also the growing awareness of others that makes the child desire their approval of him. Hence the power of social praise and blame at this stage. But these are not the only influences at work. The child is beginning, however clumsily, to put into practice the rules learnt through heteronomy.

At about 11 years we see the dawning of the final stage of autonomy – that is, self-rule. It is marked by the progressive interiorisation of the rules learnt under the sway of heteronomy, and therefore by the development of inner moral attitudes that are strongly toned by emotion. At 7 years, when the child is overwhelmingly dominated by heteronomy, the characteristic emotion is fear of offence and of consequent punishment, of whatever kind. At 9 years this fear is merging into an inner discomfort that is typically expressed as 'guilt'. At 11 years the term 'conscience' is becoming familiar, and at 13 years it is common.

The process of development, defined in these four stages, has three characteristics. The first is the progressive interiorisation of heteronomous precepts. The second is the increasing development of inner attitudes that are powerfully emotionally-toned, fear merging into guilt and guilt into conscience. The third is the growing exercise of putting into practice the rules of conduct learnt from heteronomy. Since these rules are so often badly taught, we observe the tortuous struggle in adolescence to remain true to the heteronomous principles that have been absorbed, and yet to adapt them to the clearly felt obligations of relationships with others.

These four broad stages in moral development were first delineated by McDougall (1908). His rather static picture is brought to life through the dynamic analysis of Piaget (1932), although, as we have seen, Piaget's overriding concern to prove his preconceived theory leads to a distortion of the evidence, and so to a false pattern of development. Yet he does provide ample empirical evidence to justify the description of development in terms of stages. He repeatedly gives caveats about the use of the term 'stages', variously defining them as 'phases' and as 'periods', and insisting that they are not to be taken as 'global'. He realises, too, that there can be differences in stage development, not only between individuals, but also within the same individual in differing moral areas. But none the less, in order to uphold his theory, he proclaims a 'law of evolution with age', and the evolution is in terms of stages. His gravest defect is to push individual variables on one side, ignoring them as 'minor oscillations' and even as 'interfering factors'. Hence the weakness and subsequent rejection of his unitary theory of development in moral judgement.

We must be very concerned with individual variables. We must, therefore, be the more guarded in our use of the term 'stages'. Four caveats are essential. First, we do not use the term in the same sense as stages on a bus-route, implying that each stage is left behind, totally and abruptly, as a new stage is entered. We use the term as descriptive of phases of development, showing differences of quality from both previous and subsequent judgements. Secondly, such stages will vary from one individual to another, according to the influences at work in his environment, as well as his native moral constitution. Thirdly, such stages will vary within one and the same individual. They may overlap, and merge together in moral judgement; so that, for example, we find a child's single response to reveal fear of detection and consequent punishment, a sense of reciprocity, and inner guilt-feelings. Moreover, judgements may well vary from one situation to another; and hence, of course, the element of specificity in moral judgement. Thus, a child may feel a strong sense of guilt about stealing, but none about lying.

Levels of judgement

The fourth caveat is the most important of all. We have insisted that a stage is not something passed through and left completely behind. We must now recognise that all four stages can and do survive into adult life. We can observe this in our own moral motivation, which is so often intricate in its complexity as well as in its variety. Thus, these stages of development survive into maturity, and we can best define them, now, as levels of judgement. Driving a car is a good example of behaving on different levels of motivation. Even on one and the same journey, a motorist may, according to circumstance, behave on different moral levels. At one time, he may be guided purely by impulse; at another, by fear of the law; at another, by respect for public opinion; at another, by his own inner principles of behaviour.

The more morally mature the individual, the more he will be guided by general and interiorised attitudes – that is, by his own autonomy. But by no means all achieve a rational and altruistic autonomy, and few achieve it in all areas of moral concern. Hence the abiding need for heteronomy, not least in the driving situation, for example. Hence, too, the continuing power of social praise and blame throughout life. If this is true of the adult, it is obviously the more true of the psychologically and morally immature child. He, like the immature adult, will be the more dependent upon the situation, the more specific, that is, in his conduct. It was for this reason that we found it essential to plumb children's judgements over a wide area of differing situations each producing its own pattern of response. It was for this reason too that, unlike Piaget, we found it essential to score children's responses by taking into account the different levels of judgement revealed in response to one and the same situation.

With such caveats in mind, and in the light of our empirical findings, we can now proceed to analyse the four broad stages of moral development.

Anomy: pre-morality

The first and lowest stage of anomy is characterised by purely instinctive behaviour. The only influences that modify it in any way are the pain and pleasure that are experienced. These, then, are its sole sanctions. Since the normal child will develop into some sort of moral being – through the processes of imitation, suggestion, identification and the formation of an ego-ideal – we may describe this more directly as the stage of pre-morality.

Since most animals learn to modify their behaviour through experience of pain and pleasure, we can characterise anomous conduct as animal. If, as we have seen reason to hold, man is essentially a moral being, such behaviour is less than human. It is certainly not moral. Young children learn from the satisfaction that is pleasure, and the discomfort that is pain. So do animals; but few animals rise above this lowest level of moral learning, whereas the normal child has a potential capacity to rise to far greater heights of moral awareness.

The border-line between anomy and the subsequent stage of heteronomy is very imprecise. Children of 7 years, for example, typically and dutifully reproduce the rules laid down by adults. But they no less cheerfully affirm that, if an offence against heteronomy was not likely to be detected, it would be perfectly all right. Piaget refuses to accept this as even a relative anomy, in his obsession with heteronomy. For the same reason he scarcely takes any notice of anomy, giving it the merest definition as the morality, if the term is appropriate, of the solitary. Above all, he finds no trace of anomy in older children, save for one boy who, judging it natural to cheat, was dismissed as an 'exception'.

But we find anomy to survive, if minimally, as a level of judgement in maturing young people. It would be typical of the psychopath, the emotionally deprived and maladjusted, and the child from the lowest of moral backgrounds. It would also obviously be expected to be more apparent in some moral situations than in others. Thus, for example, stealing – a far stronger temptation for boys than for girls – might have no moral significance for a child from a low background. The only controls would be the pleasure of gain, or the pain following upon detection. Such behaviour in the young adult is non-moral, immature in its essential childishness, lacking in any sense of responsibility or of interiorised moral attitudes.

Rousseau romantically advocated that the child should be left, in early years, to learn by the natural results of its actions, through, that is, the 'discipline of natural consequences'. Spencer went further in making such sanctions of pain and pleasure the basis of the whole of the child's moral education, seeing in nature the clearest illustration of all moral discipline. But, of course, the natural consequence of actions are, all too often, grossly disproportionate; they give the barest positive guidance for moral development; parents and teachers spend a deal of their time in seeking to protect children from the natural consequences of ignorant behaviour. The controls of pain and pleasure simply repress or reinforce instinctive tendencies. To describe such behaviour as in any sense moral is to regard animals as moral beings. Anomy is the lowest stage in development, and the lowest level of moral judgement and motivation. But it does see the beginning of some control over natural instincts; and such control is essential to any further moral progress.

Heteronomy: external morality

In the stage of heteronomy the child is dominated by rules imposed by others. The authorities cited by children are, naturally, parents, teachers, religion, and the police. Here, too, each moral situation will bring out its characteristic authority. Thus, the prohibition of lying derives characteristically from the home, of cheating from the school, and of stealing from both home and school, reinforced by fear of the police. The controls of heteronomy are the sanctions of reward and punishment. Here, again, each situation brings one or other into prominence. Hope of reward is strong in seeking to save life, and in taking a purse found in the street to the police. Fear of punishment is a strong deterrent against cheating in the classroom, and against taking the property of others.

Fear of punishment, which itself defines offences, further develops control of immediate impulses; for fear inhibits action. In the early stage of raw heteronomy such punishment is characteristically physical, if slight. Later, it is administered through deprivations and, later still, verbally. Children speak overwhelmingly of fear of punishment, and but minimally of rewards; the stick clearly predominates over the carrot, so psychologically weak is much heteronomy.

Yet heteronomy is, as we have seen, a vital stage in moral development. It is only through learning that he 'must' that the child can ever come to know that he 'ought'. It is only through imposed discipline that he can come to achieve self-discipline. Here we part company completely with Piaget. Far from seeing heteronomy, with Kant, as an essential moral apprenticeship to achieve moral mastery, Piaget saw it only as an obstacle to moral growth. We find ample evidence that it is precisely the opposite. Piaget sees the first signs of autonomy in the realisation – born, of course, of reciprocity – that truth-telling is essential to personal relationships. We, on the contrary, find young children of 7 years typically quoting their parents as the source of such awareness: 'My Mummy says that if you tell lies people won't believe you.' Further, we find maturing young people consciously and explicitly aware that their moral attitudes derived from the heteronomy of childhood: 'My parents drummed it into me that you mustn't steal.'

We can, however, sympathise with Piaget in his condemnation of so much crude adult heteronomy, typified, no doubt, in his study of working-class children in Geneva. Where heteronomy is practised as an end in itself – whether by individuals or by educational or religious institutions – it obviously becomes an obstacle to moral progress. Such authoritarianism, whether consciously or unconsciously, does not want the individual to develop towards moral maturity. Its aim is to condition or to indoctrinate him into conforming servitude; for heteronomy is characteristically the morality of the slave. Fear of punishment is its supreme sanction and, of course, it is a negative control. Hence the minimal reference, in children's responses, to rewards; for rewards seek positively to encourage and to develop, not to enslave. In punishments and rewards we see characteristic expressions of the two broad types of discipline that we shall need to analyse in depth – the physical and the psychological.

True heteronomy is never an end in itself. It is, rather, a means to an end – the fuller moral development of the child. Nothing has been learnt where offence is followed by physical assault, and the matter thereby concluded. Where the offence is reasoned, moral learning has occurred. An affectionate relationship, as the context of heteronomy, is clearly powerfully influential. But it, too, will seek to free, not to enslave, if it is to have a worthy end.

Heteronomy remains an imposed morality. Such outward conformity cannot be truly moral. It may, of course, degenerate into hypocritical subservience. Every prohibition may be observed, every law obeyed, but without any content of morality in such conformity. Yet the paradox remains. There can be no freedom without discipline; there can be no autonomy without heteronomy.

Socionomy: external-internal morality

Moral growth begins even within the stage of heteronomy. It is seen in the extension of the heteronomous precept so that it develops into a universal law, however rigid and overbearing in its claims. It is in the stage of socionomy that we observe dramatic development within the individual, so that the external morality of heteronomy is increasingly internalised to become part of the child himself. No longer is he wholly controlled by the crude, external sanctions of reward and punishment. The controls, now, are increasingly social praise and social blame – in a word, the voice of public opinion. Here is a further essential stage on the road to the fully internalised morality of autonomy.

Why should public opinion have such immense power? Why should such deference, going beyond all reason, be paid to it? For many, if not most, adults it is their supreme moral control. But already we see it at work in the growing child. Two factors are involved in its development. The first is the child's own concept of himself – his self-respect, or self-regarding sentiment. It includes that submission to the powerful authority of the adult which underlies the processes of imitation and suggestion, and which therefore makes the child receptive to the claims of authority. Such submission and receptivity, thus implanted in childhood, are similarly evoked by the collective voice of public opinion. In short, the powerful voice of parental authority is succeeded by the powerful voice of public opinion. Here is indeed a close and subtle relationship between heteronomy and socionomy, forming a solid bridge between them.

Other influences reinforce the power of social approval and disapproval. They include fear, deriving from the earlier fear of punishment; the active sympathy that finds its greatest dread in social isolation; and altruistic motives, of varying quality, ranging from reciprocal affection to the veiled egoism that derives pleasure from giving pleasure to others.

To the first factor of self-respect we must add the second factor of mutual respect, in seeking to account for the power of public opinion. Piaget, ignoring self-respect and the part played by heteronomy in its growth, is able to lay overwhelming stress upon mutual respect. For him, it is the source of reciprocity; and such reciprocity, in its turn, the source of autonomy. For the child now experiences from within himself the active desire to treat others as he would wish them to treat him; and awareness of the Golden Rule progressively and automatically extends it into a universal morality of love. We need not accept such dizzy optimism to agree that the sense of mutuality is a vital factor in any progress towards autonomy. Indeed, awareness of others, feeling for others, and therefore concern for others are the basic hall-marks of all morality. It is living in society that gives rise to morality and makes it necessary. Here, then, is a further sense in which morality has a social genesis.

The stage of socionomy thus has two essential characteristics. There is development within the child, in growing awareness of others, and of responsibilities towards them. There is development outwards towards others, expressed most clearly in sensitivity to their opinions and attitudes – that is, to the voice of public opinion. Here is dramatic development indeed.

Can we, then, hold socionomy to be the highest level of moral judgement? It is certainly that of, probably, most adults; and it must certainly play some part in the moral motivation of all adults. For any pragmatist denying ultimate ideals, socionomy must be the highest level of morality. Thus both in practice and in theory socionomy is held in high esteem. The primary aim of education throughout history has been to socialise the child, moulding him into a conforming member of the group. Many would still hold this to be its goal, especially today, when decay in attachment to ultimate ideals leads to increasing emphasis upon social relations. All such outlooks identify the moral with the social. They thereby fail the acid test of accounting for the autonomous, individual conscience that challenges and condemns the prevailing social morality, and thereby remains, as it has always been, the source of all man's moral progress.

The limitations of socionomy are manifest. Such a morality is, essentially, egoistic, however tinged with altruism. Its controls, secondly, lose their force when there is no danger of being found out and particularly when the individual is out of range of them. Above all, such a morality is limited to the code of a particular society, or sub-grouping of society. Moral codes differ, as we should expect. The code to which allegiance is given, in socionomy, may be limited, defective, even absurd. Finally, socionomy must tend towards rigidity in moral judgement; there are certainly no seeds of moral progress within it.

Despite these defects, socionomy remains a vital stage, and certainly a prerequisite of autonomy. It advances beyond heteronomy in three respects. First, at its very lowest it is itself evidence of decreasing egocentricity, and thus of moral development. The co-operation thus made possible implies, secondly, the individual's developing awareness of himself as a member of a community. Above all, thirdly, self-respect increasingly replaces fear as the basis of moral conduct.

Autonomy: internal morality

The highest stage of moral development must be that in which the individual has his own inner ideals of conduct. He is no longer dependent upon fear of authority or fear of public opinion. He is not dependent for his moral controls upon the praise or blame of others. His sanctions are his own, inner self-praise and self-blame. Such a morality has no such limitations as those of socionomy. The individual takes his ingrained moral attitudes with him wherever he goes. He is not limited to the code of his society, so that there is at least the potentiality of moral progress. It is through such autonomous individuals, the very salt of the earth, that all moral progress has been made.

But the self-rule of autonomy may vary enormously in quality from one individual to another. Piaget, absorbed in the process rather than the goal, gives autonomy such sparse definition that it becomes no more than a blanket term. The climacteric period of development towards autonomy is between 11 and 13 years, that is, with the onset of puberty. Adolescence is, therefore, the key period in the development of autonomy; and we recall that Piaget did not extend his researches into adolescence.

We may distinguish between three aspects of this developing autonomy. There is, first, emotional autonomy, characterised by the typical adolescent urge to throw off the familial ties that bound him in childhood. Many ancient myths centre upon this essential function of adolescence, and bear witness to its importance. For the adolescent, increasingly aware of himself as an individual, cannot achieve selfhood save by seeking to stand on his own feet, emotionally above all.

Adolescence is also characterised, secondly, by a regrouping of values so as to achieve value autonomy. No longer are imposed values accepted without question, or followed without rebellion. Much may be rejected, and rightly so, in so far as heteronomous values have been puerile. New values may well be acquired in this regrouping. The process is essential to the achievement of selfhood; for what the individual retains is his own, the framework of his own character.

As these values are put into practice it follows, thirdly, that there is behavioural autonomy. No longer will the adolescent permit adults to make decisions for him; he must make his own, and adult guidance, if it is to have any hope of being heeded, must indeed be discreet. The hard core of the individual's values will be those absorbed through his identifications and, above all, through heteronomy. Now comes the hard struggle, of which we shall find ample evidence, to remain true to the ingrained moral precepts derived from heteronomy, and yet to be loyal to newly acquired values stemming from relationships with others. Heteronomy, for example, taught that lying is wrong, and there is a deeply interiorised principle of truth-telling. But may not lying be legitimate – indeed, morally higher – if it is wholly altruistic, motivated by reasons of friendship or love? Here is the creative tension of adolescence as behavioural autonomy struggles to be born. 'It all depends' is its watchword.

McDougall holds that autonomy is born from the creative tension between differing moral codes. Piaget sees the concept of justice developing into autonomy through equity – the increasing concern for circumstances, motives and relationships that makes equality not less but more effective. For both it is moral fluidity, then, that gives birth to autonomy. But such fluidity may be no more than moral uncertainty, a mask for behavioural confusion as the adolescent struggles to decide on what factors moral judgement must depend. Here is indeed evidence of the need for a moral education that seeks to develop moral skills in giving experience of making decisions within concrete moral situations.

Autonomy may vary greatly in its quality. On the one hand, it may be no more than the exercise of a harsh and rigid super-ego expressed either in the intra-punitive guilt that castigates the self, or in the extra-punitive guilt that fiercely condemns others. On the other hand, it may be a compound of inner attitudes that are rational rather than irrational, and altruistic rather than basically self-concerned. It is the latter type of conscience that has characterised the moral leaders of mankind.

Is autonomy the highest moral ideal? Such an assertion may well be branded as a subjective judgement. Certainly some human societies make shame the basis of morality; others found it upon guilt. For the former, the moral stature of the individual is the image of himself as others see him; for the latter, he is his own moral judge. The contrast is, broadly, between socionomy and autonomy. In a democratic, inherently tolerant, morally confused, and increasingly permissive society the individual must be dependent upon his own inner values, unless he is to be held fast throughout life either in a heteronomous strait-jacket or in the rigid and static code of a particular social sub-group. There can surely be little doubt as to which is the higher level of moral judgement.

Sequential stage development

It is in terms of these four stages of development that we pattern the moral growth of the child. They follow each other in sequence; none can be by-passed if there is to be moral progress.

All four stages are closely linked with each other, and, as we have stressed, frequently overlap. Thus, the natural pain and pleasure sanctions of anomy bear close relation to the human and artificial sanctions of punishment and reward in heteronomy. Again, the powerful voice of parental authority in heteronomy is increasingly replaced by that of public opinion in socionomy; and the same inner response is brought into action. Similarly, too, the precepts learnt from heteronomy, increasingly universalised and interiorised, bear fruit in autonomy. Meantime, the awareness of, and sensitivity to, others that characterises socionomy contains within itself the seeds of that altruism which distinguishes autonomy at its highest.

The stages are linked, too, in their emotional overtones. Moral judgements, we find, are both cognitive and orectic, both rational and emotional; moral concepts and attitudes are heavily weighted with emotion. Such feeling has its roots in the fear born of the imposition of heteronomy. Increasing internalising of moral precepts develops fear into a sense of guilt, and hence ultimately the genesis of conscience.

All four stages were found to be apparent over a wide area of moral situations. But, of course, each differing situation brings out its own pattern of response. Each stage remains as a level of judgement in maturity, to a lesser or greater degree, and is applied as appropriate within differing situations. Hence the essential need to test children over a wide range of moral areas, if a realistic and genuine pattern of development is to be achieved. Hence, too, the need for experience of decision-making in varying situations, such as could be gained from direct moral education.

Variable factors

Given the reality of broad stages patterning moral development, can we assume inexorable progress from one to the other, such as Piaget's theories conclude? It was, paradoxically, the inspiration of Piaget's own work that led to the undermining of its conclusions. While maturational growth, seen in broad stages of development, remains a reality, the attainment of such stages was increasingly seen to be profoundly influenced by those factors that vary from one individual to another. Piaget's overwhelming emphasis upon nature was found to be gross distortion. Such factors as socio-economic background, ordinal position, sex, ethnicity, intelligence, religious background and, above all, familial discipline were increasingly recognised to be key factors in moral development.

Socio-economic background

Piaget, deriving his whole thesis from testing children from 'the poorer parts of Geneva', was aware that different results would certainly have derived from children of a different social stratum, if only in terms of age differences. Within two years of the publication of his findings, a follow-up research in London, testing children from a similar working-class background with a matching control group from cultured and well-to-do homes, found serious defects in Piaget's conclusions (Harrower, 1934). While similar results were derived from working-class children, the results from the subjects of high socio-economic class were very different both in quality and quantity, with markedly maturer responses from the younger subjects, and no evidence of Piaget's age evolution. The home background was patently a powerfully influential factor. Further studies confirmed this conclusion. Moral realism declined earlier in children from higher status homes; they showed far less tendency to think of moral principles as immutable and external.

Cross-cultural studies – for example, of white American, Chinese-American, American-Indian and African children – provided further evidence of both social class and ethnic differences, and of interesting subtleties. Thus the higher judgements of Chinese-American children, as compared with white American, could be attributed to the moralising influence of a Confucian background. American-Indian children, attending a white school, while fluid in their attitudes to white games, such as baseball, regarded the rules of their tribal games as sacrosanct and unchangeable.

Sociology makes us increasingly aware of the influence of social classes, each sub-grouping having its characteristic *mores*. If, as we have insisted throughout, morality is a social construct, and therefore conscience has a social genesis, the influence of the socio-economic background is manifestly powerful. Children from higher-status homes have an interwoven complex of advantages over those from a poor background. Their greater security, both economically and emotionally, gives them freedom from temptations that beset less fortunate children. It is the child from a low-status background who is tempted to steal what he needs, to be punitive in his judgements, to seek to compensate by cheating for the mental disadvantages he so often suffers. It is such children who, in our responses, make references to the police, to Borstal, to approved schools that are clearly part of their normal background.

The home

It is in the home that social class differences are focused. Not least among them are disciplinary practices. The broad distinction is between the working-class tendency to punitiveness and typical middle-class moderation, with the use of reasoning and the effort to inculcate guilt feelings. From 7 years to 17 years we find expressive evidence of both physical and psychological discipline. The former is directed aggression, the expression of adult power, overwhelmingly from the father. The child learns nothing, save that the particular offence results in punishment, and that, if repeated, care must be taken to avoid detection. Psychological discipline is, by contrast, reasoned, consistent, and aiming to develop internal controls. Mutual affection between adults and child aids this process; so that the withdrawal of affection, as an aspect of disciplining, may help the internalizing of parental values.

The contrast, then, is between discipline that tends towards internal conscience, inner-directed morality, and autonomy: and the aggressive verbal or physical discipline that tends towards external controls, other-direction and heteronomy. Studies made from a psychoanalytic standpoint amplify this distinction.

But the influence of parents goes beyond the discipline that they impose, and in a number of ways. They cannot help but serve as models for the child; and the subconscious process of identification tends towards making their values his own. Piaget ignores such powerful influence in his castigation of most parents as poor psychologists, of heteronomy as an obstacle to development, and of many children's judgements as but the parrot repetition of 'adult sermons' and 'family lectures'. Yet such heteronomous precepts form the body of explicit moral teaching which the child receives in the home, and which, we find, becomes progressively internalised through the processes at work within him. Nor, again, can we ignore the moral assumptions prevailing in the home, largely derived from its socio-economic background, which are the more powerful for being unconsciously absorbed. Influential, too, is the psychological atmosphere of the home, expressed, not only in the type of discipline imposed, but also in relationships between the members of the family and in their attitudes to each other.

Such learning experiences in the home play a far greater part in the child's moral development than the processes of maturation – and not least because they will pattern them, and either promote or impede them. The contrast is succinctly expressed by a boy of 17 years in the context of truth-telling: 'If his father was vicious, he would lie; if his father was understanding, he'd tell the truth.' The child who has a warm relationship with his parents, in a context of psychological discipline, will the more easily assimilate parental values. A boy of 13 years shows such insight: 'Father would punish me more, so I'd feel more conscience about lying to my mother.' In an atmosphere of physical discipline, it is the child who is punished. How much more powerful is a context of psychological discipline and of close parental relationships in which the child realises that it is parents who suffer from his moral offence. 'It would hurt them both; they'd think it was their fault,' is the characteristic response from such children. It is a warm, living relationship that is broken, not merely a cold, external rule.

A child can, of course, identify no less strongly with a punitive parent; and hence the fierce adult super-ego which is but the echo of the stern parental voice and which keeps up punishment, whether directed against self or others. But there is a world of difference in quality in such an infantile morality.

Religious influence

A third influence that may impinge on the child from his background is that of religion. Difficulties abound in seeking to identify and isolate it, and to assess its significance. The yardstick of Church affiliation may seem crude, but it is that used by the organised Churches; and we find strong, positive association between it and internalised religious attitudes. Again, church attendance is by no means universal. In our own sample, the maximal figure of 60% weekly attendance at 7 years drops progressively to 18% at 17 years.

Moreover, the relationship between religion and morality has received minimal definition. There are three possible attitudes. The traditional, transcendental code holds that morality is indissolubly wedded to religion, which not only provides its content but also its authority; and hence decay in religious faith must lead to the abandonment of morality. We have already observed the danger of tying morality to religion, not least because much of infinite worth – derived from long human experience and reason, not from revelation – has become associated with religion and is abandoned with it. Moreover, such transcendental morality, inherently conservative, is not only thereby static but is also grossly inadequate for the moral complexities of life. The Bible was never intended to be a moral handbook. The early Christians naturally assimilated moral precepts from their environment. Jesus was a prophet, proclaiming timeless truths, not a law-giver laying down moral codes. Each generation must seek to apply them to its situation.

In reaction to such a position, contemporary humanism rejects transcendental morality. Broadly atheistic, it is concerned with man, not with the supernatural. Morality derives neither its content nor its authority from revelation. Indeed, religion is held to be the enemy of moral progress; and it is not difficult to adduce evidence to support such an argument. Humanism holds the highest moral ideals, such as the sacredness of the human personality and the brotherhood of man; and, therefore, in most areas of social life the Christian and the Humanist can and do work together with common ideals. The ultimate question still remains as to the source and the authority of such ideals; and the nagging doubt as to whether the atheistic Humanist may not be indebted to the religion he rejects for the high values he proclaims.

Morality is clearly rooted in natural human capacities. Thus, McDougall sees the origin of all altruism in the maternal instinct; and Piaget sees the sense of reciprocity developing from the play of mutual sympathy and antipathy. Religion is not, therefore, essential to morality. Seneca, the pagan moralist, was a favourite author of the early Christians; and the cardinal virtues, characteristic of our whole moral inheritance from the classical world, had a pagan origin. In Plato's *Republic* their root origin is found in the division of labour within the state. Wisdom is the quality of the ruler, as is Fortitude that of the soldier. Temperance is the acceptance by each class of its function, and Justice is its fulfilment of that function. Socrates goes on to analyse how these virtues relate to the constitution of the individual, and so come to define moral excellence, that is, goodness.

But if morality can and does exist without religion, there is no doubting that religious faith can give it powerful motivation; this is its true function. Such religious authority for moral behaviour may be puerile and repressive. But at its best it is the inspiration of self-giving, sacrificial love, the highest moral quality known to mankind. This, surely, is the true Christian ethic, the so-called new morality that is as old as the Gospels. It is Christian humanism, an ethic of love, timeless in its relevance and unconditional in its demand. It is relevant to every encounter between persons in all ages and in all societies. There is, therefore, no such thing as a static, immutable body of Christian ethics. The single love-ethic is the principle to be applied to every moral concern. It is therefore eternally relevant, eternally changing in its application. There must, of course, be moral rules and moral habits that save endless decision-making. But love alone is absolute, not rules; and rules must always be tested by love. Morality was made for man, not man for morality; rules are always subordinate to persons. Law is the schoolmaster, guiding towards love; heteronomy is the means guiding towards autonomy, never an end in itself.

Such is the background against which we must analyse children's moral judgements, in terms of their religious content. Pre-adolescent children, particularly girls, personify the inner moral struggle as between God and the devil. Verbalisms naturally abound, given the traditional modes of religious education. But, with development, the conflict between God and the devil becomes a conflict between the good and the bad parts of the individual. With adolescence, specific religious references become quite minimal. Responses are increasingly and overwhelmingly humanistic in their expression. It is, moreover, increasingly and explicitly recognised that conscience is a social construct, built up in the main by parents and teachers: 'If you didn't grow up with other people you wouldn't have one.' Humanism is seen, above all, in the subordination of laws to persons; thus the prohibition of lying, a deeply ingrained attitude in many subjects, may be broken for reasons of friendship and love.

Such humanism is truly Christian in its overriding concern for the highest good of others. But it is not expressed in Christian terms, any more than in atheistic terms. It certainly has immense Christian potential; but it is difficult indeed to trace its religious roots, if any. An irreligious adolescent may well be unconsciously indebted to religious influence in childhood for his moral attitudes. Parents, too, however outwardly indifferent to religion, may owe a similar debt to their childhood, no less unrecognised.

Previous studies portray the same kind of difficulty. Piaget, for his part, identifies religion with all the crude trappings of the morality of constraint: sin is disobedience; punishment is expiatory; responsibility is collective, in terms of the harsh dogma of original sin, which is nothing more than the tension produced by constraint. Many subsequent studies ignore the potential influence of religion as an individual variable. Those that seek to trace it find the supreme difficulty in isolating it. We saw some slight evidence of the influence of a Confucian background upon the moral judgements of Chinese-American children. There is similar evidence from another study of the possible influence of a Catholic upbringing, teaching children from the age of 7 years to distinguish between accidental and sinful actions, and so to evaluate a deed for its motivation. To such small evidences of religious influence must be added the contrary fact that, in terms of offenders against the law, there is considerable overlap of religious and irreligious individuals; by no means all delinquents and criminals have no religious affiliation.

The broad conclusion must be that, as the Character Education Enquiry found, religious influence is a strand, difficult indeed to isolate, in the familial background and the atmosphere of the home. It may, of course, be repressive or liberating in its influence upon moral growth. But such evidence as there is for higher moral conduct in children attending church suggests that it is due, not to the fact of attendance, but to the homes promoting such attendance. Yet again, therefore, we observe the paramount significance of the home in the moral development of the child.

Sex differences

When we turn more directly to the child himself, a possibly potent factor is that of sex. Piaget, overwhelmingly concerned with the cognitive element in moral judgement, characteristically took boys for his subjects because of their more developed legal sense. Many subsequent studies did likewise. In the following twenty-five years, only three took possible sex differences into account. Such evidence as has been found has suggested trends rather than statistically significant differences between the sexes. The question remained open.

By testing an equal number of boys and girls at every age we were able to observe the sex factor in every area, and in both written and verbal tests. We observed an immense sex difference. Girls were found to be in advance of boys in their moral judgements in every area examined. Four factors must be taken into account: the earlier maturation of girls; the possibility of an earlier, parallel development in intelligence; the greater facility of girls to verbalise, so that their subtlety of expression might appear to give added quality to their responses; and what some previous research has regarded as the more strict judgements of girls. The fact remains, however, that after detailed analysis of the possible relevance of these factors, the sex difference remained clear-cut.

Girls have the innate advantages, revealed in various moral situations, of greater initial sympathy, of stronger feeling for others, and therefore of far more profound sensitivity to personal relationships and social attitudes. They soar ahead of boys in their insights and attitudes, and not least in those areas, such as lying, which pierce to the heart of personal relationships. Boys progress stolidly, far less spectacularly; they excel girls only in their residual anomy, and in their greater dependence upon heteronomy. Girls show far stronger socionomy, and much earlier progress towards autonomy. Only at 17 years of age have boys plodded to within striking distance of girls in their moral judgements. But even then, when our evidence suggests that development as such is broadly completed, the gap remains.

Boys excel in the concrete situation, girls in the subtleties, both good and bad, of personal relationships. Girls are mainly concerned with the psychological and personal, boys with the physical; girls with being, boys with doing. Girls expound subtle niceties of personal relationships of which boys are blissfully unaware. Boys have temptations – for example, stealing, cruelty to animals, damage to property, self-indulgence – that leave girls serenely untroubled. It is girls who are profoundly concerned with lying, deceit, unkindness, selfishness.

The stronger innate sympathy of girls develops into an earlier sense of reciprocity, and reciprocity, in turn, into greater socionomy. While socionomy remains strong in girls, even in maturity, they achieve autonomy earlier than boys, strikingly so in terms of truth-telling. Indeed, so strong is the advance of girls to autonomy by 13 years that they show small development thereafter. It is not until 17 years that boys achieve a similar level of autonomy, in this situation.

It was only in the stark issue of life and death that boys kept anything like in step with girls in their judgements. For the rest, girls are early developers, boys are late developers. But it is not simply in terms of development that the sex difference is patent. It is there, in one form or another, from 7 years to 17 years, above all in relationships between persons. If concern for others is the heart of all morality, as indeed it must be, the female is inherently more truly moral than the male.

Intelligence

We find ample evidence for insisting that moral judgements are both cognitive and orectic, involving both intelligence and emotion. Moral concepts are strongly affective in their constitution. The moral attitudes revealed in our testing are deeply felt, as we would expect if fear merging into guilt is the emotional accompaniment of developing conscience. A boy of 9 years gives a graphic definition of feeling guilty: 'Your mind goes all sort of beating fast.'

In many areas we find intelligence to be the key variable in its relationship with moral judgement, more markedly so in girls. Here is evidence of the cognitive in moral judgement. Without the capacity for reasoning, there can be no moral judgement. But moral knowledge is by no means necessarily reflected in moral action. The complete psychopath, the moral imbecile, is not necessarily lacking in power to reason. The place of intelligence is, then, by no means clear-cut.

Piaget, oddly ambiguous in his attitude to intelligence, dismisses it as one of the 'interfering factors' in his pattern of development in moral judgement. While absorbed with the cognitive, and aware that intelligence might be an influential factor, he so patterned his testing as to produce responses that stemmed from mental activity rather than from deeply held attitudes. Further studies showed intelligence to be positively associated with moral judgements. But here again we must stress its relevance to the cognitive, as distinct from the emotional. The inner self-criticism of a guilty conscience is a far more powerful moral control than the cold light of reason. Intelligence is not the only factor at work; and certainly our responses were by no means objective and impersonal judicial decisions.

The function of intelligence is manifest. It is a factor in the development of the sense of reciprocity. It can both foresee the likely consequences of future actions, and pass judgement upon past actions. It can foresee remote goals, and so the value of forgoing immediate pleasures for the sake of distant, but more satisfying, ends. It is an important factor in all moral learning; and no less in resolving conflicts, since conflict lies at the heart of the moral life. In all these functions, intelligence is an important, but not the only, factor. On the other hand, it has its own temptations. It can understand the behaviour best calculated to gaining approval; but this can lead to hypocrisy. It can certainly be a powerful aid to upright behaviour, in that the able individual has far less need to descend to immoral expedients to gain his ends; but such conduct may have small moral content. It can see the folly of such vices as lying, since they lead to more trouble in the end; but the intelligent child may become the more plausible in his excuses, the more agile and facile in his lying.

A moral code must above all be founded upon reason; and hence the weakness of any authoritarian code that patently conflicts with reason. But intelligence is only one factor in moral judgement. Imagination can be a powerful support to reason; sympathy, and therefore concern, for others is the heart of the matter; the inner control of conscience motivates far more strongly than intellect; far more values are absorbed through identification than are conceived in the intellect.

Motivation, not intelligence, is the key factor in moral action. To realise that 'right conduct is simply intelligent conduct' is undoubtedly a powerful asset. But the right may be known without being put into practice. There is, as we have seen, both generality and specificity in moral conduct; it is never wholly predictable. Children in particular frequently do what they know is wrong, and from various motives – for example, to assert independence, to win social esteem, to avoid social disapproval, and, of course, in seeking to avoid punishment.

In so far as we consider the cognitive element in moral judgement in isolation, intelligence is a key variable; and higher intelligence is, at least potentially, a strong asset to moral living. But it does not of itself promote higher levels of conduct. It is generally found, moreover, as one of a group of factors in the higher-status home that tend to give its children moral advantages not generally enjoyed by those of lesser ability.

The place of variables

Increasing evidence of the place of such individual variables in moral judgement has destroyed Piaget's unitary theory of development. The significance of such factors, and the complexity of their contribution to moral growth, must make any such generalised pattern doomed to do less than justice to the influences at work, and thereby erroneous.

It is this complexity of factors involved in moral growth that make it essential to be on constant guard against using terms in such a way that they become no more than blanket definitions. We have to use such key terms as reciprocity, autonomy, home influence, and moral judgement itself. But they require analysis if they are to be used in a meaningful way.

It is with this caveat in mind that we seek to trace a pattern in the development of moral judgement. Children's responses are themselves complex and subtle. Yet there is an emerging pattern; and it can be broadly delineated in the stage sequence of anomy, heteronomy, socionomy and autonomy.

Chapter 3
The research project

Purpose

This research project had a humble origin as a minor aspect of a weekly study practice with students training in a college of education. From such simple experimental beginnings, and a study of research literature, three things became clear. First, the vastness of the moral field made it soon apparent that a narrow investigation in a limited area would not give the broad view of moral development that we sought. Secondly, the complexity of the moral field indicated that such a narrow investigation would not do justice to the many facets of moral thinking. Thirdly, the very complexity of children's judgement made it no less apparent that investigation on a narrow front would be so limited and inadequate as to produce an over-simplified and erroneous picture.

It was therefore decided to attempt investigation on a broad front and with a battery of tests. Secondly, if development in moral judgement was to be effectively traced, it was necessary to take a broad age-span, including the period of adolescence ignored by Piaget. Thirdly, if the influences at work in such development were as significant as post-Piagetian research had shown them to be, we needed to take account of the main individual variables.

Our aims were therefore three. First, this research project set out to investigate the moral judgement of children over a wide age-range and with a variegated battery of tests. Secondly, it aimed to trace such development, as might be found in moral judgements, over a wide area and in terms of a four-stage scale – anomy, heteronomy, socionomy and autonomy. Thirdly, it took into account five key variables – chronological age, sex, intelligence, socio-economic class and religious background; and sought such evidence as might be found of relationship between them and moral judgements.

Methodology

Concrete moral situations were patently essential for the investigation of moral concepts, for the use of abstract ideas with the concretistic pre-adolescent would, as Piaget has clearly shown, be beyond his conceptual capacity; and research has increasingly shown that effective moral judgement can only be made in the context of the concrete situation. The approach must be inductive and not deductive, empirical and not theoretical. Above all, we needed to know what the subject thought that a child in the given situation *would* do – and not, as with Piaget, what he *should* do. Projective tests were indicated here, as both disguising our purpose and avoiding direct questioning – not least in so personal and intimate an area as that of moral behaviour.

The age-range decided upon was from 7 to 17 years inclusive. Our tests would therefore need to be simple enough for the former, but sufficiently evocative to be taken seriously by the latter. The two methods available were written tests and personal interview. The limitations of written tests, both in themselves, and particularly in the case of younger subjects with limited reading and writing skills, are substantial (Goldman, 1962, 33f.). In the event, it was decided to use both methods.

Written tests were administered to all subjects, save the 7-year age-group, and will be discussed later (Chapter 10). Their use was justified, first, on the ground that they produced further evidence that could not have been derived from personal interviews without making them both exhaustive and exhausting. Secondly, the written tests were given to the whole group corporately, as a preliminary to the individual interviews, and thus helped to establish rapport on a friendly basis with the investigator. Thirdly, while written answers cannot be explored in depth, reasons for answers were always required; and where the reason given differed from the simple answer, the reason was used in assessment. Fourthly, the six written tests were quite different from each other, thus avoiding any boredom arising from monotony; and, since the tests could be given in sequence or separately, as convenient, fatigue was avoided.

The personal interview followed the written tests, the subject being already acquainted with the investigator and familiar with the purpose of the investigation. The individual interview has many obvious advantages over the written test: the opportunity to question in depth; to use follow-up questions; to establish rapport; to evoke interest – and so to improve motivation. Above all, the use of visual, rather than verbal, testing devices proved a great stimulus.

The overwhelming majority of the 360 subjects tested were interested, responsive, at ease, and happy, not to say eager, to express themselves. Frankness was the outstanding impression throughout – in particular, in the revelation of personal peccadilloes. Many were obviously flattered at having their own views sought. Outstanding, too, if disquieting, was the obvious novelty of thinking and talking about moral behaviour in a variety of concrete, familiar situations. There was, it may be added, a refreshing absence of any equivalent of the constant 'Monsieur' in Piaget's responses.

Stress was laid on anonymity from the first meeting with each group for completing the written tests. Each group was given code letters, and each subject within the group his or her code number. Since this completely impersonal identification had to be used on each of the six written tests, every subject was repeatedly reminded of anonymity. At the individual interview the subject's code number was again used on each response sheet, and the 'personal details' sheet left until last, so as to maintain anonymity throughout the testing. How far this procedure motivated frankness it is difficult to say, since the issue never arose. At times, it must be said, anonymity seemed not merely superfluous but artificial – and even disappointing to some subjects. But at least it drove home the repeated assurance that the tests had nothing to do with school work, even less with examinations; that the results would not be seen by any member of the school staff; and that no one would know the identity of any subject.

Projection tests

Five visual projection tests were devised for the personal interview, and carefully designed so that the subject had only one child with whom to identify. Questions followed the pattern of 'What is he/she going to do?' The aim was therefore that the subject should project himself or herself into the situation depicted.

While the concept of projection originated with Freud, the evaluation of projective techniques is by no means limited to psychoanalytic – or, indeed, behaviouristic – interpretations. Projective psychology is, in fact, 'strongly committed to a dynamic rather than static approach to behavior' (Abt & Bellak, 1959). Projective tests have four characteristics that made them most appropriate for this research. First, a primary assumption is that 'the individual will "project" his characteristic modes of response into such a task' (Anastasi, 1961, 17). Secondly, such tests 'are expected to elicit responses involving not only cognitive factors (that is, those that relate to what is present to the senses and to which meaning is given), but also affective factors (that is, feelings about what is there)' (Freeman, 1963, 612f.). Thirdly, since such tests are disguised, in that their purpose cannot be identified by the subject, deliberate deception, if only to make a good impression, becomes difficult – especially since 'the subject is rarely aware of the type of psychological interpretation that will be made of his responses' (Anastasi, op. cit., 564). This fact was particularly relevant to the moral field, where the obvious pat answer ('It is wrong to . . .') may bear no relation to inner attitudes.

A final characteristic of projective techniques, seen by Anastasi as their 'chief distinguishing feature', is 'their assignment of a relatively unstructured task' (op. cit., 564). Responses are thus 'neither right nor wrong', but rather 'the subject's own spontaneous interpretations or creations. . . . The term "unstructured", as used in projective testing, means that the elements or attributes of the situation do not form a uniform and clearly defined pattern for all who encounter it'; and thus 'the stimulus situation can elicit a variety of responses from an individual. Projective tests . . . differ in the degree to which they are unstructured' (Freeman, op. cit., 613, footnote). Minimal structuring of our test devices was found to be absolutely essential in order to rule out the devious byways, produced by agile brains and fertile imaginations, that distracted attention from centring squarely upon the moral dilemma.

Projection broke down with two types of subjects, though they were few in number. Some self-righteous subjects made a fierce verbal condemnation of the child portrayed. The comment, 'He would, but I wouldn't', had to be met with the question, 'What would you have done, then?' as an introduction to analysis of the situation. A few older adolescents, secondly, saw through the projection device with some such comment as 'You really want to know what I think, don't you'. Here it was legitimate to explain that this was so, and that projection was a device to help younger children express themselves freely and unselfconsciously. The subjects concerned were just as happy to give their own consciously personal reactions. Some, indeed, at all ages, fell naturally into the first person.

Criticism of projection tests centres upon lack of norms, defective validity, and subjectivity. Norms are indeed hard enough to come by in the whole area of personality measurement, while our summary of research has shown them to be conspicuously absent in the moral field. Whether, and on what basis, norms are to be sought for in developing moral judgement remains an open question. Since our main concern was developmental, our four ascending levels of moral judgement provided an adequate yardstick. Validity was sought by experimenting with a number of visual projection devices, wholly unstructured, during a lengthy period of pre-testing. Those were retained which, with minimal structuring, satisfied the acid test of validity in really testing what we wished to test (Goldman, op. cit., 45). The element of subjectivity may enter into administration – as Piaget so disarmingly admitted (op. cit., 208) – as well as into the assessment and scoring of responses. We have from the outset stressed the subjectivity inherent in any such study as this. The practical limitations of this research, preventing *inter alia* the use of a panel of judges, may have added to it. We sought to limit it by standardised structuring and a standardised *pro forma* for each test, developed during pre-testing. For the rest, responses must speak for themselves.

Scoring

The four levels of moral judgement – anomy, heteronomy, socionomy and autonomy – gave us an ascending scale of A, B, C, D, to be scored 1, 2, 3, 4 respectively. A sophistication that proved absolutely essential was the use of half-scores, since a subject's overall responses to a given test were often indicative of two overlapping levels of judgement. Thus anomy (A-1) might be found mingling with heteronomy (B-2), producing a score of 1½. With Piaget, who insists that his 'stages' overlap, we may not only accept such mixed responses, but, indeed, expect them. But unlike Piaget, who preferred to analyse his responses in terms of 'broad stages', and who happily found negligible qualifications among them, we found the recognition of such mixed responses not only to be essential in itself, but also to promote exactitude in assessment and precision in scoring. In addition, the use of half-scores was a further limitation on any unconscious tendency to interpret responses subjectively.

Verbalism

Goldman, concerned with the development of religious thinking, and in the context of projective methods, saw three aspects of the problem of verbalism in testing: 'How far is the test merely one of verbal facility? . . . How far can the child convey a higher ability than he actually possesses? . . . How far can the child consciously deceive?' (Goldman, op. cit., 46). Verbalism is no less possible in the moral sphere. But we were struck, first, by the obvious novelty, to many subjects, of conscious and explicit discussion of moral situations; and this was true even of adolescents. A second strong impression was that the moral knowledge of children is overwhelmingly negative, rather than positive. They are armed with a string of negative shibboleths, maxims, precepts, injunctions. These may be good and useful, so far as they go – save for the dubious morality of such tags as 'Honesty is the best policy'. But by and large, children were uncertain when confronted with a moral situation which no known maxim quite fits – and the more so when confronted with the necessity to say *why* a certain line of action is right or wrong.

We sought to avoid verbalism in various ways. First was the establishment of good rapport, already noted. Emphasis was laid, too, upon the fact that there were no 'right' or 'wrong' answers, that the tests had nothing to do with the school, and, above all, that we simply wanted to know what children think. Again, follow-up questions probed apparently superficial verbalisms. Another device was to reverse the formally correct judgement made. Thus: 'You think he would not steal, because it is wrong. Let's suppose he did take something. How would he feel? . . .' Such a reversal of the situation opened up further analysis, revealing more genuine attitudes.

Goldman further notes the 'five types of reaction revealed by clinical interview' as analysed by Piaget (1929, *The Child's Conception of the World*). They are: 'answers at random, romancing answers, suggested conviction answers, liberated conviction answers and spontaneous conviction answers. The two latter are sought for by any interviewer who seeks to liberate ideas about problems already thought through or to evolve spontaneous thought about a problem obviously new to the child' (Goldman, op. cit., 46). Our methodology was dominated throughout by this aim. The main problem lay, of course, with suggested conviction responses. How far is it possible to distinguish between the parrot repetition of an adult shibboleth and an at least partially interiorised precept? Piaget, of course, had no hesitation in tossing aside 'little sermons'. We sought to be less subjective. Projective devices certainly helped here, as did follow-up questioning directed towards justification of the response made. Moreover, the *pro forma* for each visual test provided for probing more than one aspect of the situation. For example, cheating was examined not only in terms of the classroom situation, but also in the context of games. Hence the possibility of securing a comprehensive response pattern, when responses to one single aspect of the situation might have been quite unrepresentative.

Constructing visual tests

Established tests in the moral field are few, and wholly verbal, and this was found to be as true of the American market, in psychological tests, as of the English. Given, therefore, our experience of the great value of visual tests, we had to devise our own. A number of criteria governed our choice and construction of them.

First, experience gained from the early, experimental testing clearly indicated two necessities if interviews were not to become diffuse and circumlocutory discussions. First, each situation had to be minimally structured in order to rule out irrelevancies that side-stepped direct confrontation with the moral dilemma. Secondly, we needed a standardised *pro forma*, with a set pattern of questions, that also concentrated upon the moral situation and probed reactions to it. Both these necessities were evolved and stabilised during the process of pre-testing.

A second criterion was the need for strict neutrality, or ambiguity, in the visual presentation of each moral situation, so that the child portrayed in the visual device might act in entirely different ways.

Again, testing devices needed to be relevant to the child's life and concerns, if they were to be evocative. They must be true to familiar background – home, school, friends, pets, and so on. That they achieved such relevance was indicated by such comments as 'It happened to me once'; 'I once had my purse stolen'; 'I can't lie to my Mum. She always knows'. Closely allied to relevance was the criterion of meaning. Each situation had to be meaningful and significant, if projection was to be achieved. Any element of artificiality would have clearly prevented it.

A supreme criterion was, of course, universality. The moral situations to be used had to be universally applicable to our wide age-range of from 7 to 17 years. It was on this ground that two experimental visual tests were rejected and a third adapted. Those finally used retained their significance for all age-groups. Two, indeed, concerned with the value of life and with lying, became more evocative with increasing age.

But while each test situation was thus universal in theme, its actual depiction needed to be appropriate to both the sex and age of the individual subject, in order to facilitate projection. For each test scene we had therefore eight variant visuals. Four showed a boy, and four showed a girl, in the identical situation. The ages depicted in each set of four were – a younger and an older primary child, a younger and an older secondary child. The ages aimed at were about 8 years, 11 years, 13 years, 16 years.

A final criterion was simplicity. In each visual situation there must be only one child with whom the subject might identify himself or herself; there should be no distracting background, other than that essential to the situation; and the situation depicted should be clear, simple, direct.

Such were the positive criteria in our construction of visual testing devices. Negative criteria, though important, need not be elaborated. We had at all costs to avoid the artificial, the abnormal, the fanciful. No less important was the necessity to avoid any scenes that might arouse uneasiness or suspicion, embarrassment or fear, bearing in mind that we were testing a wide age-range and both sexes.

Selection of moral situations

A study of the outstanding visual projection tests – the Rorschach Ink-blots, the Thematic Apperception Test, the Children's Apperception Test, the Blacky Pictures, the Make a Picture Story, and the Rosenzweigh Picture-frustration Study – did not materially assist our planning. The essential criterion of universality, for example, ruled out the attractive possibility of portraying animals, appropriate only to younger children. We had to find moral situations of supreme significance to both primary and secondary age-groups. Fortunately, research indicated that they coincide.

Pringle and Edwards (1964), in examining 'Some Moral Concepts and Judgements of Junior School Children', used a 'Moral Wickedness Test', derived from an earlier study by Macaulay and Watkins (1926, *An Investigation into the Development of the Moral Concepts of Children*, Parts 1 & 2, The Forum of Education, IV). The 226 subjects tested – the entire fourth year in two junior schools in the Midlands, 109 boys and 117 girls – had to list in descending order the actions they regarded as most wicked. The results showed 'considerable unanimity over the six most wicked actions, and also on their respective degrees of wickedness'. The six actions were: (1) murder; (2) physical cruelty; (3) stealing; (4) cruelty to animals; (5) lying; (6) damage to property. Cheating was amongst the lengthy list of wicked actions mentioned by less than 8%. The sexes were 'very unanimous', save that 'more girls than boys thought stealing, cruelty to animals, lying and swearing to be wicked' (Pringle & Edwards, 1964).

The same 'Moral Wickedness Test' was used, among others, by Edwards (1965) in a study of 'Some Moral Attitudes of Boys in a Secondary Modern School'. His subjects were 234 boys, 102 aged 11 years and 132 aged 14 to 15 years, in the first and last years of a secondary modern boys' school in the Midlands. The six actions judged to be most wicked were:

	No.	%
1. Murder	192	32·8
2. Torture, physical cruelty	108	18·4
3. Steal, rob	89	15·2
4. Cruelty to animals	66	11·2
5. Blackmail	44	7·5
6. H-bomb war	17	2·9

'Both younger and older agree on the main types', Edwards concluded. Cheating, one of our later concerns, was not mentioned.

These two researches produce the following close correspondence in child-judgement on the most wicked actions:

Primary	*Secondary*
1. Murder	1. Murder
2. Physical cruelty	2. Physical cruelty, torture
3. Stealing	3. Steal, rob
4. Cruelty to animals	4. Cruelty to animals
5. Lying	5. Blackmail
6. Damage to property	6. H-bomb war

No other similar studies were found. But such close correspondence strongly suggested that these were the universal and outstanding evils to the young. Such proved to be the case; we did, moreover, confirm their significance from our own use of the 'Moral Wickedness Test' among our written tests (Chapter 10).

The first four and identical items were obviously essential. Murder and physical cruelty could be taken as one theme – the value of life. Stealing and cruelty to animals provided our second and third situations. For our fourth we took lying – fifth in the primary list, and only tenth in the secondary boys list with a mere 1·02%. But we can agree with Piaget that, not only is lying well-nigh universal among young children: it also goes to the very heart of all personal relationships, so that 'we see the first signs' of autonomy when the child 'discovers that truthfulness is necessary to the relations of sympathy and mutual respect' (Piaget, op. cit., 194).

For the theme of our fifth and final visual test we chose cheating. It was insignificant in the judgements of primary children and non-existent in the judgements of the secondary boys. It carries, therefore, little or no moral significance for children. But cheating is a familiar enough temptation in the competitive English classroom – as contrasted, for example, with the Soviet education system (e.g. Bronfenbrenner, 1962*b*). It arises, moreover, in play. Judgements on cheating would, we might think, be cognitive rather than affective; and this fact alone gave reason for using it.

We thus arrived at five moral themes for our visual, projective testing devices: the value of life, stealing, cruelty to animals, lying, cheating.

Depicting the five moral themes

The five visual testing devices, used to portray these five selected themes, may be briefly described in the order in which they were used.

The visual concerned with cruelty to animals provided a pleasant and interesting opening to the individual interview, as well as helping to establish rapport. It presented no direct moral challenge of deep personal concern. It was not so deeply evocative as the other visuals, primarily, no doubt, as not involving personal relationships. In the event, it was decided not to use responses to this test in our developmental analysis. It therefore has no further place in this study. We may simply note that it was easy enough to depict – a child with a stick in his or her raised hand, the dog waiting expectantly. The stick might be used to hit the pet or to throw in play. An interesting analysis, beyond the scope of this study, could be made of anthropomorphism in children's concepts of animals from the responses to this test.

The second visual used was that concerned with the value of life, embracing the child's universal concern with both murder and physical cruelty. As a rare, rather than daily, moral concern it made far less personal challenge than stealing or lying. In the event, it proved powerfully evocative, not least in delineating the development of conscience. We needed to avoid violence or aggression, bearing in mind younger and more sensitive subjects, as well as any hackneyed contest between 'goodies' and 'baddies'. We depicted a drowning scene – a child in the water, crying for help, with a lone child on the bank as the only possible source of help. Limited but precise structuring of this scene proved absolutely essential to rule out any other possible source of help. Strong attitudes were evinced – increasing, rather than diminishing, with age.

The cheating situation was used third, before the more challenging concerns of stealing and lying. The visual showed two children sitting side by side in the classroom, one looking over towards the other of necessity so as to suggest the possibility of cheating. It was stressed, in structuring the scene, that the child 'might simply be looking that way'.

That the majority of subjects inferred cheating might be attributed to a lack of complete ambiguity in the scene. But, as already seen, cheating is an artificial, rather than intrinsic, moral offence to children, fabricated as it is by a competitive educational system. It is, moreover, well-nigh universal, and in some circumstances may be motivated by the morality of loyalty, rather than by the immorality of self-interest.

The fourth visual test led the interview on to the far more significant and serious choice between honesty and dishonesty regarding property. As Piaget notes, stealing is a far less common temptation than lying; but the possibility is always there. Three visual devices were rejected as proving insufficiently evocative. That finally chosen showed a child in the school cloakroom, alone and totally unobserved, with a half-open satchel or bag, according to age, offering the possibility of stealing. This scene proved far more evocative than the best of the rejected visuals depicting stealing from a sweet-shop. This, we deduced, was due to its involving personal, rather than impersonal, theft.

The fifth and final visual test concerned lying. The constant choice between lying and truth-telling was left until last as being the most personal, intimate and intense of our moral situations. The cloakroom stealing scene, having proved so evocative, was also used for the lying situation in preference to any of the three discarded stealing visuals. All that we needed in addition were two portraits of adults – one of a man, representing either teacher or father, for use with boys; and one of a woman, representing teacher or mother, for use with girls. The cloakroom scene, together with the adult portrait, made up a moral situation in which the child is being questioned by either parent or teacher – it now being assumed that he or she had taken something from the cloakroom. Pre-testing experience showed that interpreting the adult as parent, rather than as teacher, was infinitely more evocative of deeply personal responses.

The individual interview

The personal interview was thus standardised, carefully constructed and patterned. The five visual tests, presented in the order given, made for gradual progression from pets to the most intimate personal moral situations.

It remained to conclude the interview by completing the *pro forma* of personal details, including code number, sex, age, school and class, father's work, and details of religious background.

Anonymity was preserved throughout both written tests and personal interview by the use of code numbers. It is by these alone that we can identify the 360 subjects tested.

Personal details sheet

Number in class register______________________________

Boy or girl____

Age____________years____________months__________

School____

Class or form______________________________________

Father's work______________________________________

Church or chapel on Sunday__________________________

Name of Church or Chapel____________________________

*What you attend*____________________________________

Sunday School______________Other____________________

Bible Class________________Who you go with____________

Service____________________Who you go with____________

*How often you go*___________________________________

Once a week_______________________________________

Once a month______________________________________

Sometimes____

Hardly ever____

Never____

____

____

____

Pre-testing

In the process of pre-testing we had three main concerns. The first was to assess how far the visual tests we had devised were significant and evocative in terms of their moral concerns, and how far they effectively focused upon them. The five finally selected satisfied our criteria. Three others were rejected as unsatisfactory. Our second concern was with structuring each scene, as minimally but as essentially necessary, and with standardising our questioning so as to achieve parallel focus upon the moral situation. So similar were the responses made, indicative of the four levels of moral judgement forming the basis of our assessment, that they could be included on each *pro forma* and so reduce note-taking during the interview to the more individualistic responses. This advantage affected our third and methodological concern. Initially a tape-recorder was used to record interviews, with later transcription, on the assumption that this would help concentration upon the subject by avoiding the interruption of writing. But the development of a standardised *pro forma*, enabling the interviewer simply to underline familiar responses, made for greater ease in recording distinctive responses.

Pre-testing of the visual devices took place in 2 infant schools, 3 primary schools, 1 mixed secondary modern school and 1 boys' grammar school. The subjects: 6 infants, 18 junior and 12 secondary pupils – ranged in age from 5 years 11 months to 17 plus years. They consisted of 15 girls and 21 boys, and were representative of above-average, average and below-average ability. The experience gained standardised our tests and procedures, and gave confidence in them.

Pilot testing

The overall picture of developing moral judgement that we sought required a broad age-span. It was decided to test subjects from 7 to 17 years inclusive, and that an adequate picture could be obtained by testing subjects of every other, rather than of every, year of age. We thus arrived at 6 age groups: 7, 9, 11, 13, 15 and 17 years. Pilot testing was therefore conducted with all 6 age groups, using 2 boys and 2 girls from each. The age span was from 6·11 to 17·2, and the range of I.Q. from 77 to 125. 5 primary and 4 secondary schools were used, and, for the 17-year age-group, 1 art college and 1 technical college.

Pilot testing suggested only minor amendments to our testing procedure. Previous conclusions were substantially confirmed, and experience of interviewing gained. Familiarity with the testing procedure facilitated concentration upon the subject and upon creating a friendly atmosphere. In particular, we learned how to vary our approach with reticent and less able subjects, and to change a line of questioning so as to get beneath routine responses and to tap underlying attitudes.

Testing procedure was thus standardised for the final testing. The average length of interviews was from 30 to 45 minutes, but as much as between 60 and 90 minutes with very reticent and backward subjects. Boredom was avoided by the change from one visual to another, and fatigue similarly minimised by the change from one scene to another helping to sustain interest.

Neither hostility nor apathy was encountered, and shyness was rare. 'When will it be my turn?' was the kind of comment. We cannot overstress the novelty for our subjects of dealing with moral situations; nor the immense value of visual-testing devices. The overwhelming impressions were of friendliness and, above all, frankness.

The final sample

Experimental testing began in 1964 and pre-testing in the autumn of 1965. The bulk of the testing was completed during 1966. All the schools used were urban schools in the south-west, involving the generous cooperation of three local education authorities. The geographical area from which our subjects were derived extended from the Bristol Channel to the English Channel.

In all, 6 infant and primary schools, 8 secondary schools, 1 art college and 1 technical college were used in the final testing. In no case was reference to parents proposed or necessitated. We may add, in this context, that, given the gross limitation of the term 'moral' to sexual relationships, it was stressed from the outset that we had no concern with sexual morality, as our age-span amply indicates.

Given our six age-groups – 7, 9, 11, 13, 15, and 17 years – we required an adequate, but not too onerous, sample from each. Given, too, our concern with the sex variable, we required an equal number of subjects from each sex. It was decided that 60 subjects, 30 of each sex, would be adequately representative of each age-group. Our final sample consisted therefore of 360 subjects.

For testing the three primary age-groups of 7, 9 and 11 years it was possible to take two unstreamed classes, each from a different school, for each age-group. The use of cohorts of unstreamed classes ensured randomness, so far as is humanly possible. The six schools used represented four different urban areas and three local education authorities. Save that one was a voluntary controlled school, none had any special features, and most were socially mixed.

Samples from the 13- and 15-year age-groups had clearly to be derived from both modern and grammar schools in the three local education authorities concerned. Since in all three an average of 25% of pupils are selected for grammar schools, we needed, theoretically, 75% of the sample in both these two age-groups from modern schools, and 25% from grammar schools. Since we needed an equal number of boys and girls in each age-group sample of 60, this theoretical figure was adapted. It was decided to test 44 modern pupils and 16 grammar pupils – 22 and 8 respectively of each sex – in each of these two age-groups. In all, 7 schools were used – 2 modern boys' and 2 modern girls' schools, 1 boys' and 1 girls' grammar school, and 1 mixed grammar school. Subjects were selected at random from class registers, small classes being brought together where necessary.

The 17-year age-group raised difficulties in terms of randomness. A theoretical 25% from grammar school would no longer be representative, given the fact that only a proportion of pupils stay on to that age. We therefore reduced the number of grammar school subjects from 16 to 10, with 5 of each sex, chosen at random. We now required 50 subjects from a modern school background who could not be derived from schools. An attempt to secure them from youth clubs failed. Suitable adolescents proved unreliable; reliable adolescents tended to have a grammar school background. We therefore had no alternative to using further education institutions. We were able to use the printing department of an art college for the 25 males required and the business studies department of a technical college for the 25 females required. In both cases we asked for a random group of subjects with a secondary modern background. The obvious limitation was that, having opted for further education, these 50 subjects represented the higher elements among secondary modern pupils rather than a random selection – save that some of the males were on day-release from local industry. This defect in randomness, in the 17-year age-group, must be recognised, although in all other respects, in terms of variables, this age-group sample was representative.

Age

At each of our six age-levels we had a theoretical range of six months either side of the year. Since final testing took place over almost a calendar year, minor differences were inevitable. But actual ranges, in the event, fell broadly within these theoretical ranges, in the separate sex-groups at each age-level. Two exceptions must, however, be noted.

First, in the 7-year age-group the boys ranged from 6.2 to 7.9, and the girls from 6.3 to 7.9. This wider range was due to deliberately taking half the sample from the top year of an infants' school and half from the first year of a primary school. The resulting widening of age-range was thought valuable for two reasons. First, it gave us a broader picture at the minimum limit of our age-group. Secondly, it compensated somewhat for the impossibility of administering written tests to such young children, in giving somewhat fuller evidence of moral thinking in the younger child. The resulting mean age for the whole age-group of 7 years 0·1 month was, in the event, an identical mean with that of the 9- and 11-year age-groups.

The second exception involved males in the 17-year age-group, at the other extreme. Here the theoretical age-span was extended fortuitously, rather than intentionally. However, 83% of the sample fell within the agreed age-span, and the mean age for this male group was 18 years 1·1 month.

Mean ages for the six groups were:

7 years, 0·1 month
9 years, 0·1 month
11 years, 0·1 month
13 years, 2·1 months
15 years, 2·9 months
16 years, 11·5 months

Intelligence (I.Q.)

Age	*Boys Group Range N-30*	*Girls Group Range N-30*	*Mean I.Q. Boys N-30*	*Mean I.Q. Girls N-30*	*Mean I.Q. Group N-30*
7	80 minus 128	87 125 plus	108·2	108·8	108·5
9	80 minus 125 plus	80 minus 125 plus	110·8	107·8	109·3
11	77 120	74 118	96·9	105·8	101·3
13	77 130	87 125	98·5	106·3	102·4
15	93 128	95 137	104·6	108·5	106·5
17	89 124	96 119	106·4	108·2	107·3

Given our concern with intelligence, as a potentially significant variable in moral judgement, a measure of ability was necessary if relationship between intelligence and moral judgement was to be traced. Intelligence quotient, rather than mental age, was necessary for statistical analysis.

The I.Q. was normally derived from the school. Where it was not available, generally in the lower half of the primary school, the I.Q. was obtained by the use of Raven's Coloured Matrices in conjunction with the Chrichton Vocabulary Scale. This combined test is considered unreliable at either extreme. The one can only be scored at 80 minus, the other at 125 plus.

The range of ability was reasonably comprehensive for the sex groups at each age-level. The mean I.Q. for each complete age-group was:

7-year	108·5
9-year	109·3
11-year	101·3
13-year	102·4
15-year	106·5
17-year	107·3

The means seemed the more reasonably representative if, as some hold, the pragmatic norm for I.Q. is nearer 105 than 100.

Socio-economic class

The five-class scale, adopted for statistical purposes, was derived from the 1951 Census 'Classification of Occupations' (General Register Office, H.M.S.O., 1956), with adjustments made in the light of the 1961 Census, more particularly in details of classification within the five classes. These were confirmed with a Ministry of Labour official.

To maintain uniformity with our other ascending scales, the Census descending scale was inverted to become:

Class 1: Unskilled	Score 1
Class 2: Partly skilled	Score 2
Class 3: Skilled	Score 3
Class 4: Intermediate	Score 4
Class 5: Professional	Score 5

As compared with a derived median of 3·0, the resulting mean score for our six age-groups was:

7-year	2·80
9-year	2·66
11-year	2·73
13-year	2·90
15-year	2·74
17-year	2·93

Our age samples thus inclined slightly towards lower, rather than higher, socio-economic class.

This conclusion is confirmed by a comparison of our over-all percentages, falling within each class, with the 'Heads of Households' percentage figures in the 1951 Census:

	1951 Census	*Research Sample*	*Plus/minus*
Class 1	12·4%	7·21%	minus 5·19%
Class 2	16·5%	26·41%	plus 9·91%
Class 3	49·5%	47·78%	minus 1·72%
Class 4	18·3%	15·30%	minus 3·0%
Class 5	3·3%	3·3%	same

The comparison shows a slight shift of 3% in our sample towards lower socio-economic class, as compared with the national figures. While this need not be significant, it may be remarked that a weighting towards higher socio-economic class might well be considered the more unrepresentative and atypical.

Religious class

Since religious background was another of the variables with which this study was concerned, we needed some criterion to use as a statistical measure. Two criteria were, in fact, used.

The first and obvious measure is church attendance, serving as a yardstick of both Church affiliation and of exposure to religious influence. It is, in fact, the measure used by the Churches themselves. A five-point scale of church attendance, as used for example by Goldman (1962), was inverted to form an ascending scale:

Class 1	Never	Score 1
Class 2	Hardly ever	Score 2
Class 3	Sometimes	Score 3
Class 4	Once a month	Score 4
Class 5	Once a week	Score 5

Where a subject was a keen member of an evangelical group, such as Crusaders, meeting on a week-night, he was scored as in Class 5.

Church attendance may, however, be thought a crude criterion. We recall, too, the conclusion of such studies as that of Hartshorne & May (1930) that church attendance may be seen as part of a familial way of life, rather than as an influence *per se*. Again, we find in our samples a development with age towards decreasing weekly church attendance thus:

Age 7 years	60·0%
Age 9 years	41·6%
Age 11 years	50·0%
Age 13 years	48·3%
Age 15 years	23·3%
Age 17 years	18·3%

It follows that a subject who never goes to church, at a given age, may have attended regularly in earlier and formative years. Conversely, a regular attender may not be necessarily powerfully influenced. We have previously noted, too, the possibility that religious influence, particularly in the case of an authoritarian religious ethos, may hold the individual in the clamp of heteronomy.

Church attendance

Age-group percentages

Age-group	*Class 1, never*	*Classes 1 and 2, never and hardly ever*	*Class 5, weekly*	*Classes 4 and 5, weekly and monthly*
7-year	35·0%	35·0%	60·0%	65·0%
9-year	43·3%	45·0%	41·6%	45·0%
11-year	35·0%	40·0%	50·0%	53·3%
13-year	21·6%	25·0%	48·3%	68·3%
15-year	50·0%	55·0%	23·3%	36·6%
17-year	48·3%	58·3%	18·3%	28·3%

Analysis

1. At age 7 years, the peak year for church attendance, 35% have no church connection.
2. There is a developing decline in attendance from 7 years to 17 years of age.
3. The peak decline is between 13 years and 15 years of age.
4. The overall decline between the ages of 7 and 17 years is between 36·7% and 41·7%, of subjects who originally attended.

Religious attitudes

For these and, no doubt, other reasons, church attendance may be thought a crude criterion of religious background. We therefore derived another measure from one of the written tests, the Sentence Completion Test (see pp. 272ff.). It contained sixty items, of which fourteen were concerned with religion. Rejecting four of these as unsatisfactory, we derived ten religious items from this test, and scored each on a simple ascending five-point scale:

Score 1: Very negative
Score 2: Negative
Score 3: Neutral
Score 4: Positive
Score 5: Very positive

From the scored responses to these ten items a mean score was derived for each subject, which might be reasonably accepted as a measure of interiorised religious attitudes. This mean score could be correlated with both moral judgement scores, and also with the score derived from church attendance. Strong positive correlations were, in fact, found between church attendance and religious attitudes.

The ten religious items in the Sentence Completion Test were concerned with: saying prayers, singing hymns, going to church, reading the Bible, God, Jesus, Heaven, school assembly, seeing a church, being in church. They were carefully interspersed with items concerned with the environment, home relationships, morality, personal attitudes, and open items.

This second measure, of religious attitudes, augmented our first measure, of church attendance, in seeking to trace relationship, if any, between religious background and moral judgements.

The research project

Such, in brief, was the evolution of this research project both in purpose and in methodology. Every effort had been made to ensure that subjects were being tested on moral themes of key significance to children of all ages; that the visual devices and the pattern of testing focused effectively upon these themes; that the samples taken at each age were as random as we could make them; and that measures were available for seeking such relationship as might be found between moral judgements and the variables with which we were concerned.

Accepting the legitimacy of this methodology, as well as such limitations and defects as have been exposed, we may now analyse the levels of moral judgement revealed in responses to the four visual tests, used in individual interview, that formed the basis of this study.

Chapter 4
The value of life

The test

The drowning scene was designed to incorporate the two evils of primary significance to children of all ages – murder and physical cruelty. The achievement of its purpose may be attested by the numerous responses using the terms 'murder' and 'cruelty'. It sought, secondly, to focus attention upon this supreme value of physical life in a setting that involved no violence and that would be in no way frightening or disturbing. No such emotions were aroused, despite the immediacy and depth of projection. This test proved, in the event, the most evocative of all.

The test sheet provided for assessing responses in terms of our four levels, with half-scores for mixed responses; for exploring the concepts of guilt and conscience, should the terms arise; and for plumbing concepts in depth by the use of two further questions: Why should you try to save another person's life? Is saving an animal more important/less important/the same as saving a child? Needless to say, all such questions were simplified and adapted as necessary. The value of putting these two further questions will be evidenced by responses.

The value of life

Here is a picture of a boy/girl of about the same age as you. He/she has gone for a walk in the country far from home. He/she is all alone. Suddenly the boy/girl hears a cry for help, and sees someone struggling in the lake nearby. He/she does not know the boy/girl who is in danger of drowning. There are no other people there, and there's no phone-box for miles. What is the boy/girl going to do?

ABANDON

1. Tell anyone?

e.g. parents; teachers; friends; others____________________

What will they think or say?____________________

2. Not tell anyone

Anomy__________

Heteronomy__________

Socionomy__________

Autonomy__________

3. How would he/she feel?

Afraid; ashamed; conscience; guilty; happy; indifferent; don't care; miserable; proud; sad; sorry

Guilty?__________

Conscience?__________

(*a*) Where does it come from?__________

(*b*) What makes it grow?__________

(*c*) When does it start?__________

SAVE

A. Anomy e.g. get found out; get into trouble; might drown yourself;__________

B. Heteronomy e.g. parents; teachers; police; others;__________

C. Socionomy e.g. friends__________

reciprocity__________

D. Autonomy e.g. duty; conscience; guilt__________

Why save life?__________

Saving animal more important/less important/same as saving child?

____

Is saving life instinctive?

This test might be criticised on the ground that saving life is instinctive. Such a view would imply that the urge to save life is innate, and that no deliberate moral decision would be necessary in such a situation. Moral judgements upon it would, therefore, be superfluous, if not invalid.

Two answers may be made. First, it is broadly true that, for the adult, it is 'instinctive' to save life; and the actual term was, in fact, used by some of our older subjects. But it is quite another thing to assume, therefore, that such a 'natural' reaction is present from the earliest years of life. Sympathy may be innate from early childhood; we see it evident at 7 years in over half the boys' responses and in over two-thirds of the girls' responses. But sympathy is not automatically translated into selfless action. Nor can we assume that the moral equipment of the adult is inborn. Certainly, as Piaget holds, 'compassion' is one of the 'instinctive tendencies' (op. cit., 227). He goes on to claim that 'The play of sympathy and antipathy is a sufficient cause for practical reason to become conscious of reciprocity' (op. cit., 229). By ignoring or rejecting the 'My Mum told me' type of response, Piaget concludes that both sympathy and reciprocity develop independently of adult influence. We do not find this to be true. It is true, however, that it is not until the subject sees himself struggling in the water that action is motivated ('I'd want someone to save me if I was him'). Sympathy merges into reciprocity: and reciprocity may merge into autonomy. Thus, as with every other aspect of moral judgement, we find, not an inborn 'instinct', but rather a process of development; and to its end-product, autonomous moral judgement, the obligation to save life may have become so much 'second nature' as to seem 'instinctive'.

Such a conclusion is supported, secondly, by the empirical evidence of our responses. In the earlier age-groups we find evidence of anomy and, far more substantially, of heteronomy. Both naturally decrease with increasing age. But if we add together the percentage responses of anomy and heteronomy, at each age-level, we find these totals:

Anomy and Heteronomy

Age-group	*Boys*	*Girls*	*Age-group*	*Boys*	*Girls*
7	46·6%	25·0%	13	13·3%	0·0%
9	40·0%	30·0%	15	11·6%	1·7%
11	23·3%	18·3%	17	1·6%	3·3%

HELP!
S.T.
HELP!
S.T.
HELP!
S.T.
HELP!
S.T.

HELP!
S.T.
HELP!
S.T.
HELP!
S.T.
HELP!
S.T.

Since these figures represent the responses of subjects for whom it is *not* instinctive to save life, we have evidence for explicitly rejecting such an argument. Rather do we see a similar development to that which we shall find in our other areas of moral concern.

Sympathy and the maternal instinct

Sex differences are already apparent in the above figures. Girls show a greater initial measure of sympathy and reciprocity than boys, as indicated by these percentage totals for the first three age-groups:

Sympathy and reciprocity

Age-group	*Boys*	*Girls*
7	53·3%	75·0%
9	60·0%	68·3%
11	68·3%	73·3%

This evidence would seem to be consonant with McDougall's dictum that '. . . all altruistic conduct has its root and origin in the maternal instinct' (op. cit., 175) – a contrast indeed with Piaget's almost total unawareness of the sex factor as of his finding the 'root' in the cognitive.

It would certainly be in such a situation, that of saving life, above all others, that such an instinct as the maternal would be involved. This might seem, therefore, an adequate explanation for the higher level of girls' responses. But we shall, in fact, find girls in advance of boys in our other moral situations – cheating, stealing, lying – where no such instinct would seem to be involved.

7-YEAR AGE-GROUP: BOYS

While there were no fully anomous responses in the youngest boys, we find such mixed responses as:

> 'He'd get beaten up by the boy's friends if he was found out. It would be unkind to let him drown. God and Jesus would save him if he didn't.'

Typical of this age is a preoccupation with rewards; and, while rewards, with punishments, are the sanctions of the heteronomous level, they are not easily distinguishable from the pain and pleasure criteria of anomy. Thus:

'The boy's Mummy might give him some money.'

Three subjects speak with one voice:

'You get a reward and become famous.'

'You become famous and get a reward.'

'You get a medal for being brave.'

Heteronomy is emphatic at this age. The authority may be divine:

(Why save life?) ' 'Cos God says you should. Jesus might have told him to.'

The religiosity of this response was emphasised by the addition of

' . . . who lives up in heaven' (subject pointing upwards).

Or again:

' 'Cos God doesn't like them to die. The spirit of heaven would make him go in. It's something which comes and helps you, from heaven, from where God lives.'

The authority may be school:

'We are taught at school that we must help others.'

Or Sunday school:

'You must help people. We learn that at Sunday school.'

Or parents:

'Mum and Dad told me that I ought to help people.'

'His Mummy and Daddy would be annoyed that he hadn't tried to help.'

Authority and poignant sympathy are combined in:

'The boy might drown. It would be all lonely for him under the water. He won't see his Mum and Dad any more. . . . His Dad could punish the boy for not saving him.'

That it would be 'unkind' to abandon the child in the water is a frequent response. Sympathy is expressed in other ways too:

'He would feel so sorry for him.'

'His mother might be worried.'

'He wouldn't want him to drown. His Mummy would want him back.'

Sympathy merges into reciprocity in:

(Why save life?) 'I just think that you should.'

'I wouldn't like to drown.'

'I'd expect someone to save me.'

7-YEAR AGE-GROUP: GIRLS

For some girls, too, rewards are important in this age-group:

'She would like to get a reward.'

Fame is a similar spur:

'She would get her name in the papers and be famous.'

'She would get a medal and her friends would cheer her. She would like that.'

Heteronomy is expressed by:

'Her Mummy would tell her off if she let her drown.'

' 'Cos the girl's in danger. It would be naughty to let her drown.'

But over two-thirds of the girls' responses indicate sympathy. in one form or another:

'She felt sorry for the person in the water and wanted to help. She just wanted to – she's a kind girl.'

'She wouldn't like to see anyone drown.'

'It's not kind to let her drown.'

'She wants to save her from drowning, even though she doesn't know her.'

And the religious note appears in:

'It would be cruel to leave her. She would do it for Jesus, for God.'

Sympathy merges into reciprocity in:

'She thinks how she would feel if she was in the water.'

Reciprocity may be positive:

'If I was drowning I would want to be saved.'

Or negative:

'She wouldn't want to drown. She never hurt her. It would be unkind to leave her.'

Two responses suggest something beyond reciprocity:

'She wants to help. It is natural to her.'

'She just feels inside her that she wants to help.'

9-YEAR AGE-GROUP: BOYS

The hope of reward, while less prominent in this age-group, still appears:

'The boy's parents may reward him.'

'It would be the right thing to do. He'd get a reward. He'd be a good boy. He'd show off his life-saving.'

Hope of reward is mingled with authority in:

'God would tell me to, in my mind.' (Why save life?) 'You might get a reward.'

And with more authority in:

'The police would blame him if he didn't. He was the only person around.' (Why save life?) 'He might get a reward.'

Hope of reward is mixed with reciprocity, as well as authority, in:

'If the boy didn't drown and told the police, he'd get into trouble.' (Why save life?) 'He might be rewarded – that's what he's hoping.' 'He would want someone to save him.'

Fear of punishment is allied with reciprocity in:

'He'd only get found out, anyway.' (Why save life?) 'He'd want to be saved if he was drowning.'

And again:

'He would expect to be saved.' (Why save life?) 'Because if the boy *did* manage to get out, he would hit you if you hadn't helped.' *You* might need to be saved one day.'

Heteronomy is decreasing but still appears, as in:

'It's good to save life. Mother and Father told me.'

It is apparent, too, in the response, 'It's the right thing to do'; especially so when no reason can be given for saving life.

It is now that the term 'murder' or the equivalent, 'killing', makes its first appearance:

'If you did leave him it would be just like murder.'

'It would be horrible to see a person drown. It's like murder. All life is good.'

'It would be just like killing him.'

Direct socionomy is apparent in:

'Other people wouldn't think much of him if he left him to drown.'

A sense of the value of life now becomes much more explicit:

'He'd save him because it's a person. He could make friends with him after.' (Why save life?) 'If you didn't, there'd be nobody left in the world.' (More important to save animal or child?) 'You can get another dog, but not another person.'

Or again, if more odd:

'He wouldn't like to see people die; he'd be sad.' (Why save life?) 'To save taking up space to bury them . . . His parents would miss him. . . . An animal could have babies.'

Reciprocity now becomes more and more prominent, as in:

'I would want someone to save me if I was drowning.'

'If you're in danger, somebody might come along and help you.'

'You don't want to die. You don't want to die yourself.'

'If he was in the water and couldn't swim, he'd want to be saved.'

Religious colouring appears in:

'If he went away, it would be turning from God and being with the devil.' (Why save life?) 'If you're kind to them, they'll be kind to you.'

'Someone might have saved you, and you would know what it's like to be killed. God made us to live, and not to be killed.'

9-YEAR AGE-GROUP: GIRLS

Three responses illustrate the usefulness of the subordinate question contrasting human life and animal life:

'She might get a reward. . . . Teacher told her at school that she must do it. . . . An animal has a few more lives.'

'It wouldn't be right to let him drown. . . . She might get a reward. There are plenty more dogs in shops. You can't buy little girls in shops.'

'She'd get found out. . . . It wouldn't be very nice if she was the one out there drowning. . . . A girl can be more use than animals.'

Heteronomy is clear-cut in:

'Teacher told us that it is the right thing to do.'

'She wouldn't want to be blamed for letting her drown.'

Heteronomy is combined with reciprocity in:

'She has been told that it's the right thing to do by Teacher. . . . She would want to be saved if she was drowning.'

Confused religious verbalism appears in:

'It's the right thing to do. She feels she wants to help her. Something in her body tells her that she must – it's the devil.' (Why save life?) 'You're doing it for God. He wouldn't love you if you left someone to drown.'

As with the boys, reciprocity grows out of sympathy:

'If she was in the water the person would save her.' (Why save life?) 'Because it's kind. The saved person would be nice to them.'

'If she were in there she would go and help her.'

'She'd want to be saved if she was drowning.'

'She would want saving herself if it was her. I wouldn't like to drown myself.'

'You wouldn't like to see somebody walking by.'

'If she fell in, somebody might not help her.'

'It could have been you in there.'

Three responses stand out. One hints at saving life as being instinctive:

'It's the best thing. . . . It's the only thing any human would do.'

Religious motivation is shown by:

'One day she might be in difficulty herself, and if the same person saw her he would save her in return.' (Why save life?) 'Because you're helping God if you help others.'

An interiorised attitude is suggested by:

'If she was the one that was drowning, she'd want to be saved. She'd feel guilty about it if she didn't help.'

11-YEAR AGE-GROUP: BOYS

One low-level response is found in:

'He might get a reward.' (Why save life?) 'There'd be more people alive.' (Animal or child more important?) 'Animals. We get food from them. If we let them drown there'd be no food for us.'

A very mixed response is:

'He might get a reward. . . . His mother and father told him to. It would be unkind to leave him to drown. He'd like to be saved himself.'

The term 'murder' appears again. But much more significant is the explicit appearance of the term 'conscience' in this age-group, even if it may be initially little more than a verbalism. Thus:

'He'd have a guilty conscience.' (Why save life?) 'If you didn't there wouldn't be any people left.'

The concept, without the term, is suggested by:

'God knows everything. You would feel ashamed about it. You must save people. I learnt it in Sunday school. If you didn't save the person, it would stay in your heart all the time.'

It is in this age-group that reciprocity reaches its peak. We find sympathy merging into reciprocity in:

'It's being kind and gentle. . . . If he saves a life, he will be saved if he is in trouble.'

Reciprocity is clear-cut in:

'He would expect to be saved if it was him.'

'It could be *him* in the water instead.'

'If it was me, I'd want somebody to save me.'

And the first glimmerings of autonomy in:

'He'd have it on his mind. It's a human being in danger. He'd be very upset if he had left him.'

11-YEAR AGE-GROUP: GIRLS

Low and high levels are mingled in:

'She'd get found out if she didn't try to save the girl.' (Why save life?) 'If she didn't, her conscience would be bothered.'

'She'd be sure to get found out if she didn't.' (Why save life?) 'The girl might die and it would be on her mind.'

Heteronomy is expressed by such phrases as 'My mother said . . .'; 'She'd get into awful trouble'; 'She could go to court'. Heteronomy is mixed with reciprocity in:

'She might get into trouble if she didn't do anything.' (Why save life?) 'It's good to. I'd want to be saved.'

Such responses echo those of the boys in this age-group. But the strong sympathy of girls is indicated by such responses as:

'She's a human drowning, it would be unkind not to help. . . . Somebody might love her very much. They'd be sad.'

'She would think it's not very nice to leave her. I'd think so, too. Poor girl. . . .'

'It would be cruel to leave her. Life is precious to most people.'

'It would be like torturing someone if she didn't. Life is very valuable. It's all you've got.'

Reciprocity responses parallel those of the boys in number and in strength. Thus:

'She wouldn't like to drown, so she helps others.'

'If you want your life saved, then you must help others.'

'Others would help her, so she feels she must help somebody else.'

Such suggestions of the Golden Rule become explicit in:

'You must do as you would be done by. . . . Jesus saves us, so we must save others.'

'It's the right thing to do. You must do as you would be done by.'

Such similar responses, from subjects of the same school, suggest identical teaching of the Golden Rule. But the principle of it is even clearer in the responses from another school quoted above. Conscience is cited in two responses:

'If she didn't, she'd have it on her conscience.'

'Her conscience would worry her.'

A genuine religious response is suggested by:

'She might die. It's a human thing, a kind of brother, an equal. God made all of us. He wants us to live in peace, and save others.'

13-YEAR AGE-GROUP: BOYS

With the large-scale growth of autonomy, first solidly found in this age-group, low-level responses become minimal. But we still find such mixed responses as:

'He might get a reward. It's not nice to see anyone drown. Every life matters. Jesus said that in the Bible. You can't just throw away human life.'

'He might get a reward. . . . He might get into trouble. He'd have it on his conscience.'

The debt owed to heteronomy is consciously realised in:

'He's a human being. You should help a fellow-human.' (Why save life?) 'You learn it in books, and being told.'

'There's a bond between human beings. They belong to the same race. It's wrong to take human life; you should only save it. I got the idea from the Bible and from Sunday school.'

'Teachers would have told him always to give a helping hand when needed. His parents would be upset. It could happen to you.'

Reciprocity, while yielding place to conscience, is still evident, as in:

'It's another person. He would care. It might be him in there.'

'It's another life, like him. He'd expect the same treatment.' (Why save life?) 'It would be horrible and cruel not to. The world is a beautiful place, and people should be allowed to enjoy it to the full.'

But reciprocity merges into conscience as the motivating factor:

'You'd want to be saved yourself. He'd save the boy. His conscience would make him.'

'You'd put yourself in the other person's position. Conscience would bother you. If you didn't, you'd have the thought on your mind for the rest of your life.'

The term 'instinctive' now appears for the first time:

'He'd save him. It would be instinctive, a feeling that he should save him.'

Autonomy is clearly evidenced in such response as:

'You'd feel guilty. You'd have it on your conscience – you'd keep remembering.'

'He'd save the boy. He'd feel proud. I'd never forgive myself if I let him drown. I'd never forget it.'

'No one in their right mind could stand and see someone drown. They'd have it on their conscience.'

13-YEAR AGE-GROUP: GIRLS

This group is marked by a massive increase in autonomy and a complete absence of low-level responses. Reciprocity is much more emphatic, too, as in:

'She'd want someone to save her if she was in the water. It's important to help people in need. They depend on you.'

'The drowning girl has as much right to live as she has.'

Reciprocity has religious sanction in:

'If she were in the water she'd want someone to save her.' (Why save life?) 'God made us and wants us to help each other.'

'If I were there I'd want to be saved.' (Why save life?) 'They want to live, to enjoy life. . . . Human beings are much more important to God [than animals] because He made them.'

Reciprocity and conscience are linked in such responses as:

'If she was in the same position she'd like to be saved.' (If she didn't?) 'She'd feel awful; she'd have a bad conscience; she couldn't forget.'

'If she were in the water she'd want them to save her. God made us all. We are all the same, and we should love each other. I don't think God would have made us otherwise.'

With the development to autonomy the term 'instinctive' becomes familiar in responses. It is linked with reciprocity in:

'She'd save the girl's life. It would be instinctive. She'd expect to be treated in the same way.'

It is combined with conscience in:

'She'd have it on her conscience if she didn't.' (Why save life?) 'It's an instinct.'

'She'd do it just by instinct. She'd have it on her conscience if she didn't.' (Why save life?) 'It's such a wonderful thing.'

Of the 30 responses in this group of 13-year girls, 19 use the term 'conscience', providing definitions that substantiate the concept held.

15-YEAR AGE-GROUP: BOYS

Unique among all our responses, for their powerful anomy, are those of a boy in this group (I.Q. 113; S.E. 1; R.E. 1). His response is quoted for contrast, as being totally unrepresentative:

'He wouldn't risk his own life. He'd be too frightened. His life is far more important to him. He is a human, too. He wouldn't want to lose his own life for someone else's. . . . His parents would tell him off for not going in. They'd like to think their child was a good type. . . . He'd feel pretty sick; it's hard to leave someone to drown, because he is a fellow-human. But he would have to, really, to save himself. If anyone dies you are sad – especially when you have seen it.'

The link between heteronomy and autonomy is conscious in:

'It's the right thing to do. It's what we have been taught by parents and school. He'd have it on his conscience. You can't let something living drown.'

Socionomy is patent in:

'It's a human; it could be him. People would think bad about you if you let him drown. It would weigh on his mind more.'

'His friends would talk about him if he didn't. They'd say he should have saved him. They'd have thought he killed the boy.'

As with the girls, reciprocity is more emphatic. For example:

'If the boy's in danger he should help. If he didn't it would be on his mind, that he had killed him. He has a duty to the boy's family. It might be him.'

Similar, too, is the merging of reciprocity and conscience:

'He'd want to be saved. He'd have it on his conscience, if he didn't help. It's just instinct to save your own kind.'

'You can't just let people die. He would like to be saved. He'd have a bad conscience if he didn't.'

Of the 30 responses in this group, 16 cite conscience as the sole authority, and a further 3 quote 'instinct'. One response holds life as sacred, but on purely humanistic grounds:

'He's a fellow-human in trouble: he'd feel obliged to help. It's natural. You're born with this, and it's influenced by your parents and teachers. Life is sacred – it's either that or total annihilation. But I don't believe in any after-life.'

For one subject, who had a similar personal experience himself, it would be 'a natural instinct' to save life; and for another 'his first reaction'. Typical of the responses citing conscience are:

'It's just instinctive. It's just like killing him if you left him. You'd have a conscience and keep thinking about it.'

'It's the natural thing to do. You'd have a bad conscience if you didn't – you'd be thinking you should have done something. It would be even worse if you didn't know the boy.'

'You'd save him. It doesn't matter who it is. You'd have it on your mind if you didn't. To save him would give you great satisfaction.'

Noteworthy, in these two last responses, is the spontaneous introduction of stress on the fact that the drowning boy is unknown.

15-YEAR AGE-GROUP: GIRLS

Only 1 response in this group is tinged with heteronomy. 10 responses cite reciprocity alone. Thus:

'If she were in trouble she'd want help.' (Why save life?) 'If people don't help one another we should be in a mess.'

'She would want to be saved if she were drowning.' (Why save life?) 'We should all love one another – all be one family.'

'One point would be that if I were in there, I'd want to be saved. I'd just do it, instinctively.'

Only 1 response cites both reciprocity and conscience, save that autonomy is suggested by the term 'instinctive'. Of the remaining 17 responses, 4 use the term 'instinctive'; and of the 13 who explicitly cite conscience 4 also think of such action as 'instinctive' or, its equivalent, 'natural'. Typical of these autonomous responses are:

'It would be inhuman if she didn't – almost murder. It's just natural – the automatic thing to do.'

'It's instinctive to save the life of other people. If I didn't, I'd keep thinking about it. It would be on my mind all the time.'

A solitary response has religious motivation:

'If I didn't save him I would feel guilty. It would be indirect murder. You think of Jesus dying on the Cross, so you should do your bit.'

17-YEAR AGE-GROUP: BOYS

Save for a half-heteronomous response, all responses in this group fall within the two highest levels of socionomy and autonomy. Typical of socionomy is:

'He'd be afraid of what people would say.'

And of deepening reciprocity:

'It would be almost murder to stand and watch him drowning.' (Why save life?) 'Pity – the fact that you wouldn't like to be there yourself.'

Socionomy and autonomy combine in:

'His conscience would make him do it. His friends would praise him.'

Reciprocity and conscience combine in:

'He would help. There's no one else to. The boy might drown. If it was him he'd like to be saved. I'd have it on my conscience if I didn't. I've been brought up to think of others, to some extent.'

'He'll jump in and try to save him. He'd have a bad conscience if he didn't – thinking about it all the time.' (Why save life?) 'You've only got one life. If you don't help others, others won't help you.'

Conscience is the sole motivating factor in 14 of the 30 responses. Typical responses are:

'If he didn't, he'd have it on his conscience for the rest of his life.'

'I'd go in and try to help. If you didn't, you'd be a murderer. It would be on your mind for the rest of your life.'

17-YEAR AGE-GROUP: GIRLS

The problem of inability to swim, in this situation, had not been raised hitherto. But for 4 girls in this group it posed a serious moral dilemma.

The outstanding example is:

'I suppose she'd try to save her, if she could swim. If you're like me and can't, I don't know. I'd spend hours thinking about it. I think I'd tell the police at the nearest telephone-box.' (What will others think?) 'You did your best – you couldn't endanger yourself. They wouldn't want me to risk drowning for somebody I didn't know. You'd feel sorry. You'd wish you could have done more.'

And again:

'If she could swim she'd go in. She wouldn't like to be in the same position, with nobody helping her. I can't swim. I'd tell the first person I found, and my parents. I'd go and tell the police to show it was a genuine accident.'

'You should go in without thinking. But I don't really know. I'm petrified of water. I'd tell my sister. She'd feel sorry because she'd know what I was going through. I could never get rid of the memory. I'd feel guilty – of having aided death, as it were.'

'I would go in, but I have all my life-saving certificates. I wouldn't if I couldn't swim. If she couldn't, she'd feel ashamed because she ought to be able to swim. She'd feel guilty because it was her fault.'

Reciprocity is the motivation in 3 responses. For example:

'I'd put myself in the same situation. I'd want to help.' (Why save life?) 'She's got as much right to live as I.'

Reciprocity and conscience mingle in such responses as:

'If you didn't help you'd have a guilty conscience.'

'If I was in that situation I'd hope somebody would help me. Everybody has an equal right to live.'

'I'd have a bad conscience if I didn't. I'd be thinking "That might have been me." I know what I'd feel like if they just walked off.'

Conscience is clear-cut in such responses as:

'I wouldn't want anyone's death on my conscience.'

'She'd try and help, whether she could swim or not. She might use her coat or a stick to pull her in. It would play on her conscience if she died and she might have saved her.'

'All lives are of the same value. No one is more important than another. You wouldn't think of yourself. Conscience would make you do it.'

Conclusions

The typical responses quoted suggest the effectiveness of this test, as a projection device, and the genuineness of the judgements thereby revealed. Such a situation, involving the stark issue of life and death, might well be expected to produce far deeper and firmer judgements than those derived from less significant areas of moral concern. But this makes them more, rather than less, revealing.

1. LEVELS OF JUDGEMENT

Mixed responses are to be found at every age: such is the complexity of moral judgement. While pure anomy is rare, in judgements on so vital an issue, elements of this lowest level are to be found, if minimally, at all ages and chiefly among boys.

In our youngest age-groups we find typical expressions of heteronomy – a strong interest in rewards and consequent fame, and the citation of authority, both human and divine.

We have clear and self-conscious evidence, too, in older subjects of how the attitudes from which judgement derives have been formed under the influence of heteronomy. Side by side with such heteronomy, in the younger age-groups, is a strong element of sympathy, particularly pronounced, as already noted, in girls.

The typical sanctions of socionomy – social praise and blame – are evidenced in some responses. But far stronger is the merging of sympathy into reciprocity, within this area of social relations. Such reciprocity may seem, in some responses, to be a purely ontogenetic development, as Piaget holds. But here, too, we have evidence of attitudes shaped by heteronomy – for example, the value and equality of life, the duty of kindness and of active help, and the citation of the principle of the Golden Rule, even if it is rarely quoted as such.

Such reciprocity strengthens and deepens, merging finally into the motivation of autonomous conscience. Piaget, we recall, holds such a process to be automatic. But we have already noted the heteronomous seed-bed of developing attitudes; and we note, too, the strong sense of duty, in maturing responses, that is bound up with deepening reciprocity. Certainly no test would be more likely to confirm Piaget's thesis of automatic development than one focusing upon the stark issue of life itself. But the evidence of heteronomous influence seems far too strong to support it. And, moreover, autonomy, which Piaget scarcely even attempts to define, is the flowering of a plant which, our evidence suggests, has its roots in heteronomous soil.

2. DEVELOPMENTAL CHANGES

A clear development can be traced in moral judgement between the ages

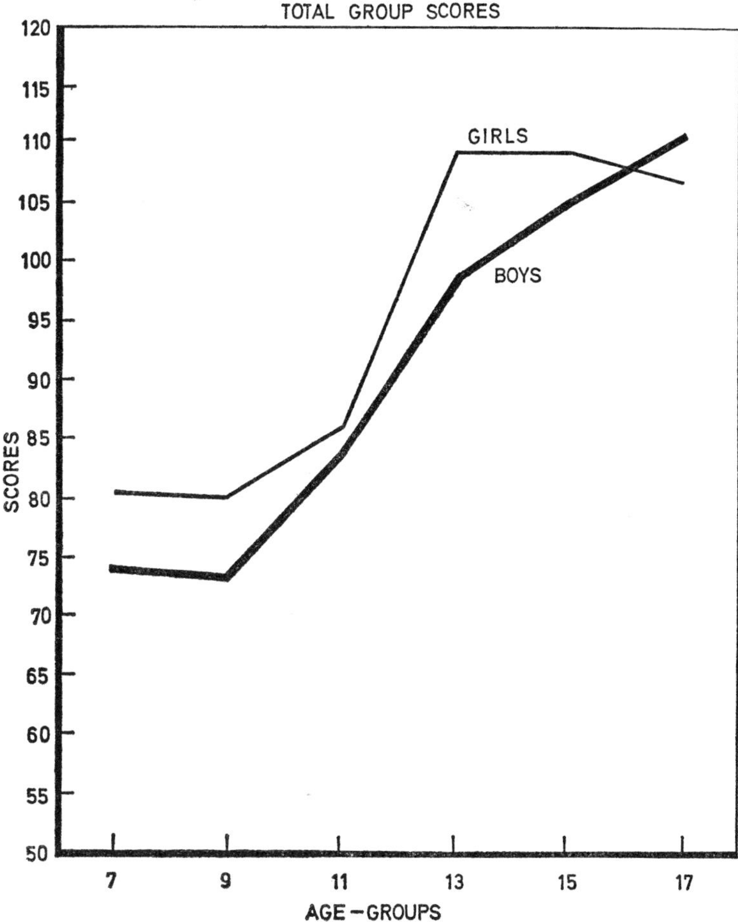
TOTAL GROUP SCORES
SCORES
120
115
110
105
100
95
90
85
80
75
70
65
60
55
50
GIRLS
BOYS
7
9
11
13
15
17
AGE – GROUPS

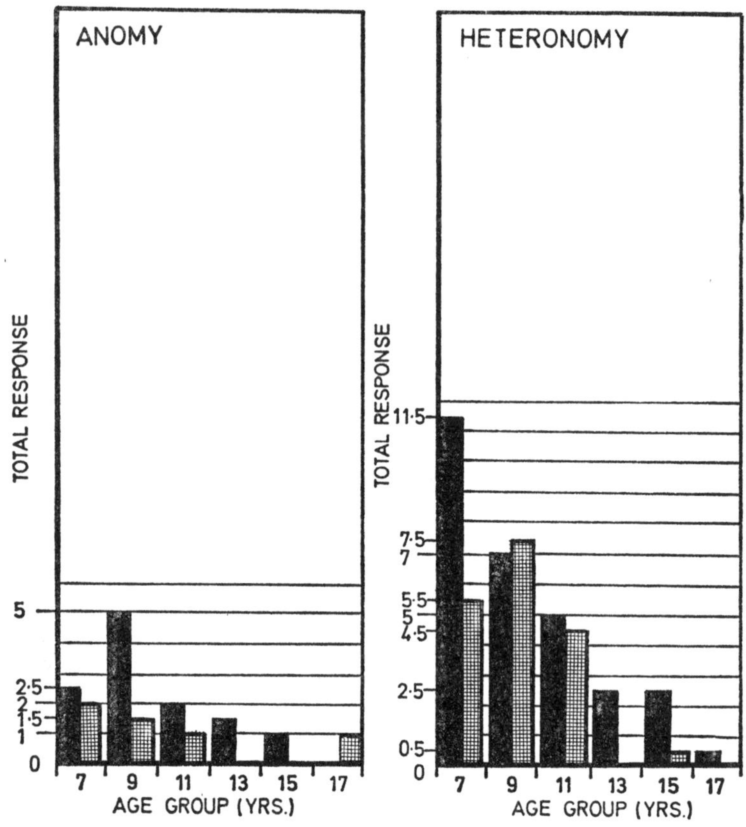

TABLE OF I.Q. VALUES

AGE-GROUP		7	9	11	13	15	17
MEAN I.Q.	BOYS	108·2	110·8	96·9	98·5	104·6	106·4
	GIRLS	108·8	107·8	105·8	105·3	108·5	108·2

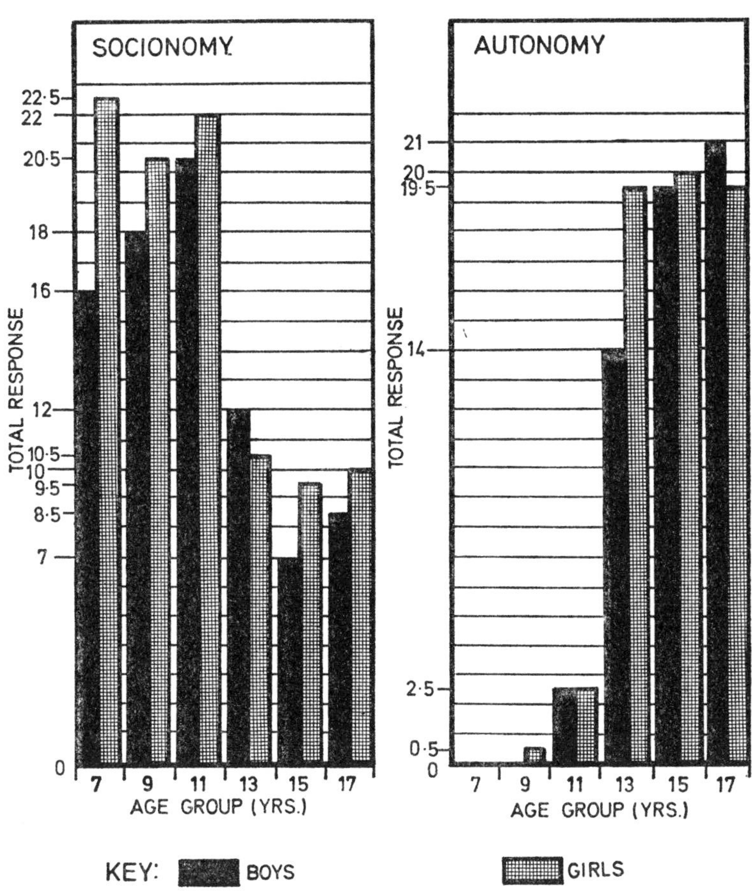

NOTE: N = 60 PER AGE-GROUP (30 BOYS + 30 GIRLS)

of 7 and 17 years. We can delineate it best in terms of the evidence of autonomy in our responses: and in terms of total responses, including half-scores, rather than of individuals.

Autonomy

Age-group	*Boys*	*Girls*
7	0	0
9	0	½
11	2½	2½
13	14	19½
15	19½	20
17	21	19½

There are partial glimmerings of autonomy at 11 years, in terms of half-scores. The climacteric development comes between 11 and 13 years, with girls clearly in advance of boys. By 15 years, an age-group later, the boys have caught up the girls. Thereafter there is little change.

3. SEX DIFFERENCES

The evidence of this test thus indicates earlier development, in moral judgement, in girls than in boys. We shall seek confirmation of such a conclusion from our other tests.

We may at the outset, however, suggest factors that must be borne in mind in terms of sex differences. First, we have already noted the evidence of stronger sympathy, merging into reciprocity, in the girls' responses; and this would give them a clear advantage in such a test situation as this. Sampling, secondly, may be a factor, in terms of the varying moral ethos of schools – though it is a factor that would be difficult to control. More important, thirdly, may be the influence of intelligence; for earlier mental development may accompany the earlier physical maturation of girls. Finally, the stronger facility of girls for verbalisation may give their responses a flexibility and subtlety lacking in the more prosaic responses of boys.

4. STABILITY IN JUDGEMENT

We observe that the total of autonomous responses from girls remains almost identical from 13 to 17 years. Those from the boys broadly equate with the girls' total at 15 years, with a slight increase of 17 years made up from formerly heteronomous responses, now reduced to one-half. In both sexes, therefore, further advance would seem unlikely, and stability may be assumed. The pattern at 17 years, in terms of percentages of total responses, would thus indicate maturity.

17-Year Response Percentages

Anomy, heteronomy	— 2·5%
Socionomy (mainly reciprocity) .	—30·8%
Autonomy	—66·7%

We would not expect such a high level of autonomous responses to be derived from less significant moral situations. This pattern would, therefore, be maximal in its picture of mature moral judgement.

5. THE SACREDNESS OF LIFE

Explicit religious references decrease markedly in the responses of older age-groups, and a humanistic attitude to life increases. But it is possible that religious influence has helped to shape attitudes now consciously expressed in non-religious terms. On the other hand, at least a measure of religious verbalism is evident in the religious references of younger subjects.

Through all responses there runs the instinctive awareness of the value of life *per se*: 'It's all you've got.' In mature responses there is, in addition, a developing sense of the equal value of all life. Life is sacred, not in the precise sense of being a divine gift for which account must one day be rendered, but rather in the transcendent value that attaches to it. To seek to save life, heedless of one's own, therefore becomes 'natural', 'automatic', 'instinctive'.

The motivation for such action is strongly rooted in reciprocity, and, ultimately, for the majority in conscience. Both concepts were overwhelmingly evoked by this test, as compared with the others. Both require analysis, therefore, before examining further evidence from our other moral situations.

Chapter 5
Reciprocity and conscience

The nature of reciprocity

Reciprocity, in its broadest sense, is the common coinage of man's relationship with his fellow-men; and the Golden Rule, its universal definition, is to be found in every human creed and philosophy, whether positively or negatively expressed. It is the more striking, therefore, that so little discussion has been devoted to it, whether from the point of view of philosophy, ethics, or psychology.

Three distinctions must first be made so as to avoid those misinterpretations of the Golden Rule that give rise to criticism of it. First, it is a moral principle, not a moral 'rule' as such. It certainly does not, therefore, do away with the need for a concrete moral code. Indeed, if it is to be expressed in moral conduct, it requires specific application to concrete moral situations. It has, secondly, two distinct forms – the particular and the general. The general form of the Golden Rule is expressed as: '*What* ye would that men should do to you do ye even so to them.' The general form is: '*As* ye would. . . .' The particular form, to be a universal principle, would require the patently untrue assumption that there is uniformity in human nature, that human needs and desires and tastes are identical. It is, of course, the general form of the Golden Rule that is of universal validity. Again, there is a distinction of both moral and psychological importance between the positive and negative forms of the Golden Rule. The negative form – do not do to others what you would not have them do to you – is limited. It could be fulfilled by passive inaction; it makes no positive demands. It is the positive form that requires constant and active expression in the daily intercourse of personal relationships.

The merit of the Golden Rule is that it defines the basic principle of all human justice – that the same standards must be used in judging the conduct of everyone. A typical response to the drowning scene puts it succinctly: 'He has as much right to live as I have. I'd want help if I was in his position.' The right or the wrong must be the same for a like person in a like situation.

The demerits of the Golden Rule are four. First, as we have seen, it is abstract and nebulous until it is applied to concrete moral behaviour. It must be interpreted in terms of actual conduct. It does not, therefore, do away with the need for a moral code. It may inspire moral rules; it cannot replace them.

More important, secondly, is the moral motivation for practising the Golden Rule. It does not of itself stand up as a motive for conduct; it requires justification. Some see it rooted in reason – in the awareness that the individual must respect for others the rights that he requires for himself. Its appearance in every major creed indicates the religious motivation that has universally undergirded it. The key question is: Why should I treat others thus? Justification in terms of enlightened self-interest is not really compelling. In many situations, such as our drowning test, it may not be obviously a matter of self-interest to act according to the Golden Rule.

Again, the Golden Rule cannot be sustained as the moral ideal, however valuable its contribution. This would require the assumption that we always desire the highest good for ourselves. The human condition belies any such romantic optimism. Certainly the Golden Rule may be the expression of the *agape* of the Christian love-ethic. It may inspire the precept 'to love your neighbour as one like yourself', in Buber's precise rendering of the Hebrew text of Leviticus xix. 18 (Buber, 1947, 51). It is consonant with the Christian way of life, and hence its citation in the Gospels. While its root is human sympathy, it may be stimulated, motivated and extended by religion into a universal. But the fact remains that the Golden Rule does not of itself go the whole way. It does not of itself require the 'extra mile' of active benevolence, of an *agape* to whose demands no bounds can be set.

Such love is a goodwill towards others which contains no thought of self. It seeks only their highest good; it gives, and seeks no return. Such Christian love is thereby distinguished from reciprocity; for at the heart of reciprocity there is always an element of self-interest. As a terse male response to the drowning test puts it: 'You help them, they'll help you.' Here, then, is a further limitation of reciprocity, as expressed in the Golden Rule. We shall see interesting evidence that, while reciprocity is adequate for the more impersonal moral situation, it is inadequate for the intimate and intense personal situation. This is natural if reciprocity has an element of calculated self-interest in its make-up. When it is applied in moral situations among peers, we shall sometimes find it characterised by a rather chilly self-righteousness too.

In short, the Golden Rule is a good working principle for moral conduct, a common coinage for human exchanges. It would not, however, qualify as the highest human moral ideal.

The Golden Rule

BUDDHISM	Hurt not others with that which pains yourself (*Udanavarga*, 5.18).
CHRISTIANITY	As ye would that men should do to you, do ye also to them likewise (*Luke* vi.31).
CONFUCIANISM	Is there any one maxim which ought to be acted upon throughout one's whole life? Surely the maxim of loving-kindness is such. Do not unto others what you would not they should do unto you (*Analects*, 15.23).
JUDAISM	What is hurtful to yourself do not to your fellow man. That is the whole of the Torah and the rest is the commentary. Go learn it (Rabbi Hillel, *Talmud*).
HINDUISM	This is the sum of duty: do naught to others which, if done to thee, would cause thee pain. (*Mahabharata*, 5.1517).
ISLAM	No one of you is a believer until he loves for his brother what he loves for himself (*Traditions*).
JAINISM	In happiness and suffering, in joy and grief, we should regard all creatures as we regard our own self, and should therefore refrain from inflicting upon others such injury as would appear undesirable to us if inflicted upon ourselves (*Yogashastra*).
SIKHISM	As thou deemest thyself so deem others (*Kabir*).
TAOISM	Regard your neighbours gain as your own gain: regard your neighbour's loss as your own loss (*T'ai Shang Kan Ying P'ien*).
ZOROASTRIANISM	That nature only is good when it shall not do unto another whatever is not good for its own self (*Dadistan-i-dinik*, 94.5).

The range of reciprocity

An analysis of reciprocity requires, as always, exact definition of the term.

Its massive range is indicated in our responses, and hence the danger of its becoming but a blanket term. At one extreme, some responses cite approvingly the *lex talionis*, the Iron Rule, of 'an eye for an eye, a tooth for a tooth'. In its time – as in the codes of Hammurabi and of Moses – it represented moral advance in its limitation of revenge. But its citation by children in the stage of reciprocity, melancholy proof of their scriptural knowledge and despite the Gospels' specific rejection of it (Matthew v.38f.), is clear evidence of their moral immaturity. At the other extreme, some responses interpret reciprocity in terms of love: 'She would want to be saved if she was drowning. We should all love one another.' Such, then, is the vast range of reciprocity.

Piaget is fully aware of this range of meaning in the operations of reciprocity. He sees it, in its initial and lowest form, as a crude law of revenge demanding strict, mathematical vengeance; and our evidence agrees. What we cannot accept is his credal conviction that such reciprocity matures of itself into the highest morality of love. Certainly, in the Value of Life Test, we find reciprocity merging into autonomy as the motivating factor of judgement. In the light of such significance attaching to reciprocity, as well as of Piaget's theoretical claims for it, we may summarise here the total evidence that we find for reciprocity.

Including parallel citations in all four tests, we find a total of 134½ responses that base judgement on reciprocity. Of these, 103, or 76%, derive from the Value of Life Test. Stealing, the next most evocative test, produced only 26½ reciprocity responses, or 20% of the total. The Cheating and Lying Tests together produce but 4% of the total. Thus, had we not included the Value of Life Test, we should have lost 76% of our evidence for reciprocity as being a key motivational factor in moral judgement.

By way of contrast, the total of 134½ reciprocity responses contrasts with a total of 257 responses citing conscience as motivating judgement, including in both cases all four tests and all parallel citations. Of these responses citing conscience, 117, or 45·5%, derive from the Value of Life Test; 80 responses, or 31%, from the stealing situation, again the second most evocative test; 15% from the Lying Test; and 8·5% from the Cheating Test.

It may be suggested that the Value of Life Test, coming first of the four tests, would inevitably produce the most responses for both reciprocity and conscience. But we have included in these figures all parallel citations in the other three tests in order to balance out this possibility. Further, we observe that, while reciprocity responses are overwhelmingly derived from the Value of Life Test (76%), this is not so with the citations of conscience (45·5%). The latter derive from all four tests, including even the relatively amoral cheating situation (8·5%), in a much wider spread. Thus, while all four tests evoke conscience, in varying degrees, only the Value of Life Test substantially evokes reciprocity. Piaget's assertion that 'autonomy appears only with reciprocity' becomes highly dubious.

Even more emphatic is the evidence derived from our Lying Test, if we may briefly anticipate its findings. It is precisely in this situation, Piaget holds, that autonomy makes its first appearance. The child discovers that truth-telling is essential to relationships based on mutual respect; and therefore reciprocity is the 'determining factor' of autonomy. Since this test, comprehensive in its analysis of all aspects of child lying, produces but 3% of our total of reciprocity responses, it would appear to be a very minimal factor indeed. We can be even more specific. When asked whether it is worse to lie to children or to adults, or equally heinous, only 2 out of 360 responses made any reference to reciprocity. Again, when asked about three aspects of lying on behalf of friends, only 14 subjects, or 4% of the total sample, invoked considerations of reciprocity. These situations were concerned with peer relations *vis-à-vis* authority, rather than with free mutuality. But it is precisely such situations that should encourage the development of reciprocity; and we shall later find melancholy evidence of reciprocity at work in free relations among peers.

In terms of age, we find reciprocity strongest at 9 and 11 years, and conscience responses appearing solidly at 13 years. But reciprocity remains, and it is most evident in situations concerned with mutual co-operation among peers. Nowhere do we find evidence for Piaget's belief that reciprocity is the *sine qua non* of autonomy. The lying situation, from which he substantiates it, suggests three quite different conclusions. First, the evidence derived from it indicates the contrary thesis that development is caused by a progressive internalising of the adult proscription of lying, with its consequent extension and universalisation. Secondly, given the strength and emotional accompaniment of this process, there is little room for the free play of considerations of reciprocity. Thirdly, therefore, calculated considerations of reciprocity have no place in the intensely close mutuality of intimate personal relationships. In short, lying, as a breach of trust, falls within the sphere of close personal relationships, not least with parents, and of conscience, not of reciprocity between peers. Hence, we conclude, the strong significance of reciprocity in the impersonal drowning situation, but its minimal significance in the personal lying situation.

Reciprocity and conscience

We recall, however, that reciprocity and conscience are the key motivating factors in responses to the Value of Life Test; and that the one appears to merge into the other. What, then, can be said of the relationship between them?

We can agree with Piaget that the play of sympathy and antipathy gives birth to conscious awareness of reciprocity. In its initial, raw dominance it is a quasi-mathematical retaliation, a sort of 'legalised vengeance'. But, Piaget holds, it 'tends of itself' towards the high morality of forgiveness and benevolence. For him, reciprocity is both a fact and an ideal; through its practice, the form of reciprocal behaviour reacts upon its content; behaviour is thereby developed from within. Aware that reciprocity is not enough as the moral idea, that charity and forgiveness are far higher than equality, Piaget resolves the conflict between justice and love in this automatic, inner development. Conduct is guided, and progressively purified, by reciprocity until it reaches universality.

Here, then, are the two first articles of the Piagetian creed – autonomy grows out of reciprocity, and the process is automatic. We have found no evidence thus far to enable us to subscribe to such a creed. Can we find evidence from an analysis of the development of autonomous conscience?

The nature of conscience

Here, again, we must begin by defining our terms. The Greek term *syneidesis* comes to us from the Stoics, and not least from the pagan Roman moralist, Seneca, for that moral selfconsciousness that distinguishes man from animal. In classical Greek, it had the primary meaning of 'consciousness'; and hence, derivatively, of consciousness of past action, in awareness of having done wrong, and so suffering inner pangs of self-judgement. The Latin equivalent, *conscientia*, had the original meaning of 'knowledge with another', and derivatively of 'knowledge with oneself'. Conscience, in the ancient world, was thus a judge, weighing and judging past actions. Primitive peoples picturesquely thought of this inner function as a sharp stone within the breast, twisting and thereby hurting – as in our phrase 'my conscience pricked me' – when wrong had been done. No more succinct definition could be given than that of Ernest Hemingway: 'What's good is what I feel good after. What's bad is what I feel bad after.'

The concept is, of course, far older than the Stoics. Among the earlier

Greeks, for example, we see it in the avenging Furies, the law of Nemesis, the 'rule within' of Aristotle's ethics. Among the Jews we see a sense of moral obligation and of consequent self-condemnation running as a thread through their interpretation of history, the ethical demands of their prophets and, not least, the self-searchings of their Psalmists. While the term itself does not appear in the Christian Gospels, they are impregnated with moral insight and concern. *Syneidesis* appears 31 times in the New Testament, 21 of such citations being found in the letters of Paul. He would almost certainly be indebted to Stoicism for the term; and in a significant passage Paul implies a universal faculty of moral self-consciousness, stamped on all human nature, and therefore acting as the effective moral guide of pagans (Romans ii. 14f.).

Conscience has been variously assigned to the rational, the affective, and the volitional functioning of the individual. But moral self-judgement clearly involves the complex and intricate functioning of the whole personality. We have already found ample reason to reject the traditional view of conscience as an inborn faculty. No more tenable is the concept of conscience as evolving through racial experience. Any theory which derives conscience wholly from society is doomed by the empiric fact that moral progress has always been made by individuals and minorities, reacting and rebelling against accepted social *mores*. Both these viewpoints, both Nativism and Evolutionalism, do, however, contain an element of truth. Man must have inborn moral potentiality for conscience to become a reality. But he is no more born with a fully developed conscience than with a fully developed mind or body. Potentiality becomes actuality through society; conscience is a social construct.

The genesis of conscience

We have already seen fear, with its associated anxiety, to be the initial factor in the growth of conscience. Moral feelings are first manifest in a sense of guilt, compounded of love and hate directed towards the same person. Some, indeed, posit a 'proto-guilt' present in early infancy (e.g. Rickman, 1951). A sense of guilt, in psychoanalytic theory, arises from the process of identification of child with parent. To offend against the parent is thereby to offend against himself; and hence intropunitive guilt. Such guilt has been more highly developed in societies, broadly those affected by the Protestant Reformation, in which individual responsibility is emphasised, a sense of sin deepens personal unworthiness, and autonomous conscience is the supreme moral value.

Such societies, in which guilt plays a dominant role in determining conduct, contrast strongly with societies in which public honour and public shame are the supreme moral yardsticks (e.g. Peristiany, ed. 1965, *Honour and Shame: The Values of Mediterranean Society*). Here morality is other-directed rather than inner-directed; the individual sees himself as he is in the eyes of others, not in the light of his own conscience; shame takes the place of guilt. Hence other-directed anxiety in determining behaviour, which some see developing in traditionally Protestant societies (e.g. Riesman *et al.*, 1950).

The guilt, or proto-guilt, of the child is irrational, in that the demands of authority and the values absorbed from it are not subject to reason and criticism. But if and when maturing reason comes to accept and approve these values, a new and powerful motivation is added, the more powerful for being conscious. The 'must' of the child becomes the 'ought' of the adult. Three main changes transform the one into the other. External controls yield to internal controls; fear yields to self-respect, must to ought; obedience to external discipline yields to self-discipline.

The super-ego

An interesting comparison may be made between the tripartite definitions of the psyche of Freud and of Plato. For both, such a division is a picture of conflict. Since victory must go to the lower but more powerful aspect, Plato placed the mediating 'personal emotions' between reason and unreason, reason being the locus of moral judgement. Similarly, between the passionate id and the prohibitive super-ego Freud placed the mediating ego, the locus of reason. He thus, incidentally, preserved the concept of an ego for psychology, even if it was to be later slighted.

But for Freud the moral agency was the super-ego, not reason. It served consciously as conscience, and unconsciously as repression. Its nucleus was formed of introjected parental precepts, reinforced by the aggression that the infant had to vent upon his natural impulses whose uncontrolled expression would threaten parental love. This nucleus was augmented in later years by further identifications, by experience, and by reason. Such is the Freudian moral agency that we call 'conscience'.

The psychopathic psyche, as we have observed, lacks such a conscience, to a lesser or greater degree. It is to that degree morally irresponsible, and the complete psychopath is a moral imbecile. There must, then, be such a moral agency in the socialised individual; and we have noted the processes at work which unconsciously shape it. But there is a pathology of conscience, and it is seen in the adult burden of what is essentially infantile guilt. Such a fierce, over-developed and irrational conscience may be turned inwards, in the self-punishment that may weaken the effective functioning of the ego; or turned outwards in the bitter condemnation of others that may mar social relationships. It can, moreover, reveal itself consciously in distorted symptoms. Here, then, is a further reason why conscience is not a perfect moral guide.

Freud held that the framework of character is laid in infancy. Substantiation for this psychoanalytic doctrine comes from Bowlby (1953), among others, observing a close link between a disturbed and emotionally deprived childhood and later anti-social behaviour. Such evidence must be accepted, but not, necessarily, the deterministic interpretation of it. A scar may indeed persist, and it is seen in the pathological guilt suffered by the adult. But love remains the great healer.

The ego-ideal

Freud's rigid and negative concept has, in fact, been revised in the light of neo-Freudian insights. Freud held that the super-ego was concerned with both positive and negative morality. It prescribed both the 'do' and the 'do not' of the internalised moral agency. But a clear distinction is now recognised. The function of the super-ego is wholly negative. The urge to positive moral action is the function of the ego-ideal which, while it may lack the power of the super-ego, is of far greater potential moral significance.

The super-ego is negative, and is dominated by fear; the ego-ideal is positive, and is dominated by love. Its nucleus is the picture of himself that the child constructs and strives to live up to in order to win and to hold the love that is his deepest need. The picture develops over the years, so that it remains an ideal never fully attained. It thereby functions as a positive spur to moral development. By contrast with the enfeebling anxiety or the chilly self-righteousness of the dominating super-ego, the dominating ego-ideal is warmed and inspired by love.

Neglect of the ego-ideal as the positive moral agency stemmed from Freud's identification of it with the super-ego, thus making it very subordinate to the overbearing negative agency. But, however close their genesis, they are distinct. Fuller analysis sees, not a single ego-ideal, but, rather, a synthesis of ideals that may vary immensely in quality. It is supremely in adolescence, as we have seen, that such ideals are regrouped, forming a new and enlarged synthesis as further values are incorporated. Hence the growth of the autonomous ego, shaping its vocational ideals, and thereby sublimating its energies in striving towards them.

The concept of the self may be further understood in terms of its three aspects. There is, first, the known self, the individual as he knows and sees himself. There is, secondly, the self as seen by others, the portrait of the individual as he believes others see him. There is, thirdly, the ideal self, the ego-ideal, the picture of the individual as he would wish to be. Such an analysis underlines not only the influence of adults upon the child's moral growth, but also the immense importance of the self picture in the motivation of behaviour. There is, of course, potential danger if the gulf between the ego-ideal and the real self becomes too great; and here, too, adult influence can play an important part, for good or for ill. But there can be no doubt of the importance of ego-ideals in moral growth, even if there is as yet limited knowledge of their content and their functioning.

Conscience: a conditioned reflex?

The behaviourist approach to psychology defines conscience as no more than a conditioned reflex. Moral values are acquired by a learning process of conditioned responses, punishment following upon moral offence. Hence the immense power of anxiety in human life. The theory is substantiated from two extreme types of personality. On the one hand, the psychopath is morally unconditioned through a defective central nervous system. On the other hand, the strong anxiety of the neurotic may be ascribed to extreme conditionability. Individuals may thus be ranged on a continuum that thereby portrays parallel measures of conditionability and of behaviour patterns. The range will be from the hyper-morality of the extremely conditionable neurotic to the amorality of the extremely unconditionable psychopath.

Such a theory clearly contains an element of truth, and it is attractive in its simplicity. It acquires its scientific substantiation from experiments with animals. This is, of course, to assume the equivalence of species, and therefore of human and animal behaviour. But we have already seen that man is set apart from animals by his moral self-consciousness, his sense of moral obligation – the very hallmark of man's uniqueness in the whole realm of life. Such a theory, secondly, fails completely to account for the creative, autonomous conscience through which all moral progress has been made. The least adequate of all possible explanations would be to define it as a conditioned anxiety response. Again, thirdly, there are many different ways by which the child acquires his moral nature. We have already observed the key processes at work, and without any necessity to refer to conditioning. Thus, we have observed the vital and unconscious processes of imitation, suggestion, identification and of the formation of the ego-ideal. We have similarly seen the immense role of heteronomy in the development of morality, with its sanctions of reward and punishment. Hence the acquired respect for the voice of authority, first of the adult and then of public opinion. Nor can we leave out of account all that is learned from experience, not least in the moral practice of heteronomous precepts, and from the reasoning of morality that we have seen to be characteristic of psychological discipline.

In short, while conditioning has its place in the development of the moral self, it is not a leading factor, even less the only factor. The weakness of conditioning theory is that it ignores the whole complex of those human relationships in which identification and introjection function, and which thereby shape the child into a uniquely moral being. Man is physically part of the animal creation. But in his moral potentiality he is set apart from it.

Types of conscience

We have noted previously the typology of personality deduced by Havighurst and Taba (1949) from research at 'Prairie City'. Each of the types defined had its own distinctive difference in terms of conscience and of strength of the ego. The self-directive individual was found to possess both a strong conscience and a strong ego. The adaptive individual had a strong sense of self, but a conscience that was more permissive. The submissive type of personality had a poor sense of self, but a severe conscience. The defiant individual had both a weak conscience and a weak sense of self. The unadjusted individual was held back by environment from maturing into a self-directive, adaptive, or submissive type.

Increasing strength of conscience characterised the types of character also delineated from research at 'Prairie City' by Peck and Havighurst (1964). The types and their accompanying stages were: amoral (infancy); expedient (early childhood); conforming, and irrational-conscientious (later childhood); rational-altruistic (adolescence and adulthood). Within this sequential development there were found to be four types of conscience. The first was the punitive and repressive super-ego, typical of the amoral and expedient types, that was the echoing voice of the punitive adult. The second was the more passive and less strongly interiorised conscience that conformed to expected behaviour and had its own measure of emotional overtone. The third was the irrational and tyrannical super-ego of the neurotic, rigid in both its dominance and in its behavioural expression, that is so familiar from Freud's analysis. The fourth, typical of the rational-altruistic type, was the autonomy that integrated the ego and the super-ego in a conscience that was firm and strong, but yet open to reasoned moral ends.

Conscience in action

It is a human tendency to hypostatise conscience in such homely phrases as 'My conscience wouldn't let me,' and 'My conscience pricked me.' The individual conscience, such as it is, remains the guiding light to moral behaviour. To follow it is to develop it; to defy it is to court discomfort. Hence the maxim of the moral theologian, '*Conscientia semper sequenda*' – 'Conscience must always be followed.' As the song puts it, 'Always let your conscience be your guide'.

But the enormities of evil perpetrated by conscience – and not least in the name of religion – are ample proof of its fallibility. Conscience is fallible, not infallible; relative, not absolute; irrational, all too often, not wholly rational. Conscience can misguide; it can be divided; it can be a false judge of self and of others. Conscience thus has its weaknesses.

The individual must have a conscience, and must broadly be guided by it. But the fear, guilt and anxiety of the neurotic show what a cruel task-master it can be. It is, too, characteristically a negative function, as commonly understood. Not one of our responses speaks of a good, of a positive conscience. The contemporary weakening of our Puritan inheritance, making guilt the arbiter of morality, gives opportunity for a more positive moral education, developing and stressing positive ego-ideals rather than negative condemnations of self or of others. Such an emphasis would root morality in love, rather than in fear. Love, as a dynamic principle of life, not as emotion and even less as sentimentality, is the moral absolute.

Definitions of conscience

With such an analysis of conscience in mind we can now turn to the definitions of conscience provided by our subjects. The term itself was never introduced into personal interviews. It was only when the term was used by a subject that we took it up and sought definition of it. Conscience responses, including parallels, were evoked pre-eminently by the Value of Life Test (117), strongly by the Stealing Test (80), to a lesser degree by the Lying Test (38), and, as expected, minimally by the Cheating Test (22). Again, it might be thought that the Value of Life Test, preceding the others, naturally produced the most responses. But it was the Stealing Test that evoked more conscience responses from younger age-groups, and the Value of Life Test that evoked more from older age-groups. Moreover, many of these latter were single conscience responses, in that no other test evoked the concept.

There is thus ground for thinking that offences against property were, no doubt heteronomously, of greater significance to younger subjects, while, with maturation, there developed a greater sense of the significance of the person.

9-YEAR AGE-GROUP: BOYS

The responses of the 7-year age-group were overwhelmingly rooted in heteronomy. Save for 2 boys and 3 girls who showed evidence of dawning reciprocity, fear of detection and punishment were universal.

It is with the 9-year age-group that we find the first evidences of that sense of guilt which develops into conscience. Almost all significant responses were evoked by the Stealing Test. Thus:

'He'd feel guilty. He'd know he'd done wrong.'

'You'd know yourself, even if you weren't caught and punished.'

'He'd feel awful. He knows he shouldn't have done it.'

'He'll feel guilty. It's horrible – a feeling you're going to get found out. Your mind goes all sort of beating fast.'

'He'd be afraid. He'd feel guilty. It's when you've done wrong – something that bothers you inside.'

9 YEAR AGE-GROUP: GIRLS

The Value of Life Test produced two significant responses:

'She'd feel dreadful.'

'She'd feel guilty.'

But it is again the Stealing Test that evokes the majority of significant responses. Key terms used are 'ashamed', 'guilty', 'sorry', 'unhappy'.

In each case the term used was explained by the comment, 'You'd know you'd done wrong.'

The Lying Test included the question: 'Would it be all right to tell lies if you were not caught and punished?' Three subjects answered 'No' on the ground that

'It starts bothering you after a while.'

'It's on your mind.'

'You'd know yourself.'

11-YEAR AGE-GROUP: BOYS

It is with this age-group that the term 'conscience' begins to appear. It could, of course, be no more than a verbalism; and hence the value of seeking definition. But, on the other hand, since higher intelligence had been characteristic of 9-year subjects giving significant responses, there was the danger of suspecting a conscience response from a subject of lower intelligence, particularly if definition was sparse. Such a subject might have a degree of interiorisation, if simple, but have difficulty in giving verbal definition, apart from the familiar term.

Stealing is still the most evocative test in this age-group. A few subjects use the terms 'sorry', 'ashamed', 'afraid', but these are clearly linked with heteronomous fear. Thus 'ashamed' is linked with fear of Borstal by one (I.Q. 90; S.E. 2; Rel. 1); and another 'ashamed' response adds 'I'd tremble' (I.Q. 90; S.E. 3; Rel. 3). Guilt feelings are expressed by the frequent 'guilty' and by the phrase 'on his mind'. Our main interest is in the 10 subjects who use the term 'conscience', 2 of them more than once. Definitions are:

'It sticks in your mind. It comes from heaven. You have it when you're born.'

'He'll have a conscience. He won't feel confident. He'll be worried about getting found out.'

'It's something we think. It comes from Satan or an evil person. He *knows* he's done wrong.'

'It keeps playing on your mind. It makes you own up in the end.'

'You feel a coward. You have a guilty conscience. It's what tells you to do right and not to do wrong. It makes you blush. You're born with it.'

11-YEAR AGE-GROUP: GIRLS

As with the boys, the phrase 'on her mind' clearly expresses guilt feelings, and is, indeed, an expansion of 'guilt' in responses. We thus have 10 guilt responses, such as:

'She'd feel guilty. It's something that feels as if it's pressing on you all the time. If you've stolen something, you feel you must tell somebody.'

'You feel guilty. If you weren't punished you'd still know it yourself.'

'Guilty means knowing you've done something wrong. You feel worried.'

'She feels guilty. She'd done something wrong. She knows it. She's afraid to admit it.'

Typical of the girls' more fulsome definitions of 'conscience' are:

'It's an inside feeling, telling you you've done wrong or right. You're born with it. It comes from God.'

'It's something inside you which you can't forget. You get a conscience when you start to think. Everyone has a conscience, but they're not all the same.'

'It bothers you when you've done wrong. It's like a person nagging inside. We know we've done wrong, even if nobody else does.'

'It's two little voices: one tells you to do right, the other tells you to do wrong. The good one is from God, the bad one from Satan. Our good conscience tells us when we've done wrong.'

'It's a person inside you which tells you to do the opposite of what your mind says.'

'It's when you've done wrong and Jesus keeps telling you that you have.'

'It's a little man inside you, prodding you all the time. He's been there since you were born.'

Sex differences are apparent, quite apart from the greater verbal facility of girls. 10 boys, as compared with 6 girls, fail to reveal any trace of interiorisation; 6 boys, as compared with 1 girl, make 'fear' responses; 4 boys, as compared with 10 girls, produce 'guilt' responses; 10 boys, as compared with 13 girls, use the term 'conscience', and 6 of the girls use it twice, one of them thrice, as compared with 2 boys. If we add guilt and conscience responses together, we find the boys produce 14 and the girls 23. Thus, at least initially, we again find girls in advance of boys in moral development.

13-YEAR AGE-GROUP: BOYS

In this age-group 3 boys give no evidence of interiorised moral sentiments. The I.Q.s are 97, 95 and 86; socio-economic classes are 2, 2, and 3; religious classes are 1, 5 (choirboy), and 1. The 6 fear responses use the various terms already met – 'sad', 'sorry', 'ashamed' and the direct 'afraid'. The 1 guilt response does not suggest dawning autonomy.

Of the 20 conscience responses, 10 use the term in response to a single test, 6 use it twice, and 4 use it thrice. It is now that more conscience responses are evoked by the Value of Life Test than by the Stealing Test, suggesting a developing sense of the value of the person, as compared with that of property. Typical definitions of conscience from subjects using the term only once are:

'It's in our mind. Rules and laws tell us it's wrong, in the first place – the Ten Commandments and the police.'

'It's a feeling from your heart. You're born with it. It's like Jesus talking to us.'

'Conscience is thoughts in your mind. It kind of creeps in whenever you relax. Babies have it, but it comes into action when they are old enough to think and act for themselves.'

'You keep thinking about the bad deed. It's formed by your upbringing.'

'It's like a little voice inside. You feel guilty – you make up the voice.'

'It's a feeling that bothers you, in your brain. It's put there by God, from birth.'

Definitions from subjects using the term twice are:

'It's a feeling inside you. It comes from your mind. God put it there when He made us.'

'It's something inside that tells you when you've done wrong. You're born with it. It grows by itself.'

'You keep remembering things you've done wrong. It's something you learn as you get older. Babies haven't got it. Primitive men have.'

Finally, 4 subjects use the term thrice:

'It stays on your mind. You dream about it. You're born with it.'

'It's a thought in your brain. It's there all the time. It probably grows.'

'You're born with it. Your parents and friends help it grow. Even if nobody found you out, you still worry.'

'You're born with it. It grows – you yourself make it grow.'

There does not appear to be any increasing depth in the concept of conscience with such increasing use of the term.

13-YEAR AGE-GROUP: GIRLS

In this age-group, 24 girls, as compared with 19 boys, give conscience responses. The Value of Life Test is again the most evocative. Of responses below the explicit level of conscience, 1 reveals no interiorisation (I.Q. 97; S.E. 3; Rel. 5); 1 is 'afraid'; and 4 express a sense of guilt in various terms, including 'unhappy'. Of the 24 conscience responses, 10 use the term once, 8 use it twice, 5 use if thrice, and 1 in response to all four tests.

Since definitions of conscience have been amply quoted, and a pattern of responses become familiar, we may now limit quotations to representative definitions, both typical and atypical. Typical examples are:

> 'It's in your heart. It grows, you feel more. You learn from parents.'
>
> 'It's inside your brain. You're born with it. You learn from parents, teachers, and friends.'
>
> 'It's inside, in your head. You can't think properly of anything else. It grows with you, through doing wrong.'

This assertion that conscience grows through wrongdoing is common in this group's responses. The idea of a 'good conscience' is absent in all our responses. While, logically, constant wrongdoing should weaken conscience until it becomes atrophied, the empirical truth of this assertion is apparent. Conscience is activated by each act of wrongdoing, and thereby exercised and developed in strength. Thus:

> 'You know you've done something wrong. You can't forget. The more wrong you do, the more you get a bad conscience.'

A variant is

> 'Conscience says whether you have done right or wrong. There's a good half and a bad half of you. Conscience grows. You get a worse conscience the worse things you do.'

The need to 'get it off your chest' is well expressed by

> 'I would have to tell someone in the end.'

There would again appear to be no significantly greater depth either of conceptualisation or interiorisation in subjects giving conscience responses to more than one test. Thus, the subject quoting conscience in response to all four tests defines it thus:

> 'She'd have a bad conscience. She'd feel guilty all the time. It's inside, in your mind. It grows through the things you've done wrong.'

15-YEAR AGE-GROUP: BOYS

Here we find 3 responses giving little or no evidence of interiorised morality – 1 controlled only by fear of punishment and another, already cited for responses suggesting abnormality, who knows only anomy. A further 4 subjects are dominated by fear, and 2 indicate some sense of guilt.

Of the remaining 21 conscience responses, 16 use the term once, 4 use it twice, and 1 uses it thrice. The Value of Life Test is now outstanding as evoking conscience responses, producing 13 of the 16 single conscience responses. Since neither stealing nor lying evoke conscience in these subjects, we have further evidence that it is the significance, rather than the priority, of the Value of Life Test that makes it the more evocative.

Definitions of conscience are now so familiar as to make quotation superfluous. Phrases such as 'you keep thinking' are common. We may quote a pseudo-sophistication but low-level response to the Cheating Test:

> 'It's a lazy way of getting marks. Your own sense of ethics should tell you that. You'd be afraid of getting caught. Fear is the proof of its being wrong.'

In answer to the question, 'Is it all right if you are not caught and punished?' the answer now is 'You punish yourself', or 'You still feel guilty', or 'You still worry', even if the offence is not known to others. Thus:

> 'It preys on your mind. You still feel guilty even if it's not known. Conscience is thinking. It grows as you grow up.'

A terse definition of conscience is

> 'Every rotten thing you do sticks in your mind.'

15-YEAR AGE-GROUP: GIRLS

The 3 low-level responses in this group are rooted in heteronomy, with rare traces of equality and reciprocity. Fear is expressed by 2 subjects in terms of 'feeling uneasy' and 'regret'. 5 subjects express guilt feelings.

Of the 20 conscience responses, 13 subjects use the term in response to one test only, 4 use it twice, and 2 thrice. 10 of the 13 single conscience responses are evoked by the Value of Life Test. Conscience is defined in such typical phrases as 'keep thinking', 'worry', 'feel awful', 'can't forget it'. Of some interest is the response:

> 'It's something you get as you grow up. If we had been brought up alone, without being with people, we wouldn't have a conscience.'

The inner compulsion to confess is expressed by

> 'Conscience is something which shows guilt. You've always had it, but it grows and grows as you get older. My conscience would force me to tell someone about it.'

17-YEAR AGE-GROUP: BOYS

Only 1 subject fails to quote conscience. He is patently abnormal, at his best knows only fear, and 'feels good' if he can get away with any crime (I.Q. 98; S.E. 2; Rel. 1).

Of the 29 subjects who use the term 'conscience', 12 use it in response to a single test, 13 use it twice, and 4 thrice. But, again, frequent use of the term is not related to depth of conceptualisation. Thus, 1 of the 3 subjects using the term thrice is unable to define it – although, of course, inability to verbalise may not preclude inner moral control.

Among the phrases used to describe the functioning of conscience are: 'It plays on your mind'; 'disturbing feeling'; 'You can't sleep, you feel rotten'; 'It bugs you all the time'; 'It's always digging at you'; 'It's like a pinprick'; 'It preys on your mind; you punish yourself'; 'A thing at the back of your head that always nags at you.'

References to religion occur in 3 responses: 2 hold the relation of conscience to religion:

> 'It's in the mind when we've done something wrong. It's a lot to do with religion.'
>
> 'It's a mental reaction. It plays on your mind and matures with it. It's a sense of right and wrong, developed by school, your upbringing, your parents. Religion would help it, if you were religious. It would make a strong conscience.'

A fierce fundamentalist background produces

> 'Conscience is an inner feeling. You're punished even if you're not found out. It's God's judgement. It's everlasting hell, the bottomless pit of fire. Conscience is a God-given faculty. You have it from birth; it grows automatically, helped by parents. It is stopped by constantly doing wrong and losing the sense of it being there.'

Familiarity with the concept of conscience in this final male age-group is indicated by its citation by 29 out of the 30 subjects; by the increase from 21 male responses at 15 years to 29 at 17 years; and by a similar increase, between 15 and 17 years, from 5 to 17 in the number of subjects who use the term in response to more than one test. The process of interiorisation, of which the first glimmerings were found at 9 years, is now complete.

17-YEAR AGE-GROUP: GIRLS

29 out of the 30 female subjects in this age-group also provide conscience responses – 17 in response to a single test, 9 in response to two tests, and 3 in responding to all four tests. The 1 abnormal subject (I.Q. 108; S.E. 5; Rel. 1) achieves calculated reciprocity in response to one test.

Found only in the female responses is the term 'awful' to describe guilt feelings: and one definition of conscience as changing 'with mood'. A strong definition is:

> 'Conscience is a high sense of guilt which haunts you all the time. It comes from religion.'

A loquacious definition is:

'When I hear people talk about conscience it makes me think of something resting on top, like a brick. If you're not used to doing these things you're bound to have a conscience. A certain amount is born in you – a part of the brain, a sense of guilt. A certain part is put into you at school. If you did these things a lot of times you wouldn't give it another thought.'

Since conscience is now substantially held to derive from upbringing, its development depends upon human society. Two subjects make this point explicit:

'Conscience is given to you by others. You'd have no conscience without other people – except about killing. It changes as you grow.'

'It's an inner part of you which pricks your mind when you've done something you shouldn't have done. If you were brought up like Kim, you wouldn't have any feelings of guilty conscience.'

As with the males of this age-group, the increase from 20 female conscience responses at 15 years to 29 at 17 years, together with a similar total of 29 conscience responses from the 30 subjects, indicates that the process of interiorisation is complete.

The development of conscience

A pattern of development of conscience can be observed in these definitive responses. This pattern, being derived from responses to a series of projection tests, may be held to be based upon genuine interiorised moral attitudes.

1. FEAR

In the subjects of 7 years, our youngest age-group, we find no evidence whatever of interiorisation. Certainly the Value of Life Test revealed strong native sympathy, merging into a sense of reciprocity in 8% of the age-group. But in terms of moral awareness – that is, of a 'system of rules' and of the 'respect' acquired for them (Piaget, op. cit., 1) – we find only strong fear of detection and of consequent punishment for the breach of adult regulations. Adding this fear of punishments to the hope of rewards revealed by the Value of Life Test, we have a clear picture of heteronomy. But such heteronomy, far from being the moral strait-jacket that Piaget conceives it to be, is increasingly revealed in later responses as the seed-bed of moral development, bound up, as it is, with strong personal relationships between child and adult.

2. GUILT

In the 9-year age-group we find the first evidence of interiorised moral feelings of disquiet at awareness of having done wrong – that is, of not having carried out the 'good' laid down by heteronomy. Fear of external sanctions now merges into inner discomfort, expressed typically as 'guilt'. We find evidence of such guilt feelings in 25% of the age-group. Terms used are various: guilty, awful, ashamed, dreadful, unhappy, sorry, something that bothers, on your mind. The essence of guilt is clear: 'It starts bothering you after a while,' for 'You'd know yourself, even if you were not caught and punished.' Here, clearly, is development beyond heteronomy. But we observe, and again in opposition to Piaget, that such development is within a heteronomous context, not outside it. Moreover, the most evocative test situation concerned stealing, reflecting, it might be thought, heteronomy's strong concern with the value of property.

Both fear and, more particularly, guilt are to be found in subsequent age-groups, although, of course, rapidly merging into conscience. Thus 23% of the 11-year age-group express guilt feelings that do not yet appear to have merged into autonomous conscience, a figure that has dwindled to 8% at 13 years.

3. CONSCIENCE

(A) 11-YEAR AGE-GROUP

The actual term 'conscience' first appears in the 11-year age-group, 38% of the subjects using it, in addition to the 25% expressing guilt feelings. Thus 61% of the 11-year age-group reveal interiorised moral sentiments.

Concepts of conscience, at its first appearance, are personified, primitive and pictorial. It is 'a little man', 'two little voices', 'a person inside you', 'a little thing that niggles', 'something inside', 'a person nagging inside', 'Jesus keeps telling you you've done wrong'. Where conscience and its obverse temptation are both mentioned, the one is the voice of God, the other the voice of Satan; but only 5 of the 23 conscience responses make religious reference.

In the 11-year age-group, conscience responses are evoked most strongly by the Stealing Test, and particularly so with boys. Every aspect of the analysis of this age-group indicates girls to be in advance of boys in both quantity and quality of interiorisation.

(B) 13-YEAR AGE-GROUP

Conscience responses are almost doubled in the 13-year age-group, with 73% of subjects using and defining the term as compared with 38% at 11 years. Adding guilt and conscience responses together, 81% of the 13-year age-group reveal interiorised moral attitudes as compared with 61% at 11 years. The term is now used by some subjects in response to more than one test. But we find no evidence that frequency of reference to conscience is indicative of stronger conceptualisation. In general, however, conscience is more clearly defined: it is located predominantly in the mind; it is a social construct; it is exercised and consequently strengthened by wrongdoing; relief comes only through 'getting it off one's chest'. It is now that the Value of Life Test replaces the stealing situation as most strongly evoking conscience. Of the 44 conscience responses in this 13-year age-group, only 4 use religious terms. The 'voice of God' and the 'voice of Satan' now become 'the good half and the bad half of you'. The most significant characteristic of the developing concept of conscience is that it is shaped and patterned by upbringing.

(C) 15-YEAR AGE-GROUP

After the massive advance at 13 years in awareness and definition of conscience, there is little of note revealed in the 15-year age-group. This age-group is morally standing still, or possibly, as we shall suggest elsewhere, wavering, if not regressing. Thus, the 68% of subjects citing conscience compare with 73% at 13 years, and the 12% citing guilt feelings compare with 8% at 13 years. The Value of Life Test is now outstanding in evoking conscience responses. Heteronomy is now, for the majority of subjects, totally irrelevant in that, even if wrongdoing is not detected and punished, 'you still worry', 'you still feel guilty', and so 'you punish yourself'. Conscience is increasingly recognised as the social development of the innate moral capacity present from birth. It is shaped chiefly by parents and partly by teachers.

(D) 17-YEAR AGE-GROUP

97% of this age-group give conscience responses in response to one or other test, a massive increase of 29% over the 15-year age-group. The process of interiorisation, the first indications of which were seen at 9 years, is now complete. Religious references are minimal; conscience derives from upbringing, and its development is therefore explicitly seen as dependent upon human society. Conscience 'comes from society'; 'some people seem not to have one'; 'you'd have no conscience without other people'. Conscience is, in fact, 'the idea of right and wrong put into you by parents and teachers'. While a few subjects refer to it as a 'feeling', it is universally located in the mind.

(E) THE PATTERN OF DEVELOPMENT

The pattern that emerges from these responses may be evidenced thus:

Age-group N-60	*Guilt Responses*	*Conscience Responses*	*Guilt and conscience Responses*
9-year	13	—	13
11-year	14	23	37
13-year	5	44	49
15-year	7	41	48
17-year	—	58	58

This pattern is quantitative, rather than qualitative, in that no attempt was made as such to measure depth of interiorisation – if such a measure is conceivable. Certainly frequency of citations of conscience is no such measure. Indeed, the use of a mere verbalism had to be guarded against, chiefly by seeking definition. What the pattern does reveal is the progressive interiorisation of originally heteronomous precepts – not Piaget's theory of free reciprocity producing autonomy; and the progressive realisation that conscience is the moral potential of the infant shaped and developed by society.

Factors affecting conscience

Comment may be made, finally, upon three factors relating to the growth and power of conscience.

1. RELIGION

Explicit references to religion are few in our responses. They appear thus:

Age-group N-60	*Religious references*
11-year	5
13-year	4
15-year	—
17-year	4

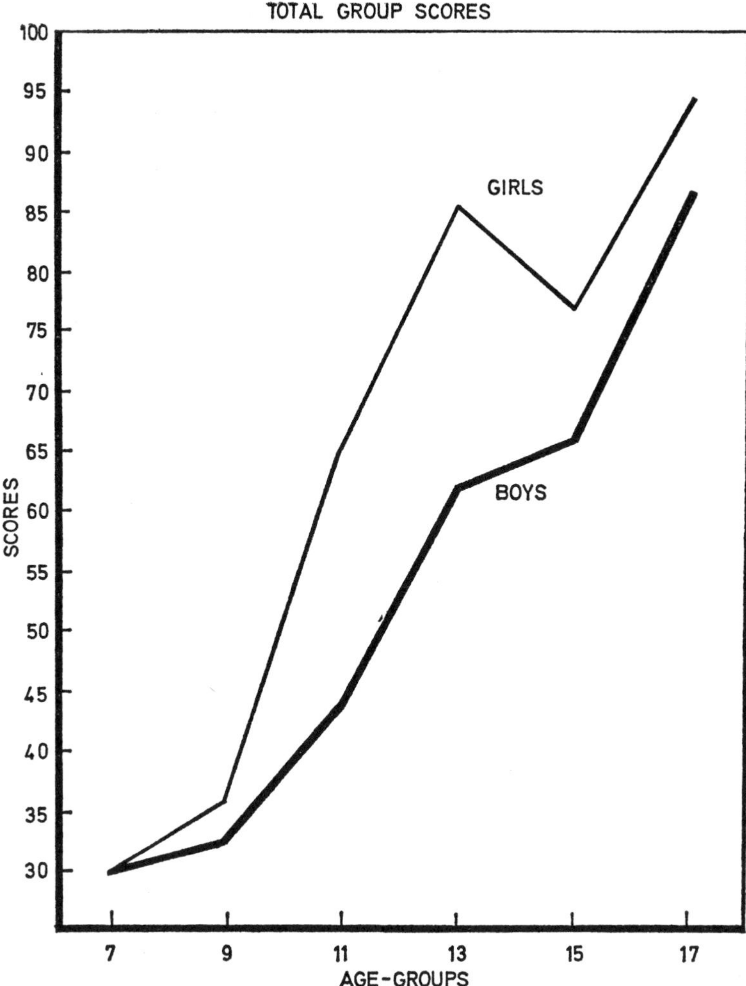
TOTAL GROUP SCORES
100
95
90
85
80
75
70
65
60
55
50
45
40
35
30
SCORES
GIRLS
BOYS
7
9
11
13
15
17
AGE-GROUPS

The thesis held from the outset of this work – that conscience is a social construct, and not a special faculty divinely implanted – is increasingly confirmed by our responses. But three points must be borne in mind. First, adolescents could not be expected to be consciously aware of the early influences upon their moral development – of which religion may well have been one. Secondly, since conscience is specifically attributed to adult guidance, it may well be indebted to the religious sentiments of the parents and teachers who shaped it. Thirdly, the contemporary neglect, if not repudiation, of religion can in no way deny that the moral values held and practised in society – for example, by atheistic humanists – may well be derived from the religious convictions of the past.

2. SEX

If we add together the total scores, in the development of conscience, for each single sex group at each age, the pattern that emerges shows girls to be clearly in advance of boys throughout. This pattern is derived from the total elements of anomy, of heteronomous fear, of a sense of guilt, and of conscience in each sex group at each age; and is thus indicative of responses, rather than of individuals. It is therefore not dependent upon the earlier maturation of girls, including intelligence, nor upon the greater facility of girls for verbalisation. Certainly the girls are most strongly ahead of boys at 11 and 13 years, the ages showing climacteric development. But they lead throughout in this quantitative measure of interiorisation. Such a sex differential is certainly consistent with evidence to be derived from the individual tests.

3. AREA OF AUTONOMY

We have remarked that the Value of Life Test was the most evocative of conscience responses, and increasingly so with age. For complete age-groups the figures are:

Age-group *N-60*	*Conscience Responses* *Value of Life Test*
11-year	6
13-year	34
15-year	33
17-year	44

This test thus produced 117 of the 257 conscience responses derived from all four tests – 45% of the total. The test certainly concerned the moral themes of pre-eminent significance at all ages – namely, murder and physical cruelty – and might therefore be expected to be the most evocative. But the fact remains that the issue was one of life and death; and it does not follow that conscience, evoked by so stark and vital an issue, will be similarly called into play by far less fundamental moral situations. Conscience may be strong in one moral area, weak in another. It may motivate saving life, but not necessarily being honest in word or deed. Conscience may be limited both qualitatively and quantitatively. It is true that conscience responses derived from the lying and stealing situations together equalled those from the Value of Life Test. But had we not used the Value of Life Test our evidence for the reality of conscience would have been greatly reduced.

It follows that, for example, when we find conscience invoked by 97% of the mature 17-year age-group in one or other test area, it would not be legitimate to infer autonomy in every moral area; and even less to do so for earlier age-groups. Given, however, our insistence upon levels of moral judgement at all ages, rather than upon stages achieved and left behind, such limitations of autonomy are precisely what we should expect. To put the same truth in other and familiar terms, there is both specificity and generality in moral judgement.

With this necessary qualification, we may accept the pattern found in our responses as definitive. We find autonomy to be rooted in heteronomy – not, as Piaget insists, in reciprocity. Fear merges into a sense of guilt, and guilt into autonomous conscience; and the process is a continuous and developing interiorisation of initially heteronomous definitions of good and evil.

Chapter 6
Cheating

Test situation

Evidence cited earlier showed that cheating is insignificant as a moral offence to both primary and secondary pupils. It is, in fact, an artificial, rather than intrinsic, offence, being fabricated by an individually competitive educational system. Indeed, positive and healthy child morality may be expressed in deliberate and illicit co-operation, as Piaget recalls from his own childhood, when 'cheating never seemed to us a sin. For years, as boys, we calmly did our homework together and arranged to help each other in class within the limits of possibility' (op. cit., 286, footnote).

Piaget fires an initial broadside against such a system – 'Instead of taking into account the child's deeper psychological tendencies which urge him to work with others – emulation being in no way opposed to co-operation – our schools condemn the pupil to work in isolation and only make use of emulation to set one individual against another' (op. cit., 286). Such a system is calculated to produce good examinees rather than good citizens. It calls forth cheating as a 'defence reaction' which may take two forms: 'Either competition prevails, with individual cheating; or comradeship wins the day, more particularly among older pupils, with organised cheating' (op. cit., 286). Piaget therefore speaks approvingly of the development of co-operative 'Activity Schools', as he would have done of the co-operative Soviet educational system (Bronfenbrenner, 1962*b*).

The universality of cheating, whether individual or fraternal, justified its use as one of the test situations in this study. Moreover, if moral judgements on cheating should be, as might be thought, primarily cognitive rather than orectic, the evidence derived from this test would be the more useful. That this was the case is suggested by the fact that only 8·5% of conscience responses were derived from the cheating situation.

Piaget concerned himself with cheating in the classroom and with cheating at games. We also tested both situations. One reason for this was to compare our results with those of Piaget. A second and more important reason was to gain fuller insight into the moral judgement of the child by balancing judgements on the primarily heteronomous situation in the classroom with those derived from free co-operation in games. Responses to the test showed clearly that to have used either aspect of cheating in isolation would have produced a one-sided, and in effect false, picture of child morality.

Cheating

Here is a picture of two girls/boys of about the same age as you. They are sitting next to each other in school. The teacher has often warned the class against cheating. One of the boys/girls is looking over towards the other. He/she might simply be looking that way. Do you think he/she is going to try to cheat and to copy from the other boy/girl?

YES

Does he/she think it's all right to cheat? ______

There's nothing wrong in cheating? ______

If caught, would he/she deserve to be punished? ______

What good would being punished do? ______

NO

What does he/she think about cheating? ______

Why does he/she think it's wrong? ______

A. Anomy e.g. you only get caught; you only get into trouble; or ______

B. Heteronomy e.g. it is forbidden; you get punished; it's wrong/naughty ______

C. Socionomy e.g. it is unfair; your friends will ______

D. Autonomy e.g. it's useless; you cheat yourself ______

______

CHEATING AND PUNISHMENT

Would it be all right for him/her to cheat if he/she could do it without getting caught and punished? ______

Why do you think so? ______

Even in an important examination? ______

CHEATING AT GAMES

Would he/she cheat at games?____________________

Why do you think so?____________________

A. Anomy____________________

B. Heteronomy____________________

C. Socionomy____________________

D. Autonomy____________________

We recall that the visual test devised showed two children sitting side by side in the classroom, one necessarily looking over towards the other to suggest the possibility of cheating. In structuring the scene, it was stressed that the child 'might simply be looking that way'. That the vast majority of subjects inferred cheating might be attributed to lack of ambiguity in the visual; or, alternatively, to the universality of cheating. Whatever the case, analysis of the situation with the subject was not affected.

Our primary question in terms of the classroom was, of course, why cheating was wrong. We asked, secondly, whether it would be all right to cheat if it could be done without detection and punishment, and the reason for the response made. We asked, thirdly, whether it would be all right to cheat even in an important examination. The value of these follow-up questions will be illustrated in responses. In terms of cheating at games, we asked whether the child would be likely to cheat at games, and the reasons for the response made.

7-YEAR AGE-GROUP: BOYS

Piaget reports one boy who thought it quite natural to cheat. Dismissing this as an 'exception', he none the less revealingly adds that 'no doubt many others thought the same without having the courage to say so' (op. cit., 288). He thus ignores anomy totally, as he does throughout.

We find elements of anomy in responses at all ages. It was indicated above all by responses to the question: 'Would it be all right to cheat if it could be done without detection and consequent punishment?' The child dominated by heteronomy would regard it as still wrong, as being prohibited and therefore deserving of punishment. Anomy, with its simple sanctions of pain and pleasure, would, on the other hand, regard cheating as good, in terms of the benefits derived from it, if it could be done without detection.

We may illustrate from 3 responses which hold cheating to be wrong since

'You only get caught.'

'He might have the wrong answers.'

'You always get it wrong.'

Piaget professes not to have met the first of these responses – which he dismissed as 'an adult sermon' – until the age of 10 years; this boy is aged 7 years 5 months. To the further question, the answers are:

'Yes. It would help me to get a star.'

'Yes. He wouldn't be seen.'

'Yes. Nobody would know.'

Such responses are indicative of anomy. A further 11 subjects show indications of anomy mixed with heteronomy. Thus:

'It is wrong. You only get into trouble'. (Q. 2) 'It would still be cheating, but I think I would do it.'

'You only get into trouble.' (Q. 2) 'I suppose so. No. It's wrong.'

'He'd do it so that he could be first. But someone would tell Miss.' (Q. 2) 'Yes. Nobody would know.'

A further 9 subjects are dominated by heteronomy, typically expressed as: 'It is wrong. Teacher tells you not to.' And heteronomy is even more confirmed when it extends to games, too. 'Rude' appears as an equivalent of 'naughty' in

'It's rude, you didn't really do the work.' (Q. 2) 'No. You have to show teacher some time, so you get found out and smacked.'

Another odd term is 'lie', as in

'It's wrong, 'cos he's been told not to.' (Q. 2) 'No. It would be a lie. It would be naughty.'

When the phrase 'it's not fair' appears, Piaget's 'adult sermon' might be suspected. But we can accept it as genuine in the context of games, as in the mixed response:

'It is forbidden. Teacher tells us not to.' (Games?) 'No. It is not really fair to the others.'

A similar and model Piagetian response is

'No. You have to follow the rules of the game, or else it isn't fair.'

But when we find the phrase 'it's not fair' applied to both aspects of cheating we see glimmerings of development, as in

'It is wrong. His teacher told him. It is unfair, and you never learn that way.' (Games?) 'No. It is not fair to the other people.'

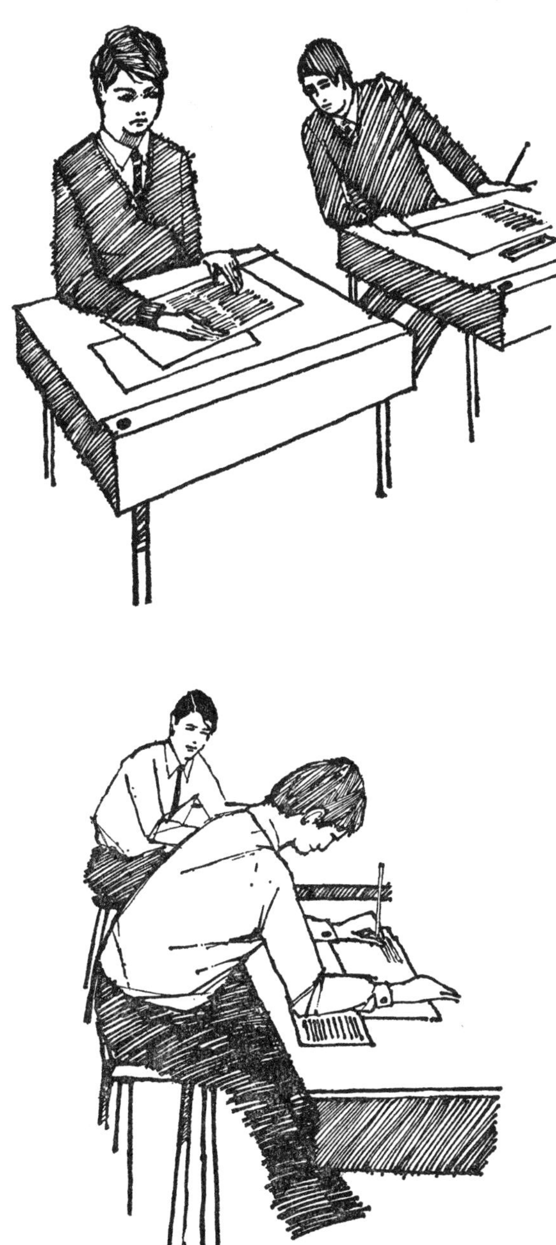

S.T.

7-YEAR AGE-GROUP: GIRLS

From 2 responses indicating anomy we may quote:

> 'It is wrong. You only get caught'. (Q. 2) 'Yes. You wouldn't get into trouble and it wouldn't matter.'

17 responses show anomy and heteronomy mixed. Thus:

> 'It's bad. She's not doing what teacher said.' (Q. 2) 'Yes. No one would see.'
>
> 'It's naughty. Teacher might see you.' (Q. 2) 'Yes. She knew no one would catch her and smack her.'
>
> 'It's bad. Teacher says so.' (Q. 2) 'Yes. Nobody knows.'

Variants of 'naughty' are 'horrible' and 'rude'. Mixed anomy and heteronomy are starkly expressed in

> 'It's naughty. You get a smack.' (Q. 2) 'Yes. You won't get a smack.'

A further 5 responses are wholly heteronomous. For example:

> 'It is wrong. Teacher tells us we mustn't.' (Q. 2) 'No. It would still be not what Teacher tells us to do.'
>
> 'Teacher tells us we mustn't because we don't learn.' (Q. 2) 'No. You mustn't, because it's wrong.'

Typically, strict heteronomy in the classroom situation combines with strict equality in games. Thus:

> 'It is wrong. You don't learn.' (Games?) 'No. It would be very unfair to the others.'

It is not easy to decide at what point the 'adult sermon' becomes part of the child's own thinking – and such common phrases as 'you don't learn' are clearly derived from the teacher. Piaget airily dismisses all such 'adult sermons'; we have to look for signs of interiorisation in the total responses. But the phrase 'it is unfair' we can accept as indicative of equality, especially when it arises in both aspects of cheating. 2 responses show heteronomy mixed with equality, and a further 4 are fully socionomous.

9-YEAR AGE-GROUP: BOYS

15, or half the responses, show anomy mixed with heteronomy. Examples are:

> 'You get punished.' (Q. 2) 'Yes. I've done it tons of times without getting caught.'
>
> 'It's wrong. The other person may have the wrong answer. You're at school to learn, not to copy.' (Q. 2) 'Yes. No one's looking. They can't tell.' (Exam.?) 'No. You'd get punished if you were caught.'

'The other boy might have the wrong answers too.' (Q. 2) 'No. But it'll be all right for him. But it's wrong really, 'cos cheating is a bad deed.'

'He hasn't really done the work. The other boy might be away and he won't be able to copy. Then Teacher would wonder why he couldn't do it.' (Q. 2) 'Yes. Teacher wouldn't find out.'

4 responses are wholly heteronomous. For example:

'Teacher told him not to. It's wrong.' (Q. 2) 'No. Because it's wrong.'

'It is stealing. You don't use your own brain.' (Q. 2) 'No. Because cheating is wrong anyway.'

'It's wrong. It's Teacher's fault. The boys shouldn't be given the chance to cheat.' (Q. 2) 'No. Cheating is like lying. It's wrong.'

Another 5 responses show anomy mixed with socionomy. Thus:

'No. He might get the wrong answer.' (Q. 2) 'No. It wouldn't be fair on the rest of the class.'

'I think it's not fair. You get rewarded for somebody else's work.' (Q. 2) 'Yes. Nobody would do anything to him.'

A real Devon response includes the moral judgement:

' 'Tidn nice.'

Heteronomy is mixed with socionomy in 4 responses. Thus:

'It's wrong, and you get caught in the end.' (Q. 2) 'No. It wouldn't be fair on the boy who is working honestly.'

2 higher responses remain, both from subjects of higher intelligence (I.Q. 125, I.Q. 120):

'It is stealing somebody else's answers, not doing your own. You only get the worst if you do.' (Q. 2) 'You still get found out. You get into the habit and do it all your life.'

'There's no point to it. It's like committing a crime.'

9-YEAR AGE-GROUP: GIRLS

12 responses show anomy and heteronomy together. Thus:

'Teacher told them again and again not to.' (Q. 2) 'Yes. The other person won't know.'

'Being punished will stop her from cheating again. You only get caught, anyway.' (Q. 2) 'Yes. You might be able to get into the top group if you copied from somebody brainier.'

'I think it's horrible. The other person might have the wrong answers, too, and then you'd lose all your marks.' (Q. 2) 'Yes. I would then, because nobody *could* find out.'

'It's wrong. It's not your own work.' (Q. 2) 'Yes. No one knows but yourself.'

A further 11 responses are purely heteronomous. For example:

'She knows it's wrong. Teacher told her not to.' (Q. 2) 'No. It's not nice to cheat.' (Games?) 'No. She has been told it's wrong.'

'It's wrong, like lying.' (Q. 2) 'No. You should be punished; then you would stop.'

Finally, 7 responses show both heteronomy and socionomy in the classroom context. Thus:

'It is wrong and it's not fair.'

'It's not fair.' (Q. 2) 'No. Teacher has said it's wrong so it's wrong.'

One includes a rare example of reciprocity:

'I think it's a horrible thing. She wouldn't want anyone to copy her work, so *she* shouldn't.'

11-YEAR AGE-GROUP: BOYS

While there are glimmerings of future development, the general pattern remains much the same as that of the 9-year boys. 2 responses indicate anomy. For example:

'It's wrong. The other boy might have it wrong.' (Q. 2) 'Yes. You can get away with it.' (Games?) 'He might if it's hard. He wouldn't if it's easy. The other boys might walk off and leave him.'

A further 10 responses show both anomy and heteronomy. The teacher's shibboleths are duly produced by anaemic heteronomy, but without much conviction. Examples are:

'It's wrong. You're using somebody else's brain. It's lazy. You won't learn by it.' (Q. 2) 'Yes. You wouldn't get punished.'

'He really knows it's wrong. Teacher tells you not to. You get punished.' (Q. 2) 'Yes. It's easier to get through your work.'

'I think it's wrong, because I got caught myself once and got punished.' (Q. 2) 'No. But do it and try to make up your mind not to do it again.'

From the 4 wholly heteronomous responses we may quote:

'It's wrong. Teacher wants to know what *you* can do, not someone else. You're supposed to do your own work.' (Q. 2) 'No. It's like being sneaky – and you might get caught in the end and *really* punished.'

'It's not doing your own work. It's a sin. It says in the Ten Commandments that you mustn't cheat. If you keep those Commandments you'll be a Christian.'

Elements of socionomy are found in 6 mixed responses, such as:

'It's not very good. You get told off if Teacher finds out.' (Q. 2) 'No. Nobody likes to be called a cheat – the other children would get to know.'

> 'Cheating's bad, but it's not really bad like cheating for money. Teacher wants his answers, and not the other boy's. It's not really fair. It takes away the chance of the others to do well.'
>
> 'It's bad. It won't get you anywhere.' (Q. 2) 'No. The other person may be wrong too.' (Games?) 'No. More people are watching him. His friends will call him a cheat and a fouler and throw him out of the team.'

A further 8 mixed responses show glimmerings of autonomy. It is suggested by the dawning realisation that you are only cheating yourself, and that therefore cheating is pointless, as well as being dishonest with yourself. Thus:

> 'It's not a honest thing to do. It's not his own work. He'd get more marks than he should.' (Q. 2) 'No. You're not being honest with your work.'
>
> 'It's wrong. I like to see for myself whether my work is right or wrong.'
>
> 'It's wrong. Someone will find out.' (Q. 2) 'He still doesn't gain anything. He might go to a school where he couldn't do the work.'

Even more clear-cut is the response:

> 'He would be punishing himself. He'd get into a class where he couldn't do the work.' (Q. 2) 'No. It wouldn't get me anywhere. One day I'll have to do my own work for myself.' (Exam.?) 'It's just silly. It wouldn't get you anywhere.'

11-YEAR AGE-GROUP: GIRLS

The pattern is similar to that of the 11-year boys, though with somewhat more socionomy. Anomy is indicated by

> 'It's not really wrong.' (Q. 2) 'Yes. She knows she won't get caught.' (Exam.?) 'No. You might get marks knocked off.' (Games?) 'Yes. To win.'

3 responses show anomy mixed with heteronomy, 7 are fully heteronomous, and a further 3 show both heteronomy and socionomy. From the 5 socionomous responses we may quote:

> 'It's not a fair way to get the answers. Why should *she* do it the easy way?'
>
> 'You shouldn't cheat at all. People won't want to sit by you because you copy their work.'

10 mixed responses show glimmerings of autonomy. Thus:

> 'She should ask Teacher, who would help her, and she'd know how to do it the next time. Cheating's wrong. Somebody else is working hard, and she just copies and gets away with it easily. She'll grow up

into the sort of person who's always trying to do things easily.' 'You'd get found out by Teacher asking questions. It may lead to trouble.' (Q. 2) 'No. Conscience would stop you – the little man inside, prodding all the time.'

'No. You wouldn't have earned the merit. Teacher wants to know what you can do.' (Q. 2) 'No. You'd have a guilty conscience – it tells you, it bothers you when you've done wrong.'

13-YEAR AGE-GROUP: BOYS

7 responses show both anomy and heteronomy. For example:

'It's an easy way. It's not wrong. But punishment would stop me.' (Q. 2) 'Yes.' (Exam.?) 'No. You're more likely to be found out.'

'You don't learn.' (Q. 2) 'No. You might get over-confident and one day get caught.' (Exam.?) 'It might be worth it if you're not caught.'

2 responses are fully heteronomous. From the 7 responses showing socionomy mixed with lower levels we may quote:

'It's dishonest, using another's brains.' (Q. 2) 'No. But I would.' (Exam.?) 'No. By that time, by O levels, I'd really know it was wrong.'

'Teacher says it's wrong. It's stealing.' (Exam.?) 'It's worse. If you pass and the other person doesn't it's unfair.'

'It's unfair to the others – it doesn't give them a chance.' (Q. 2) 'Yes. It's better than doing it all yourself.'

The 3 socionomous responses may be illustrated by

'It would be disloyal to the teacher and to the class. It would be unfair.'

7 mixed responses show signs of incipient autonomy. For example:

'Cheating is an urge you can't help. It's unfair, though, making yourself look as brainy as other people. It's unfair to yourself.' (Q. 2) 'No. He is punishing himself in a way – he's not learning and he'll never do well in his job.'

'It's unfair to the others – you're stealing off them.' (Games?) 'No. You still shouldn't cheat. Otherwise you will have no confidence in yourself.'

Finally, 2 responses are even more emphatic:

'In the wide world you cannot cheat. You must stand on your own.' (Games?) 'No. You don't get the satisfaction of knowing that you won on your own merits.'

13-YEAR AGE-GROUP: GIRLS

We now observe the strong development between 11 and 13 years that we find in response to other tests. Anomy becomes minimal, and only 2 responses are fully heteronomous. A further 6 responses show one or the other level mingled with socionomy. From the 7 fully socionomous responses we may quote:

'It is unfair. One's doing all the work.' (Games?) 'No. If you cheat and win it's unfair to the other person or team.'

'I was always taught that it's wrong. You're using other people's knowledge for gain. I now realise that it *is* wrong.' (Games?) 'Yes, if you do it in fun, but it's not really right. It's not using your own skill. It's not fair.'

'It's bad and wrong. It shows you are incapable of being left. It is unfair – using other's brains.' (Games?) 'No. It's still bad. It's being unfair to the other side.'

9 responses show autonomy side by side with lower levels of judgement. For example:

'You would feel guilty about it.' (Q. 2) 'No. Because the other girls would see you.'

'The other girl might have the wrong answers.' (Q. 2) 'No. You'd have a conscience about it.'

From the 6 responses suggesting autonomy we may quote:

'It's a waste of the test and of time. You're not showing what you can do.' (Exam.?) 'No. Your whole future is at stake. If you pass, you're not really going to be able to do your work in life. It'll be the worse for you.'

'If you start cheating you can't live for yourself. It will lead to other things.' (Q. 2) 'No. You'd have a guilty conscience.' (Games?) 'Once you start cheating at games you cheat at other things too.'

The total responses of the girls in this age-group show 10½ autonomous responses as compared with 6 from the boys; 15 girls are partly or wholly autonomous as compared with 10 boys. It is not until the next age-group that boys achieve this quantity of autonomous responses. Again, therefore, we see girls developing earlier than boys.

15-YEAR AGE-GROUP: BOYS

While fulsome responses tend to be characteristic of girls, boys are more inclined to pseudo-sophistications in this test as in others. Examples here, from the 13 mixed lower responses, are:

'I don't treat cheating as very serious myself.'

'Cheating's too small to be a matter of conscience.'

'Morally it's wrong, really.'

'I'd be afraid of getting caught. Fear is proof of it's being wrong.'

9 responses indicate partial autonomy. It is typically suggested by lack of the satisfaction of achievement, in work or play; by getting into a bad, lifelong habit; and by inadequacy in later work. In the examination context, it is realised that the whole future may depend upon the result, and that cheating may well lead to a situation in which one cannot cope. This is, of course, a parallel to those 11-year subjects, who saw that cheating might lead to an undeserved grammar-school place and to consequent inadequacy and failure. Both suggest a cognitive rather than an attitudinal judgement. In short:

'It doesn't do you any good in the long run.'

'It won't do you any good.'

'We're cheating others as well as ourselves.'

A final 5 responses show autonomy. Cheating is typically 'stupid' in the classroom and 'unsporting' at games. Moreover,

'It's the principle of the thing. If you cheat at games you're just as likely to cheat in exams.'

15-YEAR AGE-GROUP: GIRLS

Anomy is now minimal, with a total of but $1\frac{1}{2}$ responses, while heteronomy has declined to $4\frac{1}{2}$. For the 9 fully socionomous responses, cheating is typically 'unfair'. 10 responses show partial autonomy, and 5 show full autonomy. Typical of these responses are:

'You don't know your own ability.'

'You'd have a guilty conscience about it.'

'It doesn't help you.'

'You're cheating yourself.'

'It's herself she's cheating in the first place.'

'You don't get any satisfaction.'

'You're not being honest to yourself.'

And the ultimate judgement:

'If you know the work, there is no point in cheating. If you don't know it, it's no help.'

17-YEAR AGE-GROUP: BOYS

Even at this age we find anomy and heteronomy mixed in 4 responses:

'You get punished.' (Q. 2) 'Yes.' (Exam.?) 'Yes. If it's for an important job.'

'Father might find out.' (Q. 2) 'Yes. Good luck if you can get away with it.'

'You might copy wrong. You might be right if you did it yourself.' (Games?) 'It's O.K. if the referee doesn't see.'

'You can't help it if the chance is there.'

Anomy or heteronomy are mixed with socionomy in 6 responses. Two pragmatists respond:

(Q. 2) 'Yes. Everybody cheats at times.' (Games?) 'I might if I was losing.'

(Q. 2) 'Yes. No one will be hurt.'

12 responses mingle autonomy with lower levels. Thus:

'People will find out. . . . You cheat yourself.'

'It's not fair on the other person.' (Q. 2) 'No. Not if he had a conscience.'

'His friends wouldn't like him.' (Q. 2) 'No. You're cheating yourself. It will catch up with you.'

'It's no good to yourself.' (Games?) 'No. I'd be afraid of being found out.'

A final 8 responses show clear autonomy. Typical comments are:

'It's no help at all – a waste of time.'

'Your conscience would find you out.'

'I'd rather fail than cheat.'

'You're cheating yourself.'

'It's the principle. You're doing yourself no good.'

'You gain nothing, you learn nothing.'

17-YEAR AGE-GROUP: GIRLS

The only element of anomy is in the response:

'Sooner or later you'll be in a situation where you can't.' (Q. 2) 'Yes. If you can get away with it it's O.K.' (Exam.?) 'It's not right. It's unfair to others.'

Another mixed response is:

'It's using another person for one's own advantage.' (Q. 2) 'It's still wrong, but a lot of people would. I don't think I would for fear of being caught.'

5 responses indicate socionomy. Quotable comments are:

'It would be a terrible society if everybody did it. You just can't live that way.'

'People can always see it in your face. They won't like you in the end for it.'

And the fulsome definition:

'It's not all right, but it's not a deadly sin. You do more harm to yourself than to others.' (Q. 2) 'No. It doesn't make it any more right because it isn't punished.' (Games?) 'You wouldn't want to give your friends a false impression. In the classroom you cheat *with* your friends; in games you cheat *against* them.'

14 responses show autonomy mixed with lower levels. Cheating is clearly distinguished from more serious offences in

'It's not fair on other people or yourself. But it's not quite as bad as stealing.'

'It's not fair on the other person. Stealing is a crime – more important. Cheating is a sin – less important.'

Cheating is therefore permissible in certain circumstances:

'You know you don't deserve credit for cheated work. It's a bit like stealing.' (Q. 2) 'No. But you probably would if stuck – if you were afraid of being punished for poor work.'

'It's dishonest and self-deceptive.' (Q. 2) 'As long as you don't do it too often, ordinarily. But not on the big occasion.'

The greater concern of girls with personal relationships is seen here as elsewhere:

'You don't gain anything. Your friends despise you.'

'People don't believe what you say or do if you're liable to cheat. They don't trust you.'

Even romantic interests are involved in

(Games?) 'If it's a friendly game, everybody cheats. If it's a serious game it might do harm. If I did it playing tennis with my boy-friend, who thinks a lot of himself at tennis, it might do harm and break things between us.'

Finally, 9 responses show full autonomy. We may quote:

'It's like stealing.' (Games?) 'No. It's against my principles.'

'She's wasting her own talents. She's punishing herself.'

'It's self-deception.' (Games?) 'It's very annoying. But games aren't important to me. Boys take them so seriously.'

'Cheating is dishonest, whether you're caught or not.'

The pattern of development

The developmental pattern, to be seen in response to the Cheating Test, may be traced most conveniently in terms of the variable factors involved.

1. SEX DIFFERENCES

The comparative development of the sexes can be illustrated by applying to each sex group, at each age-level, the scoring scale that was applied to individual responses (A-1, B-2, C-3, D-4, with halved scores for mixed responses). The resulting figures are:

Total group scores

Age-group	*Boys N-30*	*Girls N-30*	*Comparative Girls' Score*
7 years	55·0	53·5	− 1·5
9 years	57·0	57·5	+ 0·5
11 years	65·5	74·5	+ 9·0
13 years	78·0	91·0	+13·0
15 years	81·5	92·5	+11·0
17 years	90·0	103·5	+13·5

Sex differences are minimal at 7 years and at 9 years. At 11 years, however, girls are in advance of boys through their stronger socionomy. Another, and familiar, dramatic development between 11 and 13 years increases the girls' lead. Yet again at 15 years we see little advance by either sex; at this age autonomous responses are similar, while the girls show less anomy and heteronomy and greater socionomy. At 17 years both sexes show another broadly similar and familiar, though less dramatic, advance. Thus the lead established by the girls at 11 years is increased at 13 years and thereafter remains broadly constant. It derives from the greater socionomy and developing autonomy of the girls, as contrasted with the anomy and heteronomy in the boys' responses that are still residual at 17 years.

For both sexes the main development is between 9 and 13 years. But it is far stronger in girls: and they reach a level at 13 years that is not attained by boys until 17 years. In short, therefore, once development begins after 9 years, when the sexes are almost identical in their judgements, girls show a consistently higher pattern than boys.

2. INTELLIGENCE

We have previously hypothesised that judgements on the cheating situation might be predominantly cognitive – as contrasted, for example, with the strongly orectic judgements that we have already analysed in terms of conscience. If this were so, might it not, in particular, be the key factor in the higher response pattern of girls?

We may note, first, the mean I.Q.s for each sex at each age level in our total sample:

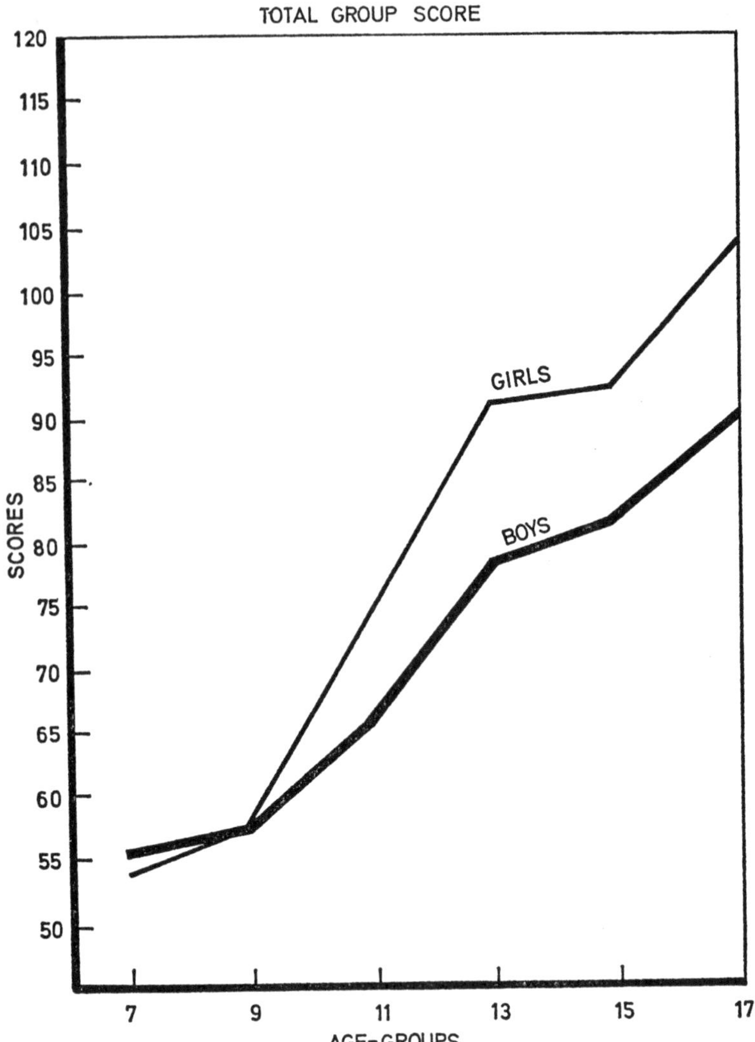
TOTAL GROUP SCORE
120
115
110
105
100
95
90
85
80
75
70
65
60
55
50
SCORES
GIRLS
BOYS
7
9
11
13
15
17
AGE-GROUPS

Mean I.Q.s

Age-group	*Boys* *N-30*	*Girls* *N-30*
7 years	108·2	108·8
9 years	110·8	107·8
11 years	96·9	105·8
13 years	98·5	106·3
15 years	104·6	108·5
17 years	106·4	108·2

While the mean intelligence of girls is in advance of boys at every age level save 9 years, the sharpest disparity is at 11 years and 13 years; and it is precisely at this age that we find climacteric development, particularly in girls, in our test situations. Such disparity might be attributed to selectivity in the sample tested. The 11-year subjects, both boys and girls, however, were from the same two unstreamed classes, each in a different school. The mean socio-economic class was 2·8 for the boys and 2·7 for the girls, while boys exceeded girls in mean chronological age by 1·3 months. Both factors therefore favoured the boys, if minimally. Yet the mean female intelligence exceeded that of the boys by 8·9. It seems impossible to attribute this to any other than innate, developmental factors. The 13-year age-group was made up of 8 boys and 8 girls, selected at random from the same class of the same mixed grammar school; the remaining 22 girls selected at random from a girls' secondary modern school, and the remaining 22 boys randomly selected from two boys' secondary modern schools. At both 11 and 13 years, therefore, the samples of each sex were as nearly equivalent as possible, and at 11 years from identical classes.

The fact remains, however, that in our age-groups from 11 to 17 years inclusive the means of the girls' I.Q.s exceeded those of the boys by 8·9, 7·8, 3·9, and 1·8 respectively. The differences are strongest at 11 and 13 years, when the girls' scores show their strongest advance. At 15 years the boys, with the hypothetical handicap of lower mean intelligence, increase in total score by 3·5 as compared with the girls' increase of 1·5. Such a difference is minimal and, in any case, we are becoming familiar with the relative 'standstill' in development at 15 years. Again, at 17 years the mean I.Q. of the girls exceeds that of boys by only 1·8, and their increase in total score exceeds that of the boys by only 2·5. Thus the earlier development of girls in intelligence, attributable to innate, maturational

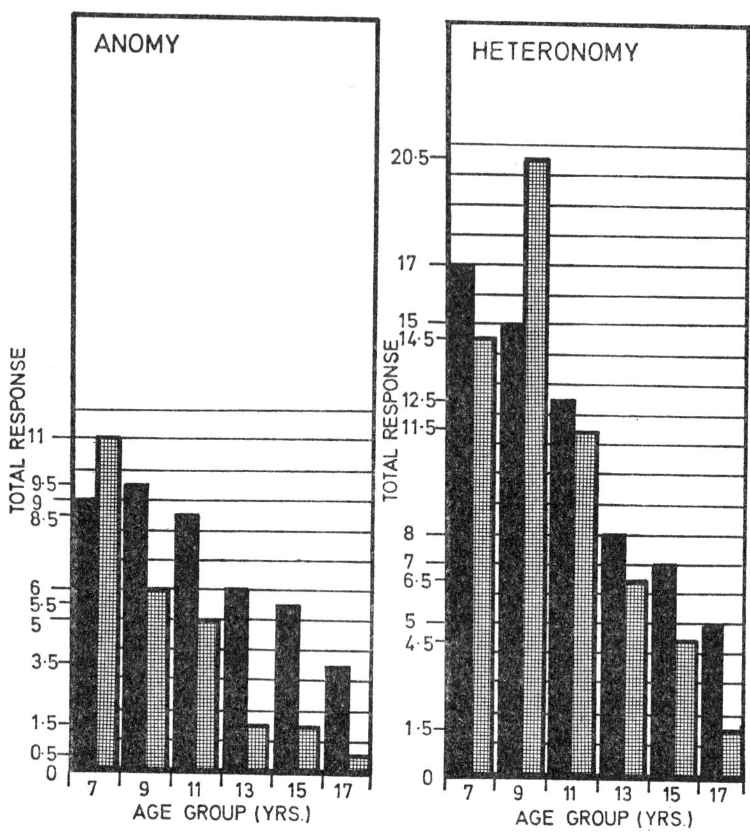

TABLE OF I.Q. VALUES

AGE-GROUP		7	9	11	13	15	17
MEAN I.Q.	BOYS	108·2	110·8	96·9	98·5	104·6	106·4
	GIRLS	108·8	107·8	105·8	106·3	108·5	108·2

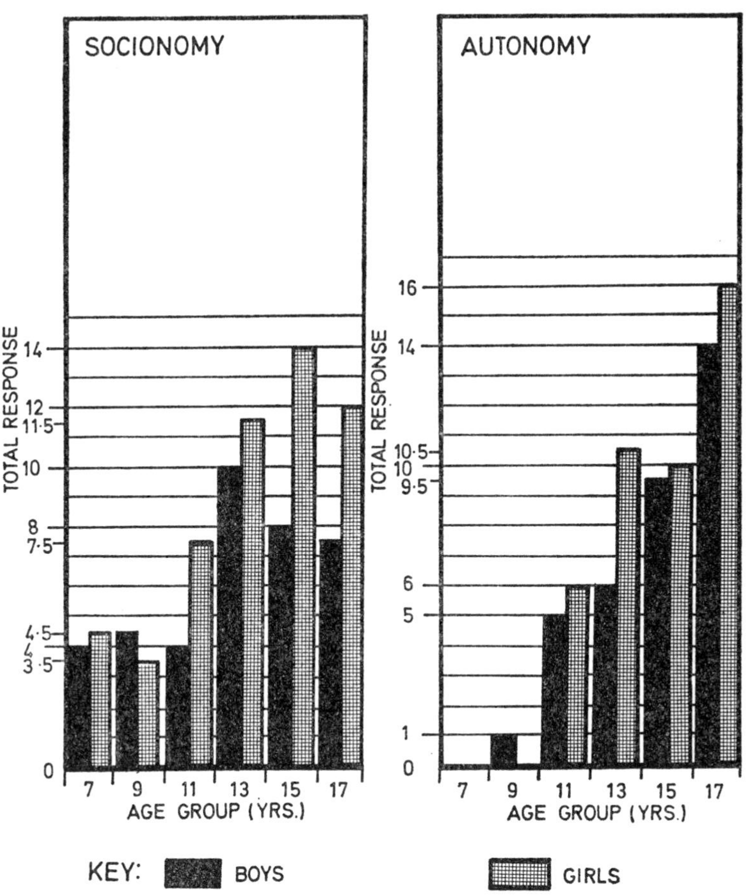

NOTE: N=60 PER AGE-GROUP (30 BOYS + 30 GIRLS)

factors, appears a key factor in their higher moral judgements with the onset of adolescence.

Such a conclusion derives support from a contrast between the girls' lead in total scores in response to the Cheating Test and the Value of Life Test. The figures are:

Girls' lead in total group scores

Age-group	*Cheating Test*	*Value of Life Test*
7 years	− 1·5	+ 7·0
9 years	+ 0·5	+ 7·0
11 years	+ 9·0	+ 2·5
13 years	+13·0	+11·0
15 years	+11·0	+ 4·0
17 years	+13·5	+ 3·5

The higher scores of girls at 7 and 9 years in the Value of Life Test were attributed to stronger innate sympathy, while thereafter girls are only minimally in advance of boys, save at 13 years, the climacteric age. Were intelligence the key factor, we might expect a similarly striking lead in the girls at 11 years, when the mean of their I.Q.s is also strikingly in advance of the boys as at 13 years (8·9 and 7·8 respectively). The fact remains, however, that from 11 years the girls' lead is consistently higher in the Cheating Test than in the Value of Life Test. We infer that, when deep issues of life and death are involved, there is no such sharp difference in the moral judgement of the sexes as in the matter of cheating. This difference may be attributed to differences in mental maturation. But we have observed in responses the greater sensitivity of girls to personal relationships, and we shall be concerned with the significance of this factor in other moral areas.

Comparison with Piaget's results: classroom

We note at the outset the difficulties of comparing our results with those of Piaget. First, he always happily secures single and clear-cut responses. The great majority of ours, however, are mixed and complex to a degree; and hence our vital sophistication of half-scores. Secondly, in his overwhelming concern with heteronomy and equality, he ignores anomy, whereas we find it at all ages. Thirdly, Piaget is cavalier in rejecting any response that smacks of the 'adult sermon', whereas we find in their progressive interiorisation the process of growth to autonomy.

Piaget found his results 'very definite'. His enquiry showed 'a gradual diminution in the preoccupation with authority and a correlative increase in the desire for equality'. His single question was: 'Why must you not copy from your friend's book?' He found three types of answer. The first judged cheating to be wrong as disobeying adult prohibition ('It is forbidden', 'It is naughty', 'It is deceit', 'It is a lie', 'You get punished', etc.). The second judged cheating wrong as being 'contrary to equality ("It does harm to a friend, it is stealing from him", etc.). The third saw cheating as being useless ("one learns nothing", "one always gets caught", etc.)' (Piaget, op. cit., 287). We shall return to Piaget's astonishing rejection of this third type of response as being no more than the reproduction of adult sermons. He is thus left with two types of response. Cheating is wrong either as being contrary to adult constraint or as being contrary to equality.

We consider first Piaget's findings of heteronomy. Since he finds no anomy, we will assume, in fairness, that it is included in his heteronomy, and tabulate two sets of figures accordingly to compare with Piaget's:

Comparative findings from the Cheating Test (I)

Age	*Heteronomy*		*Anomy and Heteronomy*
	Piaget	*Us*	*Us*
7 years	100%	52·5%	87·5%
9 years	88%	59·1%	85·0%
11 years	32%	40·0%	62·5%
12 years	15%	—	—
13 years	—	24·1%	36·7%
15 years	—	19·1%	30·8%
17 years	—	10·8%	17·5%

Our results thus differ markedly from those of Piaget. While heteronomy does, of course, decrease, its waning is nothing like so emphatic as Piaget finds. In particular, it is residual throughout adolescence and far more strongly so than Piaget's figures would imply.

We turn, secondly, to Piaget's figures for equality. His 'equality' is part of, but not the whole of, our 'socionomy'. We will, however, in fairness, regard all our responses on this level as indicating equality. We have, in addition, Piaget's third category of responses holding that cheating is 'useless ("one learns nothing", "one always gets caught", etc.)'. Piaget opines that: 'This third sort of answer is probably of adult origin: the child is merely repeating the sermon that has been preached to him when he has been caught cheating. It only appears after the age of 10' (op. cit., 287).

Comparative findings from the Cheating Test (II)

Age	*Equality* *Piaget*	*Socionomy* *Us*	*'Useless'* *Piaget*	*Autonomy* *Us*
6 years	—	—	—	—
7 years	—	—	—	—
8 years 9 years	16%	13·3%	—	—
10 years	26%	—	5%	—
11 years 12 years	62%	19·1%	4% 25%	18·3%
13 years	—	35.8%	—	27.5%
14 years	—	—	—	—
15 years	—	36.7%	—	32.5%
16 years	—	—	—	—
17 years	—	32.5%	—	50.0%

Again our results differ markedly from those of Piaget. While we agree that the broad development is from heteronomy to equality, our figures for all socionomy responses are nothing like so impressive as Piaget's figures for equality. The greatest difference is at 11 to 12 years, and it is quite unbridgeable. Even if we add together our responses for both socionomy and autonomy, they still amount to little over half Piaget's equality figure of 62%. We have certainly found reciprocity to be strongest at 9 to 11 years, but to nothing like that extent. And, even accepting that for Piaget equality merges into equity and equity into autonomy, we can still find no accommodation between his equality and our socionomy combined with autonomy.

Even more striking are Piaget's figures for his third category of responses judging cheating to be useless. He rejects these as 'adult sermons', delivered when the child is caught cheating. Why should these responses suddenly appear *en masse* at 12 years, with a dramatic rise from 4% to

25%? Are we to assume that the average child does not cheat before that age? And hears no 'adult sermons' on cheating before that age? Would not repetitions of 'adult sermons' be expected earlier, in the heyday of heteronomy – as, for example, in the teacher's shibboleths that we found repeated so frequently in our responses?

The very appearance of so dramatic an increase, as late as 12 years, strongly suggests a new development. We find that new development, of course, in the dawning of autonomy, the first glimmerings of which are seen precisely at this age. Hence, we hold, the strong correspondence between Piaget's 25% of 'useless' responses at 12 years and our 27% of autonomy responses at 13 years. Thus in his dubious and idiosyncratic determination to get beneath 'adult sermons' – which are, of course, rejected – to 'genuine' responses, we find Piaget rejecting the first significant signs of that autonomy which goes on developing through adolescence.

In short, we find a gross over-simplification of developing moral judgement in Piaget's findings. It is hard to avoid the impression that he finds figures that happily confirm his theory. Ignoring, in effect, anomy on the one hand, and autonomy of the other, and, of course, never encountering mixed responses, he finds massive support for a simple and strict dichotomy of heteronomy and equality. We, on the contrary, find the increasing interiorisation of those 'adult sermons' that Piaget spurns. It is true that judgements on cheating seem to be characteristically cognitive, but by no means wholly so; and that a sense of reciprocity, in terms of Piaget's equality, plays its part in development. But the basis of development remains the interiorisation of heteronomous precepts. We may sum up the process in the response of a girl of 13 years: 'I was always taught that it's wrong. You're using other people's knowledge for gain. I now realise it *is* wrong.'

Comparison with Piaget's results: games

We followed Piaget in also seeking judgements on cheating at games, not simply for the sake of comparing results, but also to secure more representative responses from a situation in which free co-operation replaces the broad heteronomy of the classroom; and we have already seen their value.

Piaget found four types of answer to the question: Why should one not cheat at games? They were: '(1) It is naughty (forbidden, etc.). (2) It is contrary to the rules of the game. (3) It makes co-operation impossible ("You can't play any more"). (4) It is contrary to equality' (op. cit., 305). To codify his results, Piaget divided his subjects into two groups – 6 to 9 years and 10 to 12 years, remembering that 'it was round about 9 that rules began to be stabilised' (op. cit., 305). Piaget noted 'the following changes as we pass from one group to another. Answers appealing to the authority of rules (whether of morality or games), i.e. answers of types 1 and 2, drop from 70% to 32%, whereas answers of types 3 and 4, appealing, that is, to co-operation or to equality, rise from 30% to 68%' (op. cit., 305).

Once again we may agree with Piaget that heteronomy gives ground to the realisation that cheating 'makes co-operation impossible' – it 'spoils the fun', in our responses; and to the realisation that it is contrary to equality – 'it's not fair to the others', in our responses. Once again, too, we must bear in mind the fact of a different population and country – and not least the traditional British attitude to games being notoriously different from the Continental.

It is still, however, immensely difficult to make parallels with Piaget's findings. We find categories that he does not seem to have met. Thus, at the lower end of the scoring scale we find cheating motivated simply by the overweening desire to win. In the age-groups from 7 years to 13 years, our parallel to Piaget's age-groups, the desire to win accounts for 30%, 30%, 41·6% and 18·3% respectively of our responses. The desire to win, initially the game – but, later, esteem from peers – is linked with the strong and increasing opinion that 'games are not important' and are 'just for fun' – responses also unknown to Piaget. At the other end of the scoring scale we find, from 11 years onwards, an increasing measure of autonomy, similarly absent in Piaget's analysis – unless we are to interpret his 'equality' to include its development, in Piaget's theorising, into equity which in turn is universalised into autonomy. In short, as in the classroom situation, we find Piaget ignoring both anomy, expressed in the desire to win, and autonomy in order to concentrate upon his two concerns – heteronomy and equality.

Again, it is difficult to find in our responses anything like the heteronomous type 2 of Piaget: 'It's against the rules.' We find, in fact, only 4 such responses, and those at 7 years. Similarly, we find a minimal number of his type 3 responses: 'It makes co-operation impossible.'

The nearest we can come to a comparison is to take our 7- and 9-year age-groups as the equivalent of Piaget's 6- to 9-year group; and our 11- and 13-year age-groups as the nearest equivalent to his 10- to 12-year grouping. If we then take the mean of each grouping of two age-groups combined, we have a reasonable parallel to Piaget's age-groupings. The contrast then appears thus:

Comparative Findings from the Cheating Test (III): Games

Age-group	*Against Authority Type 1*		*Against the Rules Type 2*		*Against Co-operation Type 3*		*Against Equality Type 4*	
	P-t	*Us*	*P-t*	*Us*	*P-t*	*Us*	*P-t*	*Us*
6-9 years	64%	27%	6%	1·6%	0%	5%	30%	14%
10-12 years	8%	12%	24%	—	20%	3%	48%	20%

Thus whereas, in the earlier age-grouping, Piaget's combined figures for the Types 1 and 2 decrease from 70% to 32%, our decrease is from 29% to 12%. Similarly, whereas, in the older age-grouping, Piaget's combined figures for Types 3 and 4 increase from 30% to 68%, ours merely increase from 19% to 24%. The rest of our responses in each age-group fall into categories that have no place in Piaget's analysis.

We can, therefore, only agree that heteronomy is replaced by considerations of equality, but to nothing like the extent that Piaget finds. Nowhere, not even at 7 and 9 years, do we find the awareness of rules upon which so much of Piaget's thesis hangs. If the vast difference in findings is to be attributed to ethnic and environmental differences, it follows that Piaget's theory is limited, and therefore, when generalised, erroneous.

We do, of course, find sophisticated distinctions in our older age-groups. For example, while it is quite permissible – indeed, it 'adds to the fun' for some subjects – to cheat in private games, cheating would be quite immoral in any representative games. We find, too, that cheating is rejected because it would be offensive to friends, risk quarrels, and possibly cause fights. Even conscience is invoked by some older autonomous responses.

All such distinctions are, of course, absent from Piaget's work. Perhaps his gravest deficiency is not to have continued his research into years of adolescence. His stimulating study concludes at the very moment when the first glimmerings of climacteric development are on the horizon. It thus has two weaknesses. First, such deductions as the automatic development of reciprocity into autonomy would have been seen to be fallacious. Secondly, all that Piaget has to say about autonomy

– the very lodestar of any study of moral judgement – can only be a matter of airy theorising quite unsubstantiated by fact.

Analysis of children's judgements on cheating at games gives us further evidence, therefore, for rejecting Piaget's theory of the two moralities of the child. These judgements have also been of value – as indicated by responses quoted – in contributing to a more balanced and comprehensive picture of the development of moral judgement in the context of cheating.

Chapter 7
Stealing

The test situation

Research evidence showed that, after murder and physical cruelty, stealing is universally the third most heinous offence to children of all ages. Thus offences against property are only secondary to offences against the person. The only age distinction, we recall from our Value of Life Test, is that with increasing age offences against the person become more significant; and we suggested that heteronomy may be the more characteristically concerned with offences against property.

This significance of stealing was amply confirmed from analysis of our responses, in that 31% of our conscience responses were derived from this test, second only to the 45·5% derived from the Value of Life Test. Our evidence, at 9 years and 11 years, for those feelings of guilt that merge into conscience was overwhelmingly derived from the Stealing Test. From 13 years the Value of Life Test became far more evocative of conscience responses.

Stealing, as Piaget observes, is a far less common temptation than lying, and we therefore left the latter test until last, as being the most intensely personal. The possibility of stealing, however, is always present. Of the four visual situations we had devised, experience of testing showed the most evocative to be that of a child in the cloakroom at school, entirely unobserved, confronted with the temptation of stealing from a half-open satchel or bag. We deduced its significance to lie in its being a more personal matter – stealing from a fellow member of the school – than the more impersonal stealing from a shop.

The situation was briefly, but essentially, structured so as to rule out irrelevancies or qualifications detracting from the direct moral choice. The *pro forma* provided for the two possible answers: he/she will steal, he/she will not steal. The majority of answers were increasingly 'No'. It was then feasible to probe deeper with the question, 'Suppose that he/she did take something, how would he/she feel then?' Here, of course, was a further opportunity to plumb the concept of 'guilt' or of 'conscience', and a valuable one, as already indicated.

An addendum asked, 'Would it be all right to keep something he/she found – say, a purse in the street?' This was, in fact, a verbal form of one of the rejected visual tests. It had value, as we shall see, not only as raising an entirely different situation from that in the cloakroom, but also as confirming, or otherwise, the responses already made to it.

Stealing: cloakroom

Here is a picture of a boy/girl of about the same age as you. He/she is in the cloakroom at school. He/she is all alone. No one else is there to see what he/she does. Someone has left a satchel/bag/briefcase in the cloakroom. It is open. Do you think the boy/girl will take anything out of it and keep it?

YES

Would that be stealing?________________

It's all right to take what belongs to someone else?________________

(If 'NO') Then why would he/she take it?________________

Would he/she be afraid?________________Of whom?________________

Would he/she tell anyone?________________Whom?________________

How would he/she feel about it? afraid; ashamed; conscience; guilty; happy; indifferent; don't care; miserable; proud; sad; sorry

Guilty?________________

Conscience?________________

(*a*) Where does it come from?________________

(*b*) What makes it grow?________________

(*c*) When does it start?________________

NO

Why not?________________

A. *Anomy* e.g. get found out; get into trouble;________________

____

B. *Heteronomy* e.g. God; Jesus; police; parents; others,________________

____

C. *Socionomy* e.g. friends________________

reciprocity________________

D. *Autonomy* e.g. guilty; conscience ______________________

____

Would it be all right to keep something he/she found – say, a purse in the street? ______________________

Why?/why not? ______________________

____

7-YEAR AGE-GROUP: BOYS

There are naturally elements of anomy to be found in the younger age-groups – 10 responses among the 7-year boys. Thus:

'It's too nice and he'll take it. He might be afraid of teacher or his friends. He'll feel happy. He wanted it.' (Purse?) 'Yes. I should think so.'

'No, he'll get caught.' (Purse?) 'No. But I have kept some money I found.'

'Yes. He wants it. His Mum wouldn't buy him one. He'd feel happy.' (Purse?) 'No. Give it to teacher. He'd get a team point.'

Pure heteronomy is, of course, strong, with 13 responses. The authority may be God:

'God wouldn't like it. We learn at Sunday school that we must not take things.'

'God will say inside his heart, "That's a naughty thing to do. You must put it back." So he will, the next day.'

Or teacher:

'Teacher says you mustn't.'

Or parent:

'He'll be sorry. Mummy might find out.'

Or police:

(Purse?) 'No. He'd be sent to prison if he's found out.'

7 responses show elements of socionomy. Imaginative sympathy appears in 3 subjects. Thus:

'Yes, he's a greedy boy – the sort of boy who asks his Mum to buy lots of toys every day.' (Purse?) 'No. It might be somebody's bus-fare and they couldn't get home.'

The classic 'not fair' appears in 3 subjects. For example:

'It's wrong to steal, and it would not be fair to the other people.'

And reciprocity, thus early, in

'You might get found out and punished, anyway. But I wouldn't like anyone to steal from me.'

S.T.
S.T.

Of the 30 responses, 12 judge that the child will steal. It will be recalled that, in order to get a wider spread of age at the lower end of our sample, and to compensate in some sense for the inability to give written tests at this age, we chose a top infants' class and a first-year junior class to make up this age-group of 7 years. The mean chronological ages were 6 years 6 months and 7 years 5 months – a difference of 11 months. It was the younger group that produced these 12, out of 15 responses, judging that the child will steal; no subject from the older class judges thus. But we also observe that the mean socio-economic class of the younger class was 2·7 as compared with the 3·4 of the older class. Thus environmental differences between the two schools used may also have been involved.

7-YEAR AGE-GROUP: GIRLS

Anomy is seen in

> 'It's bad, 'cos somebody might see her using it.' (Purse?) 'Yes. It doesn't belong to anybody.'
>
> 'She'd be afraid of being found out. But she'd be happy because she got what she wanted.' (Purse?) 'Yes. It's not really stealing.'

14 responses are purely heteronomous, 11 of them coming from the younger class. It is 'naughty', 'nasty', 'very, very naughty' and 'wrong' to steal, though specific authorities are not quoted.

The 6 responses suggesting elements of socionomy are, as with the boys, all from the class with higher mean chronological age and higher socio-economic class. Typical responses are:

> 'Someone might have stolen from her and she knows what it is like.'
>
> 'She wouldn't want anyone to steal from her, and she thinks about the other girl's feelings.'
>
> 'She wouldn't like anyone to steal off her.'

As with the boys, the 12 responses which envisage the child stealing are all from the younger class with lower mean socio-economic class – as compared with 1 from the older and environmentally favoured class.

Sex differences are minimal at this age. The mean I.Q.s are similar – 108·2 for boys, 108·8 for girls. The total scores are similar – boys 59·0 and girls 58·5. Here then, as in the Cheating Test, is a situation in which the sexes start almost exactly level and produce similar judgements. The girls have no such advantage, as in the Value of Life Test, of innate sympathy.

9-YEAR AGE-GROUP: BOYS

The 10 mixed lower responses show fear of detection and of authority, and hope of reward. One refers to religion:

'Yes. Because he thinks he'll get away with it because no one can see him But there is someone – God.'

11 responses are wholly heteronomous. Thus:

(Purse?) 'No. It's still stealing, no matter what.'

'He'll be sorry for himself, because he shouldn't do naughty things – take people's things.'

Guilt feelings are now revealed, and also a growing concern for the owner of the purse. For example:

'No. It's still someone else's. They might want it.'

'No. It might be all the person has.'

8 responses show socionomy mixed with lower levels. Thus:

'He would be called a thief.'

'People will call him a stealer.'

Finally, we may quote a definition of 'feeling guilty' as

'Something that bothers inside. It's when you've done something wrong.'

Two schools were used for this age-group. 11 boys from one and 10 from the other judged that the child will steal. While imaginative sympathy may be stronger, in this age-group, 21 out of the 30 subjects still envisage stealing.

9-YEAR AGE-GROUP: GIRLS

From the 12 lower and mixed responses we may quote:

'No, it's not hers.' (Purse?) 'Yes, Nobody would know about it.'

(Purse?) 'No. Take it to the police station. But she says that if there was under ten shillings in it she might not take it.'

The hope of reward is still strong in this age-group. Heteronomy is typically expressed in

'That would be stealing and it's wrong. If her teacher knew she would be punished.'

'No. Teacher's told her it's wrong.' (Purse?) 'No. It's not yours and it would be a kind of stealing.'

(Purse?) 'No. Take it to the police station. Someone would find out if you'd got it and you would be put in prison.'

A measure of socionomy appears in such responses as

'Everyone will call you a thief.' (Purse?) 'No. If she lost something she'd want it returned.'

'It's wrong to steal. You might get someone else into trouble.' (Purse?) 'No. Take it to the police so it can be claimed. My teacher told me. If it was 6*d*. I'd keep that – but it would still be wrong really.'

8 responses from one school and 7 from the other judge that the child will steal – a total of 15 as compared with 21 such responses from the boys. But the girls' total score of 56·0 is untypically lower than the 59·8 of the boys. So is their mean I.Q. at 107·8 as compared with the boys' 110·8. It is plausible to see intelligence as a factor here.

11-YEAR AGE-GROUP: BOYS

The 10 lower and mixed responses are again concerned with fear of detection, fear of punishment, and hope of reward. Thus:

'You get into trouble from teacher.' (Purse?) 'No, you might get found out.'

(Purse?) 'No. You might get found out.'

'It's dishonest because if you're caught you'll be sent to a special school.' (Purse?) 'No, best to take it to the police. Then you might get a reward.'

'I've been taught it doesn't get you anywhere. You get caught and punished.' (Purse?) 'No. It's like stealing.'

Of the 10 strongly heteronomous responses 2 refer to religion. For example:

'God told people not to steal. It's in the Commandments.' (Purse?) 'No. Take it to the police. It's still stealing.'

A rare example of Piaget's immanent justice appears in

'Jesus might punish him.' (How?) 'He might make him trip and lose his money.'

The rare phrase 'stealing by finding' appears in

He'd feel uncomfortable. He's taken something which wasn't his. He'll be afraid of punishment.' (Purse?) 'No. That's stealing by finding. He should take it to the police.'

Heteronomy is starkly defined in

'It is bad to steal, because if a teacher found out you'd be punished.'

4 responses show partial socionomy. In a final 6 we find the first appearance of conscience, suggesting autonomy, but mixed with lower levels. Typical references to conscience are:

'It's wrong to steal. It says so in the Ten Commandments.' (If he stole?) 'It's stuck in his mind. You can't get rid of it. It's conscience – it comes from Heaven.'

'You know you've done wrong. Conscience keeps on about it.'

He'd have a guilty conscience. It would keep playing on his mind. He had stolen it, and done something wrong.'

11 responses from one school and 9 from the other judge that the child will steal.

11-YEAR AGE-GROUP: GIRLS

From the 4 lower mixed responses we may quote:

'She'd take something. There's nobody around.' (Purse?) 'It would be dishonest, but O.K. so long as nobody found out.'

Typical of the 12 heteronomous responses are:

'She'd feel miserable. She knew it would be wrong. She'll get punished.'

'You might be told to leave school for doing things like that. It's wrong to steal. When you grow up, you might keep on stealing and get into trouble.'

Among the 5 responses with elements of socionomy we find reciprocity, as in

'It's somebody else's; it doesn't belong to her. I wouldn't like anybody to take mine.'

And a rare citation of the Golden Rule:

(Purse?) 'No. Take it to the police. You must do as you would be done by.'

The 9 responses indicating autonomy use either 'guilt' or 'conscience' as motivating factors, and give definitions. For example:

'She'll feel guilty. It's a feeling of being wrong. We know in ourselves that it's wrong.'

'If you've stolen something you have it on your mind, and you feel you must tell somebody. My Mummy and Dad told me it was wrong to steal, in the first place. You learn this as you grow up.'

'She'll be afraid of conscience. It's when you've done wrong and Jesus keeps telling you that you have.'

'Conscience tells us we're wrong. *We* know we've done wrong, even though nobody else does. It's like a person nagging at us.'

7 responses from one school and 10 from the other judge that the child will steal.

It is in this age-group that we find the first striking disparity in mean I.Q.s between the sexes, the girls' exceeding that of the boys by 8·9. And while the total boys' score rises only from the previous 59·0 to 63·0, that of the girls jumps from 56.0 to 74·5. Here again it is plausible to hypothesise that the dramatic girls' advance in development is linked with their striking higher development in innate intelligence.

13-YEAR AGE-GROUP: BOYS

From the 5 mixed lower responses we may quote:

'It's wrong, but there's nobody around, so nobody would know. He'd be afraid. He might get found out.' (Purse?) 'No. Somebody might recognise the purse, and there'd be trouble.'

The term 'conscience' appears as a pure verbalism in

'His conscience tells him to go into the bag and take something' (I.Q. 79; S.E. 3; Rel. 4).

Heteronomy is found in 5 responses. For example:

'It's wrong. I've been told not to do it.'

'It's not yours to take. It's wrong. My mother told me.'

Socionomy may be illustrated by

'It belongs to others. We wouldn't like it.'

'It's dishonest. They could have worked hard to pay for it and you just take it.'

'It would be hurting somebody else.'

Autonomy may be illustrated from the purse situation:

'No. Even if it's only a shilling. It's the principle of the thing.'

'No. Take it to the police, whatever the value.'

'No. Take it to the police. Even if it's a small amount, it's still wrong, taking something that doesn't belong to you. Someone might have saved and worked for it.'

A strong example of autonomy is:

'I couldn't bring myself to steal anything. It's wrong to steal. I've been taught it through the school. Even if I wasn't caught, I couldn't do it. I'd feel guilty.'

20 of the 30 responses judge that the boy will steal.

13-YEAR AGE-GROUP: GIRLS

From 5 lower responses we may quote:

'She'll be worried because she's done something wrong. She thinks stealing is wrong because you may get caught and put in prison.' (I.Q. 87; S.E. 2; Rel. 4).

A further 8 responses show elements of socionomy. Thus:

'She'll go red and worry. Her friends would be upset, and that would make her sorry. She'll feel guilty.' (Guilty?) 'It's when you've done something and feel sorry. Other people are talking about you.'

'My parents and teachers have taught me it's wrong.' (Purse?) 'No. The person who took it is stealing. It's important to the loser to have the money. It's not mine to take.'

A genuinely sophisticated response is:

'No. It's not her property. Somebody else wants it. It's not right to steal unless you're really desperate – starving, for instance. It's not right then, but its justifiable.'

17 responses show partial or full autonomy. The genesis of autonomy is clearly put in

'It's wrong to steal. My parents told me this, but I know it as well.'

'It's in the Commandments, therefore it's wrong. We find out whether a thing is right or wrong from people – or by doing it and being punished.'

A feminine sophistication appears in

(Purse?) 'No. My conscience would nag. I'd keep 6*d.* if it was *not* in a purse. But I'd return it if it was *in* a purse.'

17 girls, but only 9 boys, give responses indicating partial or full autonomy. 20 boys, as compared with 17 girls, judge that the child will steal.

The mean I.Q. of the girls exceeds that of the boys by 7·8. This advantage is paralleled by an increased total score for the girls of 11·5 (girls, 88·5; boys, 77·0), the increase being identical with that at 11 years. The total score of both sex-groups has increased by the identical figure of 14·0, the girls remaining substantially ahead, however, through their far greater advance at 11 years.

15-YEAR AGE-GROUP: BOYS

The 1 fully anomous response in this group is:

'If a boy leaves the bag open, he deserves to have it stolen. If it's money, the boy taking it will feel happy. Money is just about everything.' (Purse?) 'Yes, however much. If it was about £50 people would know about it, and there is more likelihood of your being caught.'

Mixed anomy and heteronomy in 4 responses may be illustrated by

(Purse?) 'I would share it with friends. It's wrong, but who's worried? It would depend on the value. If it was below £5 I'd return it.'

'He'd be pleased if it was valuable and he wasn't caught'. (Purse?) 'I might take it to the police. Everyone says you should.'

A further 4 responses show full heteronomy. Thus:

'He's bound to get found out and punished in the end. That will show him how wrong it is.'

Socionomy, partial or full in 7 responses, has familiar expression in

'I wouldn't like it done to me, so I wouldn't do it to them.'

'It's unfair on the other person. You wouldn't like to lose it if it was yours.'

'Your friends would call you a thief.'

Elements of autonomy are found in 14 responses. We may quote:

'I wouldn't like to break the trust of another person.'

'I'd feel guilty. Others may be blamed wrongly. Somebody else's money has bought it, saved up for it, and you take it just like that. This is wrong.'

'I wouldn't. I don't like stealing, I've never wanted to. It's not right. You should buy it yourself. They've earned it. I wouldn't like anyone stealing from me. I never would. I'd always have what I'd done on my mind.'

In this age-group, 9 subjects judge that the boy will steal – as compared with 20, 20 and 21 respectively in the three previous age-groups; and some of these say that 'it will depend on what type of boy he is'.

15-YEAR AGE-GROUP: GIRLS

Illustrative of 5 lower responses is:

'You're likely to get caught. My parents would half-kill me.'

From 14 responses showing partial or full socionomy we may quote 3 which show, not only heteronomy as the seed-bed of development, but also the link between heteronomy and reciprocity:

'My parents told me not to steal. You wouldn't like anything of your own to be taken.'

'I've been brought up not to. I wouldn't like it done to me.'

'I've been taught that it's wrong. It isn't your property, and it's unfair to the other person to touch it.'

A rare definition appears in:

(Purse?) 'No. It's stealing by finding.'

From 11 responses showing partial or full autonomy we may also quote 3 which illustrate the link between heteronomy and autonomous conscience:

'You get told stealing is wrong. I'd have it on my conscience.' (Purse?) 'No. It doesn't belong to you. If it was just 3*d*., the right thing to do would be to take it to the police, but I don't know whether I would be bothered.'

'I just know it's wrong to steal from other people. I expect I've learnt this from my parents, but it may be instinctive.'

'If I did steal my conscience would prick me to tell someone – either the girl I stole from and I would give it back, or my parents. They are very understanding, but they would be upset to think that their daughter had stolen. I've been brought up to realise that it is not right to take what doesn't belong to you.'

Of the 30 girls in this group, 9 judge that the girl will steal, as compared with 17, 17 and 15 respectively in the three previous age-groups.

17-YEAR AGE-GROUP: BOYS

From the 2 responses showing mixed anomy and heteronomy we may quote:

> 'He'd take something and feel good. He wouldn't care.' (Purse?) 'You shouldn't. I would.'

Of the 4 heteronomous responses, one gives an inadequate definition of conscience as 'something on your mind – fear of being found out.'

An interesting response among 5 showing socionomy is:

> 'It's taking advantage of another's work. I had a tape-recorder stolen, worth £30. I wouldn't do it to another.' (Purse?) 'Obtaining things others have worked for is theft.'

19 responses show partial or full autonomy. Conscience and reciprocity are linked in

> 'It's a matter of conscience – it tells you right from wrong. You don't like having your own property stolen.'

Socionomy remains strong in

> 'It's against the law and what people think. They won't trust him.'

But socionomy is not enough:

> 'The opinion of others is only part of it – not the whole reason. It's wrong. It's not yours. It's always wrong to steal. You haven't worked for it.'

A common characteristic of the responses in this 17-year male group is the strong conviction that stealing is wrong because the thief takes, not so much the property of another, as the work which earned it. He earned it, it is his: the thief did not earn it, it is not his. This may be a characteristic of young men, whose main concern is with earning a living. It may, alternatively, be seen as almost a humanistic redefinition of autonomy, expressed, not in terms of inner guilt, but rather in terms of what has been justly earned by work. A final response, at once simple and human and honest, again illustrates this characteristic:

> 'I wouldn't touch it myself. There's a risk of being caught – but it's wrong, taking other people's property. You should do a paper-round and get the money yourself.' (Purse?) 'I'd take it to the police. I would not tempt myself by looking inside it.'

Autonomy is strong in 9 responses. Thus:

> 'It's not just the law. It's a matter of conscience.'

'My parents drummed it into me. It's always wrong for anyone to steal. You don't know what hardship it is causing others.'

'Conscience says it's wrong.'

'If everyone goes around stealing we might as well have communal property.'

17-YEAR AGE-GROUP: GIRLS

There is but 1 heteronomous response in this group. Typical of the 14 responses on the level of socionomy, of which 5 quote reciprocity explicitly, are:

'I wouldn't like anybody to do it to me.'

'You'd be disliked.'

'The other person is losing for your gain.'

'It might be one of her friend's bags. On second thoughts, it wouldn't really matter whether it was a friend or not.'

'Society just can't live by stealing.'

The remaining 15 responses show partial or full autonomy. Reciprocity is linked with conscience in

'It's all to do with the conscience, which tells you when you have done wrong.' (Purse?) 'No. Take it to the police, because I wouldn't want my purse to be kept.'

An interesting new note is concern with property stolen from institutions. Such impersonal theft, increasingly common in society at large, and so easily rationalised away, could only be the concern of a strong and intelligent autonomy. 2 responses show such concern:

'Taking other people's possessions is always wrong. Even institutions have to pay for the things that are stolen.'

'It's not hers to take. Stealing is always wrong, even from institutions. It belongs to somebody else.'

Finally, self-respect is invoked in

'It wouldn't belong to me. I just know I wouldn't want to take it. I wouldn't want to lower myself.'

Only 4 responses judge that the girl will steal. One other adds:

'I might have when younger.'

In this age-group of 17 years, the mean I.Q. of the girls exceeds that of the boys by a minimal 1·8. Their total score, however, increases by 11·0, as compared with the boys' total increase of 6·5. This increase in girls' total score is very similar to that of 11·5 at 11 years, when the girls' mean I.Q. exceeded that of the boys by 7·8. Here, however, intelligence would not appear to be a significant factor.

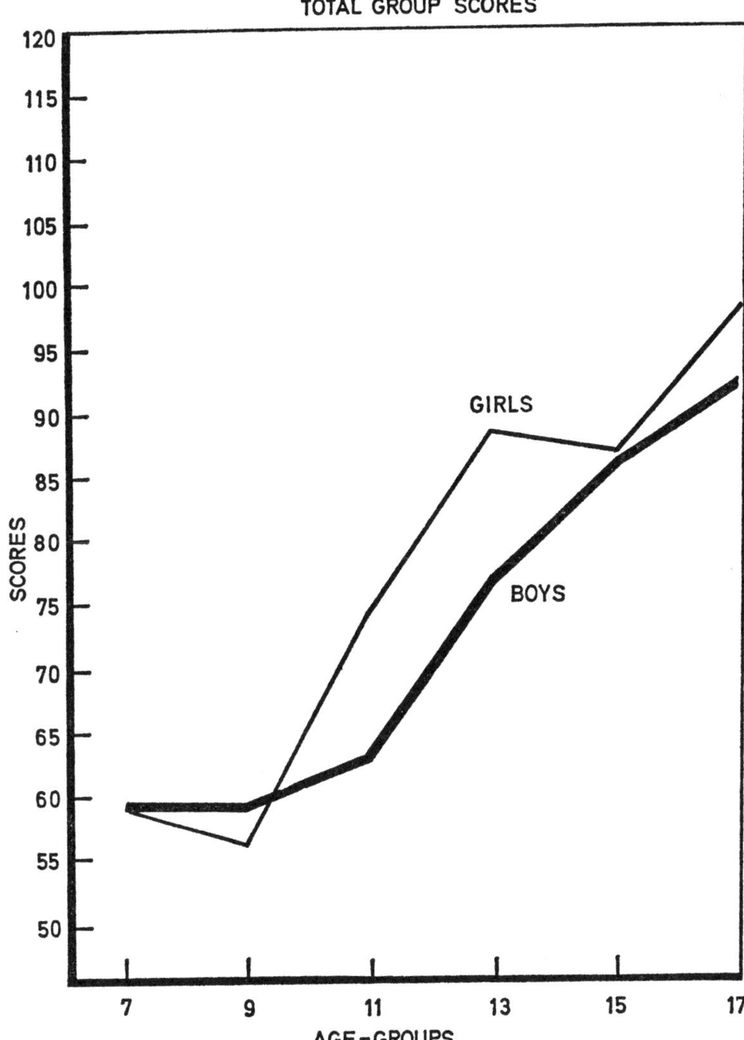
TOTAL GROUP SCORES
SCORES
120
115
110
105
100
95
90
85
80
75
70
65
60
55
50
GIRLS
BOYS
7
9
11
13
15
17
AGE-GROUPS

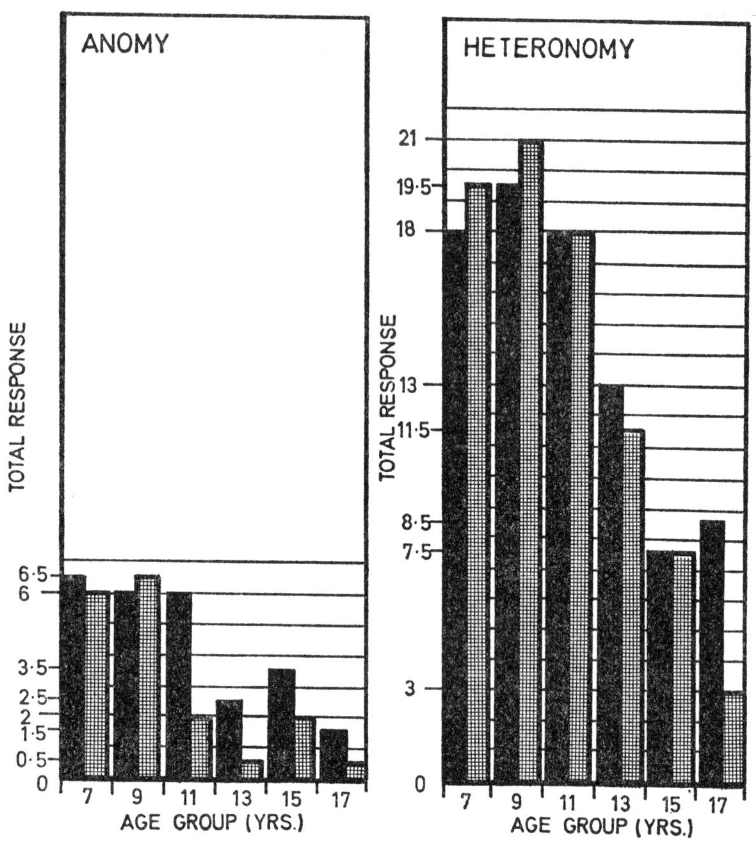

TABLE OF I.Q. VALUES

AGE-GROUP		7	9	11	13	15	17
MEAN I.Q.	BOYS	108·2	110·8	96·9	98·5	104·6	106·4
	GIRLS	108·8	107·8	105·8	106·3	108·5	108·2

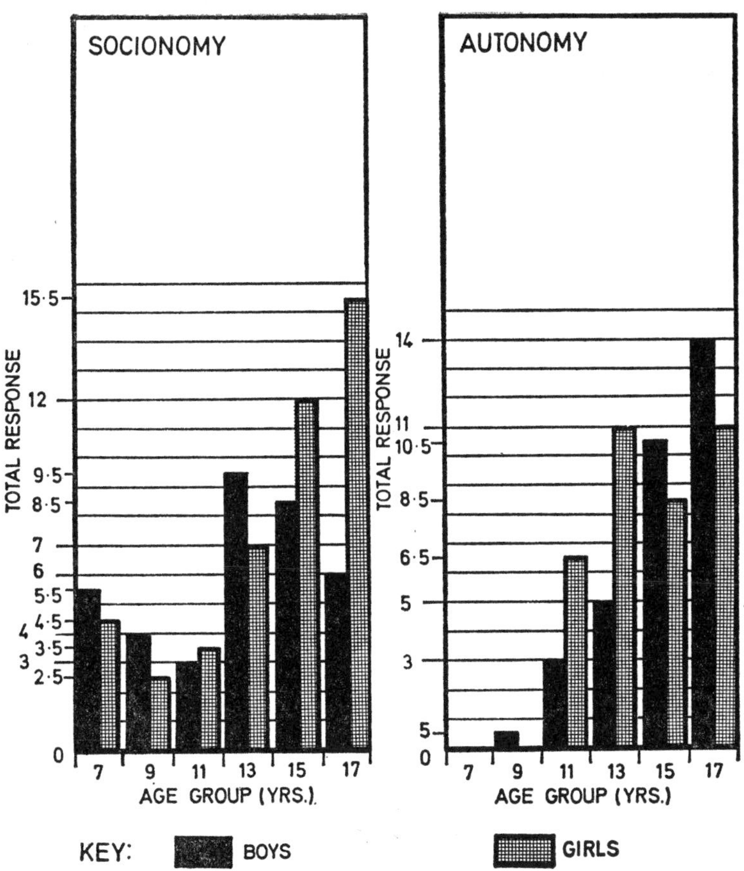

NOTE: N = 60 PER AGE-GROUP (30 BOYS + 30 GIRLS)

The greater heteronomy score of the boys indicates, even at this age, their greater need of authority. Girls, on the other hand, have a far higher socionomy score, and, in particular, a greater sense of reciprocity – indicative of their stronger sensitivity to personal relationships.

The pattern of development

Development may be patterned by tabulating the total sex group scores, at each age, noting also the lead held by the girls in total scores and in mean I.Q.

The Stealing Test: Sex-group Comparisons

Age-group N-60	*Boys' Total Score*	*Girls' Total Score*	*Girls' Lead in Score*	*Girls' Lead in Mean I.Q.*
7-year	59·0	58·5	− 0·5	+0·6
9-year	59·0	56·0	− 3·0	−3·0
11-year	63·0	74·5	+11·5	+8·9
13-year	77·0	88·5	+11·5	+7·8
15-year	86·0	87·0	+ 1·0	+3·9
17-year	92·5	98·0	+ 5·5	+1·8

At both 11 and 13 years the strong increase in girls' scores is paralleled by markedly higher mean I.Q. Yet the boys' marked development at 13 years, identical with that of the girls, is despite the hypothetical disadvantage of markedly lower mean I.Q. Sex group increases in total score are:

The Stealing Test: Increases in Total Scores

Age-group	*Boys' Increase in Score*	*Girls' Increase in Score*	*Girls' lead in Mean I.Q.*
9-year	+ 0·0	− 2·5	−3·0
11-year	+ 4·0	+18·5	+8·9
13-year	+14·0	+14·0	+7·8
15-year	+ 9·0	− 1·5	+3·9
17-year	+ 6·5	+11·0	+1·8

Again we find girls developing an age-group in advance of the boys, girls at 11 years and boys at 13 years. Boys develop steadily, if less spectacularly, from 13 years onwards, despite lower mean I.Q. At 13 years the sexes show an identical increase, despite the higher mean I.Q. of the girls. At 15 years boys make solid progress, and the girls show a slight decrease, despite their higher mean I.Q. Again, too, at 17 years girls show a marked increase, despite a minimal lead in mean I.Q. In short, the significance of intelligence is only really seen at 11 years, when it remains a hypothetical deduction.

The pattern of development, therefore, is not dictated by intelligence *per se*. Bearing in mind that 31% of conscience responses were evoked by this test – second only to the 45·5% from the Value of Life Test – we would expect orectic factors to be closely involved in judgement, and not simply the cognitive. Analysis supports this assumption.

Stealing by finding and keeping

We now turn to an analysis of responses to the additional question: Would it be all right to keep something found – say, a purse in the street? We have already quoted some responses where they helped to elucidate judgement in the broad context of stealing. We may now isolate them as responses to a separate, and more subtle, situational aspect of honesty with the property of others.

7-YEAR AGE-GROUP: BOYS

The 5 responses indicating anomy may be illustrated by

> 'Yes, I should think so.'

Heteronomy is, of course, strong with 23½ responses. Parents, teachers and police are the authorities variously cited. There is engaging frankness in

> 'No. But I have kept some money I found.'

Concern for others is evidenced in

> 'No. It might be somebody's bus-fare and then they wouldn't get home.'
>
> 'No. Somebody might be looking for it to buy food.'

7-YEAR AGE-GROUP: GIRLS

Anomy is clear-cut in

> 'Yes. It doesn't belong to anybody.'
>
> 'Yes. It's not really stealing.'

Heteronomy is strong, as with the boys. Thus:

> 'No. Take it to an adult person.'

'No. You should give it to Mummy or Teacher.'

Concern for others is similarly apparent in

'No. The owner would want it.'

'No. Somebody might want it to buy sweets with.'

'No. It's somebody else's.'

The total score of boys at 7 years is 56·5 and of girls 58·5, showing little initial sex difference. There is no suggestion at this age of keeping any part of the money found, or of keeping a small sum found.

9-YEAR AGE-GROUP: BOYS

Anomy and heteronomy are mingled in some responses. A common response is to hand the purse to the police, but with the strong motivation of getting either a reward or the purse itself if unclaimed. Heteronomy, still strong, is well illustrated by

'No. It's still stealing, no matter what.'

'No. It's stealing. It's naughty to steal.'

Concern for others appears in

'No. It's still someone else's. They might want it back.'

'No. The owner might be very poor. It might be all the money he had.'

'No. The owner might be poor.'

9-YEAR AGE-GROUP: GIRLS

Anomy is direct in

'Yes. Nobody would know about it.'

A typical response is

'No. You should take it to the police-station. You'll get it in the end.'

Heteronomy is direct in

'No. It's stealing. You have to take it to the police-station.'

Reciprocity appears in

'No. If she lost something she'd want it returned.'

Sympathetic concern for the owner is seen in

'No. It might be all the person had. She should take it to the police-station.'

In this age-group we find the first appearance of the phrase, 'It depends on what's in it'. Now, too, it is thought right to keep a small amount of money found. Generally, the maximum is 6*d*. One response says 2*s*., another 4*s*. and a very low-level response quotes 10*s*. The total score of boys in this age-group is 64·5, and of girls 57·0. Girls therefore have a rare deficit in score of 7·5. It parallels, we recall, a deficit in mean I.Q. of 3·0.

11-YEAR AGE-GROUP: BOYS

Lower responses may be illustrated by

'No. You might get found out. You'd be asked questions like, "Where did you get all this money from?"'

'No. It's best to take it to the police-station. You might get a reward.'

'No. You still get found out.'

Heteronomy is strong in such responses as

'No. You could get found out and severely punished.'

Now appears the rare definition:

'No. It's stealing by finding. Take it to the police.'

We may also quote:

'No. It doesn't belong to you. Take it to the police-station, no matter how much is in it.'

'No. It's not yours to keep.'

4 responses use the situational maxim, 'It depends on what's in it'.

11-YEAR AGE-GROUP: GIRLS

Lower responses may be illustrated by

'It would be dishonest, but it's O.K. so long as nobody found out.'

'No. It's still stealing. Take it to the police. You'll get a reward.'

The phrase 'It's stealing' or 'It's still stealing' appears in 8 responses. For another subject, it is 'a kind of stealing'. Concern for others is seen in such responses as:

'No. Somebody may need it a lot more than you.'

'No. It's not yours. It might be an old age pensioner's, who would need it. It would cause a lot of worry.'

'No. Somebody might need it badly.'

Reciprocity finds classic expression in

'No. Take it to the police. Do as you would be done by.'

Only three sums of money that may legitimately be kept are mentioned by this group: 1*s*., 2*s*., 10*s*. The girls in this age-group make a strong increase in total score of 18·5, as compared with the boys' 2·5, which parallels their increase in mean I.Q. of 8·9. Once again girls make a strong development an age-group ahead of boys.

13-YEAR AGE-GROUP: BOYS

Lower mixed responses may be illustrated by:

'If over 5*s*., it would be missed, so it would be wrong to keep it.'

'No. Somebody might recognise the purse and there would be trouble.'

'It depends on how much money is in it. Anything under £4 would be all right to keep.'

Heteronomy is seen strongly in

'No. Take it to the police-station. That's the right thing to do. My parents said so.'

Concern for others is evident in

'No. It might be somebody who needs it.'

'No. It might belong to an old lady, who might want it.'

Autonomy is evidenced by

'No. Take it to the police, even if it's a small amount. It's wrong taking something that doesn't belong to you. Someone might have saved and worked for it.'

'No. Not even if it's only 1*s*. It's the principle of the thing.'

Four responses say that 'It all depends.' Sums of money mentioned as being legitimate to keep are 2*s*., 5*s*., 10*s*. In general, it is thought all right to keep up to 10*s*.

13-YEAR AGE-GROUP: GIRLS

There is no visible anomy in this group. Heteronomy lingers in a few responses, such as:

'No. You should take it to the police, so that the person would have it again. I've been taught it's wrong to keep it by my mother and my father.'

Reciprocity is seen in

'No. Take it to the police. If I lost my purse, I'd want it returned. Even if it's only 6*d*., it's still the same.'

The 19½ responses showing autonomy may be illustrated by

'No. It doesn't belong to you. Someone else might need it, and be worried about it. It's stealing if you keep it, however small the amount.'

'No. The person who lost it would be upset about it. My conscience would prick me if I kept it.'

'No. It's still taking what isn't yours. However small, I'd take it to the police. If it was 6*d*. by itself, I might keep it. It's still wrong, but it seems silly to take 6*d*. to the police.'

As with the boys, 10*s*. is the dividing line made by the few who mention a sum between what may be kept and what should be handed in to the police.

Increase in autonomy is reflected in the girls' massive increase in total score of 28·0 as compared with the boys' increase of 11·5. Once again boys show their most emphatic developmental surge at 13 years. But this second strong advance made by the girls keeps them well ahead of the boys.

15-YEAR AGE-GROUP: BOYS

The one anomous subject in this group responds:

'Yes. I'd keep it, however much. If it was about £50 people would know about it, and there'd be more likelihood of your being caught.'

There are at least traces of heteronomy in

'Yes. I'd share it with my friends. It's wrong, but who's worried?'

'You should take it to the police. I might. Everyone says you should.'

Reciprocity is suggested by

'No. Take it to the police. The purse might be worth something. It's the right thing to do. It might be you.'

Autonomy is present in such responses as

'No. If it was a small amount I'd leave it where it was. If it was large, I'd take it to the police-station. If I spent it, it would be on my conscience.'

'No. I don't think it's right. Even a small amount might mean a lot to someone.'

'No. It's other people's property. Take it to the police, however small.'

Sums of money mentioned range from 2*s.* 6*d.* to 10*s.* or £1. Specificity is rife, by this age, with more than half the responses quoting sums of money.

15-YEAR AGE-GROUP: GIRLS

The lowest response is:

'No. It doesn't belong to me. Someone might recognise it and I would be in trouble.'

It is characteristic of girls of this age to take into account the possible value of the purse itself. Thus:

'If it was a small amount it would be O.K., unless the purse was an expensive one.'

Heteronomy typically advocates strict resort to the police. Concern for others grows. The definition 'stealing by finding' appears for the second time. Autonomy may be illustrated by

'No. It doesn't belong to you. Even if it was just 3*d.*, the right thing to do would be to take it to the police, but I don't know whether I would bother.'

'No. Someone's at a loss. However much there is in it, it would be wrong to keep it.'

Superficial sophistication appears in the response:

'It all depends. If it was from an old person it would be wrong. If it was from someone else who flings money around, I'd keep it. But that would be wrong really.'

The average sum thought reasonable to keep is 10*s*., although some boys go up to £1.

In total score we see the boys marking time, with an increase of but 0·5. Girls decrease by 13·0, but their total score is still 12·0 above that of the boys.

17-YEAR AGE-GROUP: BOYS

The lowest responses are:

'You shouldn't, but I would.'

'Not really. I'd keep up to £20.'

Specificity is typified by the response: 'It all depends how much.' Autonomy may be illustrated by

'I'd take it to the police, regardless of whether it was 2*s*. or £100.'

'I'd take it to the police. It might be the purse of a housewife, and she needs the money. I wouldn't tempt myself by looking inside.'

17-YEAR AGE-GROUP: GIRLS

We find here the only completely negative response among all our 360 subjects:

'I'd leave it there. I wouldn't like to be involved.'

Heteronomy is still present. A sense of reciprocity is always strengthened by personal experience, as in

'No. Take it to the police, because I've lost things myself and you know how people feel.'

'It's not yours to keep' is typical of autonomous responses. Most responses mentioning a sum thought fit to keep quote £1. The total boys' score increases by 7·5 and that of the girls by 8·0. But the girls' score still exceeds that of the boys by 12·5. Both anomy and socionomy are minimal. The bulk of the responses are either heteronomous or autonomous in this final age-group.

The pattern of development

It is noteworthy that only 2 out of our 360 subjects are aware of the definition, 'stealing by finding'. For the rest, the strict rule of heteronomy gradually and generally merges with the realisation that one's gain must be another's loss, and with a sense of reciprocity, to develop autonomy. Both heteronomy and autonomy are strict in their refusal to keep any money that may be found. Such strict heteronomy is characteristic of the two youngest age-groups of 7 and 9 years. Such strict autonomy develops from 13 years onwards–although its rationality is indicated by the realisation of a touch of absurdity in solemnly journeying to the police-station to hand in 3*d.* or 6*d.*

Between these two firm moral controls there is an area of specificity, evidenced typically by responses holding it legitimate to keep money that may be found up to a general limit. The fact that a limit is recognised shows the relationship between such specificity and a loose, rather than strict, heteronomy. Naturally the limit rises with age–

The General Limit of Money that may be retained

Age-group	
7-years	None
9-years	6*d.*
11-years	2*s.* 6*d.*
13-years	10*s.*
15-years	10*s.*
17-years	£1

Such specificity is associated with loose heteronomy and not with socionomy. For socionomy realises that *any* money found must be another's loss; that even a small amount may mean a lot to, say, a child, an old-age pensioner, or a housewife; that reciprocity dictates action that would be desired by oneself; and that, therefore, it is unfair to retain any money found.

Moreover, such heteronomy remains strong. At 17 years, when we have seen reason to assume that development as such is completed, we find 14 boys and 19 girls who are wholly autonomous in their judgement that to keep money found is 'stealing by finding'. Thus 55% of our final age-group are controlled by autonomy in this situation. The remaining 45% are substantially dependent on heteronomy.

The pattern of development may again be evidenced by the total scores for each sex at each age level.

Yet again we observe the first strong development in girls at 11 years, followed by an even stronger development at 13 years. Yet again we observe the climacteric development in boys at 13 years, an age-group

Comparative Total Scores

Age-group	*Boys' Total Score*	*Girls' Total Score*	*Girls' Lead*
7-year	56·5	58·5	2·0
9-year	64·5	57·0	−7·5
11-year	67·0	75·0	8·0
13-year	78·5	103·0	24·5
15-year	79·0	91·0	12·0
17-year	86·5	99·0	12·5

later. Yet again at 15 years there is a 'standstill', if not regression, in both sexes. And yet again we observe a steady, if less pronounced, development in both sexes at 17 years, and a broadly similar one. Save at 9 years, girls lead throughout and remain well ahead of boys at 17 years through their stronger autonomy, as compared with the boys' greater reliance upon heteronomy.

It would not appear that the feminine custom of carrying money in a purse makes girls the more sensitive to this situation, thereby accounting for their higher level of moral judgement upon it. Certainly one or two girls, in older age-groups, do mention the possible value of the purse. But their overriding concern is with the money itself. Totalling all responses, for all age-groups, that fall within the area of socionomy, we find 26·0 for boys and 21·5 for girls. There is, therefore, no evidence that in this situation girls are more strongly sensitive than boys to reciprocal relationships; or, indeed, that socionomy is strongly relevant to this situation. Once development commences, the broad and increasing choice is between heteronomy and autonomy.

The very fluidity of this situation may be held to be all the more evocative of genuine attitudes. While only two subjects can quote the definition 'stealing by finding', there is none who openly asserts that 'finding is keeping'. There are, of course, responses indicative of partial or full anomy at all ages, if decreasing – a total of 29 from boys and 15·5 from girls. Apart from them, there is some moral control evident in all responses. The major controls are heteronomy, which admits of a measure of specificity, and autonomy, which admits of none.

It may be observed, finally, that no attempt has been made, in our concern with stealing, to compare the results found with those of Piaget. His concern with it is, in fact, slight. He considers stealing within the

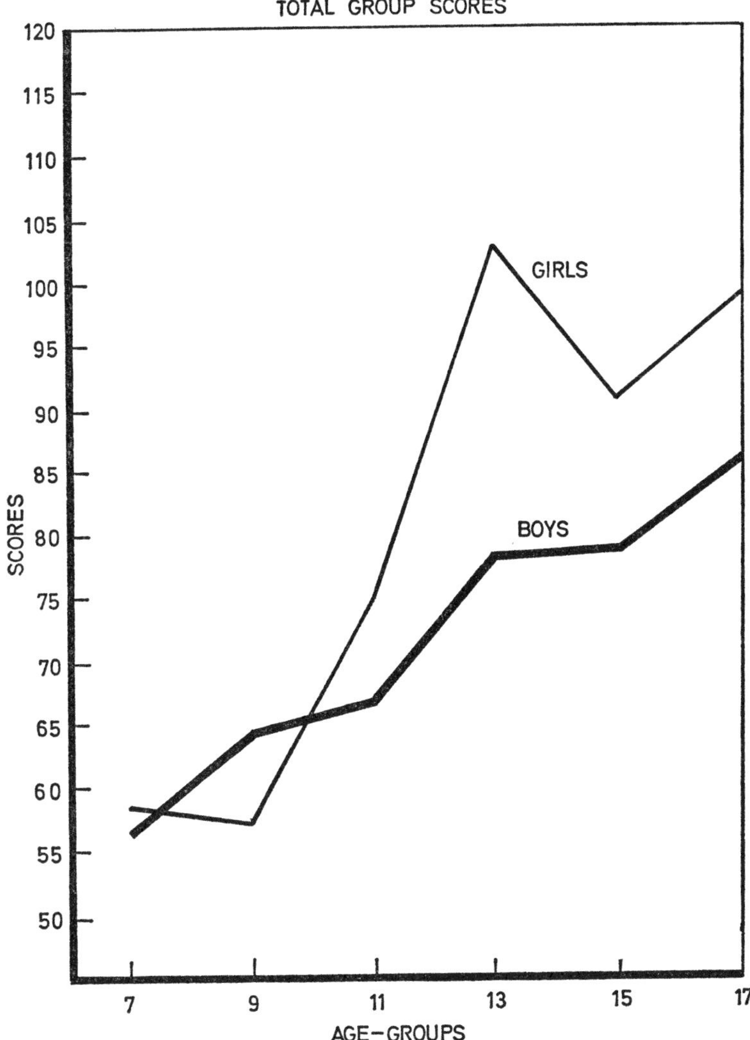
TOTAL GROUP SCORES
120
115
110
105
100
95
90
85
80
75
70
65
60
55
50
SCORES
GIRLS
BOYS
7
9
11
13
15
17
AGE-GROUPS

context of the contrast between objective responsibility, which 'judges actions according to their material consequences', and subjective responsibility which 'only takes intentions into account' (op. cit., 129). Piaget found 7 years to be the average age for the former, and 9 years for the latter (op. cit., 120). The explanation of such a development is, of course, that the 'objective conception of responsibility arises, without any doubt, as a result of the constraint exercised by the adult' (op. cit., 129); whereas 'taking intentions into account presupposes co-operation and mutual respect' (op. cit., 133).

There was thus no common approach to the stealing situation to make comparison possible. We can say, however, that if adult constraint, or heteronomy, is the source of objective responsibility, it is no less revealed in our responses as the original source of those interiorised convictions that shape autonomous conscience.

Chapter 8
Lying

The lying situation

Piaget begins his extensive examination of lying by defining the gravity of the problem of truth-telling for the child. 'This is due to the fact that the tendency to tell lies is a natural tendency, so spontaneous and universal that we can take it as an essential part of the child's egocentric thought' (op. cit., 135). He summarises the work of Stern and his followers as demonstrating conclusively that 'until the age of 7 to 8 the child finds systematic difficulty in sticking to the truth'. This is because 'without attempting to deceive anyone, and without even being definitely conscious of what he is doing, he distorts reality in accordance with his desires and his romancing' (op. cit., 160f.). Lying, in early years, is therefore essentially a feature of child egocentricity.

Piaget analyses lying under five heads: 'definition of a lie'; 'responsibility as a function of the lie's content'; 'responsibility as a function of its material consequence'; 'May children lie to one another?'; 'Why should one not lie?' (op. cit., 136). Our own extensive analysis of lying follows up some of these lines, as well as others not pursued by Piaget, and comparisons will be made where appropriate.

Research evidence, we recall, showed lying to be fifth in the primary child's order of moral evils, but only tenth, with a mere 1·02%, in that of secondary modern boys. But, given its universality in the young child, its piercing to the heart of all personal relationships, and the ever-present temptation it presents, we were confident of its close relevance to our study of developing moral judgement. As a test it proved, in the event, powerfully evocative. It produced but 15% of our conscience responses. But we recall Piaget's dictum that 'we see the first signs' of autonomy when the child 'discovers that truthfulness is necessary to the relations of sympathy and mutual respect' (op. cit., 194). Here, then, we could not only examine Piaget's thesis in depth, but also analyse intensively the child's maturation in moral judgement.

Lying: 1

Let's keep that picture of the boy/girl in the cloakroom. Now, we'll put this one beside it. It's a picture of his/her father/mother. Let's suppose the boy/girl *did* take something out of the satchel/bag/briefcase (pen/money/or . . .). When he/she gets home, his/her father/mother notice it. Here he/she is, asking where it came from. What will the boy/girl say?

TELL THE TRUTH

He/she will own up?____________________

Why will he/she do that? ____________________

Will he/she be afraid of being punished?____________________

What good would being punished do?____________________

Would he/she deserve to be punished?____________________

If *not* punished, would the boy/girl do it again?____________________

You think he/she *should* own up. *Would* he/she own up?____________________

(Let's suppose he/she *did not* own up, but told a lie instead).

TELL A LIE

How would he/she explain having it?____________________

____

That would be a lie?____________________

What is a lie?

1. Naughty word.
2. Something not true (objective error in fact).

   You mean anything that's not true?____________________

Would a mistake be a lie?____________________

3. Something deliberately intended to deceive____________________

WHY IS IT WRONG (NAUGHTY) TO TELL LIES?

A. *Anomy* e.g. you get found out; get into trouble;____________________

____

B. *Heteronomy* e.g. God; Jesus; parents don't like/forbid/punish

____

C. *Socionomy* e.g. friends____________________

reciprocity____________________

D. *Autonomy* e.g. guilt, conscience, trust____________________

____

Lying: 2

LIES AND PUNISHMENT

Would it be all right to tell a lie if he/she was not caught and no one punished him/her for it? ______

______

Would telling lies be wrong (naughty) if they were not punished?

______

TELLING LIES TO ADULTS AND CHILDREN

1. Is it worse to lie to an adult? ______
2. Is it worse to lie to a child? ______
3. Is it just as bad to lie to either? ______

Why do you think so? ______

______

TELLING LIES TO FRIENDS

Is it always wrong to tell lies? ______

Is it all right to lie to help a friend? ______

Is it all right to lie to save him/her getting into trouble? ______

______

Is it all right to lie by not telling on him/her?

______

LYING TO PARENTS

Which is worse to lie to: ______

Father? ______

Mother? ______

Both the same? ______

Why do you think so? ______

______

We left this test till last as being the most personal and intimate of all. We used the cloakroom scene that had proved so evocative in the stealing test, together with two portraits of adults—a man, more effectively representing a father rather than a teacher, for use with boys; and similarly a woman, representing a mother rather than a teacher, for use with girls. It was now assumed that the child in the visual had taken something from the satchel or bag in the cloakroom. The two visuals taken together made up the confrontation between parent and child. A searching analysis of various aspects of lying followed, making this by far the most extensive of our tests.

Telling the truth

Our preliminary question was: Will the child tell the truth or not? A total of 42, or 11·7%, of our 360 subjects judged that the child *would* tell the truth. The figures were:

Age-group	*Boys* *N*-30	*Girls* *N*-30	*Total* *N*-60
7-year	3	1	4
9-year	5	2	7
11-year	4	6	10
13-year	3	4	7
15-year	4	0	4
17-year	4	6	10
Totals	23	19	42

The assumption of lying is thus overwhelming at all ages. Moreover, even the motive for truth-telling was not always high-minded. Of the 42 truth-telling reponses, 12 were motivated by the prudential concern to lessen trouble and lighten ultimate punishment, and 14 by the inevitability of detection. Only the remaining 16 responses, 4·4% of the total sample, were high-minded, speaking of a sense of having done wrong, of feeling guilty, of having broken trust, of being impelled by honesty, and, of course, of being compelled by conscience.

Such a picture may seem black. But, as analysis will show, it is by no means the whole story. For the present, two points may be made. First, the item stolen from the cloakroom was not envisaged as being costly or valuable – a fountain-pen, for example, was frequently mentioned. Much more important, secondly, was the fact that, where there was a good relationship with parents, truth-telling was far more likely. Thus, two boys of 17 years say:

> 'If his father was vicious, he would lie. If his father was understanding, he'd tell the truth, and get advice about what to do for the best.'
>
> 'He'd be afraid of his father beating him.'

Three girls of 17 years make similar responses. For example:

> 'My mother always knows when I'm telling a lie. It's better for her to tell the truth, and her parents would find out, anyway, and then it would be even worse.'
>
> 'The truth's got to come out some time. You've got to go on living with your parents.'

Further analysis underlines the fact that harsh punishment and lack of understanding on the part of parents simply encourage lying; and, conversely, that a good and understanding relationship encourages truth-telling. Here is striking evidence for the superiority of psychological discipline to physical discipline as a moral influence.

Definition of a lie

Piaget's first concern is with the definition of a lie. He finds three developing types of definition. The first, and 'most primitive', is that a lie is a 'naughty word'. Here the child, 'while perfectly well acquainted with a lie when he meets one, identifies it completely with the oaths or indecent expressions which one is forbidden to use'; so that 'to tell a lie is to commit a moral fault by means of language' (op. cit., 136f).

A second and more developed definition, found 'between 6 and 10 on the average', asserts that a lie 'is something that isn't true'. Here, says

Piaget, 'we must ascertain whether the child confuses lying with every kind of inaccuracy (especially with mistakes)', in order to see whether awareness of intentionality is present. Piaget found that 'children of 5 to 7, while perfectly aware of the shade of difference between an intentional act and an involuntary mistake, do not tend to stress this distinction at all, and often, on the contrary, group both facts under the same name of "a lie". . . . Mistakes, although they are distinguished from lies proper, are still conceived as constituting lies. More precisely, a lie is defined in a purely objective manner, as an affirmation that does not conform with fact . . . this identification of mistakes and lies disappears towards the age of 8' (op. cit., 138ff.).

Thirdly, Piaget found a 'third type of definitions, or correct definitions of lies; any statement that is intentionally false is a lie. Not till about the age of 10 to 11 do we find this definition in an explicit form' (op. cit., 142).

Piaget's whole concern was with pre-adolescent childhood, but ours was with a far broader age-span. We were not therefore concerned directly with such definition of lying, although we shall find much evidence indirectly. We were, however, interested to see how far the identification of mistakes and lies would be found in our responses. We therefore simply asked: Would a mistake be a lie?

In the 7-year age-group, 10 boys and 10 girls held that a mistake would be a lie. Here are typical quotations from boys responding thus:

'Saying it's not yours when it was.'

'Cheating.'

'Saying something which is wrong, not true.' (Would a mistake be a lie?) 'Yes. Unless he put it right quickly, it would be a lie just for a second.'

'Tell things wrong.'

And from the girls:

'Saying no when you did.'

'It's a naughty word, being naughty by mistake.'

'It's naughty.'

'Saying they did when they didn't really.'

'When you didn't tell the truth.'

Such responses may be held to fall broadly within Piaget's second stage, and at an age consistent with his. But since 40, or 66%, of the subjects in this age-group did not identify mistakes with lies, we find poor confirmation of his second stage. The difference suggests greater maturity in our subjects than in 'children from the poorer parts of Geneva'.

We were additionally interested to see if any subjects beyond the age of 8 years – Piaget's dividing line – identified mistakes and lies. Cases were rare. They consisted of a boy of 9 who defined a lie as 'a naughty word' (I.Q. 105; S.E. 2; Rel. 3); a girl of 11 years (I.Q. 79; S.E. 1; Rel. 1); and three boys of 13 years. One of these boys simply answered in the affirmative (I.Q. 75; S.E. 2; Rel. 1); the second went on: 'it would be a sort of lie, a guilty lie' (I.Q. 79; S.E. 2; Rel. 4); and the third added: 'a naughty deed is a lie' (I.Q. 77; S.E. 1; Rel. 1). We thus found 5 cases in all after the age of 7 years, characterised particularly by low intelligence.

Why is lying wrong?

We now turn to our major concern in this test: judgements on the wrongfulness of lying. While Piaget's main thesis is not concerned with this aspect, he does pay it some attention. Typically, he finds three stages.

The first and lowest stage is seen in subjects who 'look upon lying as naughty because it is punished, and if it were not punished no guilt would attach to it. This is objective responsibility in its purest form.' Piaget refuses to admit any possibility of anomy: 'These facts, moreover, should not be interpreted as even a relative amorality . . . Lies are forbidden, though one does not quite know why . . . a lie is a fault in so far as it is forbidden by God or adults. This is heteronomy in its most naïve form' (op. cit., 164f.).

The second stage brings a higher definition: 'A lie is a fault in itself, and would remain so even if it were not punished . . . But even though they are generalised in this way, rules are none the less heteronomous. The child, it is true, takes the particular command that has been given him and raises it to the level of a universal law. This rational process of extension is probably already due to co-operation. But the rule may nevertheless persist in the form of an imperative that is external to the child's own conscience' (op. cit., 165f.).

The weaknesses in this theorising are apparent. Piaget will not follow the logic of his own argument. Thus, where there is no sense of truth or falsehood, he explicitly rejects a definition of anomy. Again, while commands from respected adults are thus universalised, we are not permitted to see any beneficent value in heteronomy. Typical, too, is the assumption that progress to universality is simply one of elaboration 'by the child's reason'. Such bland optimism is admirable, if foolhardy;

empirically we find conscience to be far more orectic than purely cognitive in make-up. Yet again we observe the weakness of the quite unsubstantiated assertion that universalisation of rules is 'probably' due to mutual co-operation.

Piaget's third stage, appearing at 10 to 12 years, holds that 'truthfulness is necessary to reciprocity and mutual agreement'. But there are, inevitably, 'adult sermons' to be identified, isolated and rejected. 'Among the alleged motives there will be found, it is true, a whole set of phrases inspired by adult talk: "We mustn't tell lies because it's no use." "We must speak the truth ... our conscience tells us to." ' Here again we observe the same grave weaknesses – or perversity – in Piaget's attempt to isolate 'adult sermons' from genuine convictions, and in his failure to continue testing into adolescence, as we found in analysis of the cheating situation. At the very age when we find clear evidence of the first glimmerings of conscience, Piaget explicitly rejects the citation of conscience as motivating truth-telling.

Having identified and rejected such 'commendable but too often meaningless formulae', Piaget finds genuine reactions holding that 'truthfulness is necessary because deceiving others destroys mutual trust'; so that 'while the younger child had regarded a lie as all the worse for being unbelievable, the older ones, on the contrary, condemn a lie in so far as it succeeds . . . in deceiving the other person' (op. cit., 166f.). Thus, summing up his thesis, Piaget traces an evolution towards reciprocity with age: 'The consciousness of lying gradually becomes interiorised and the hypothesis may be hazarded that it does so under the influence of co-operation . . . Intelligence animates co-operation and yet needs this social instrument for its own formation' (op. cit., 168).

The extension of rules into universal laws was defined as 'probably already due to co-operation'; now the 'hypothesis may be hazarded' that the interiorisation of the consciousness of lying is also due to the same mutual co-operation. Here we are in the realm of pure theorising, not of empirical research.

For Piaget, then, intelligence plus mutual co-operation are the key factors in development towards autonomy in the area of truth-telling. Analysis of our responses must determine whether we can agree.

7-YEAR AGE-GROUP: BOYS

We asked, first, why it is wrong to tell lies. But, as in the Cheating Test, additional questions were vital to probe deeper. The second question (Q. 2 in quotations) was – Would it be all right to tell a lie if you were not caught and punished for it? The third question (Q. 3 in quotations) was – Would telling lies be wrong/naughty if they were not punished?

20 of the 30 boys in this age-group were inevitably and firmly rooted in heteronomy, with elements of anomy and of socionomy on either side. From the lower, and generally mixed, responses we may quote:

'Miss might find out.' (Q. 2) 'Yes. Nobody would know.'

(Q. 2) 'Yes. Nobody knows.' (Q. 3) 'No. Mum or Dad might be playing a joke on him and pretend not to punish him. Then they'd send him to bed after.'

' 'Cos his Mum will send him to bed.' (Q. 2) 'Yes. Nobody knows.'

'It's naughty and a wrong habit. It's all wrong, 'cos you're saying all the wrong words.'

'It isn't true, and you shouldn't say what's not true because you get put in prison.'

'He'd be afraid of being smacked. His face would go red.'

Touches of socionomy appear in 6 responses, but they are very mixed. A typical example is:

'Its rude. If he tells lies to someone, they'll do the same to him.' (Q. 2) 'Yes. No one would know.'

The response, 'No one will ever believe you', might be accepted as a Piagetian 'adult sermon', which in origin it doubtless is. The question is to decide when it can be accepted as interiorised. Since our Lying Test included some 12 questions in all, ranging over various aspects of lying, we had a wide range of evidence for making a decision.

7-YEAR AGE-GROUP: GIRLS

Here, too, heteronomy is naturally strong with elements of anomy, and, surprisingly, fewer indications of socionomy than in the parallel boys. Typical of lower, mixed responses are:

'It's naughty because somebody might find out . . . because it's not the truth.' (Q. 2) 'Yes. She knew nobody would find out.'

'It's very rude. You get smacked.' (Q. 2) 'Yes. You're not smacked.'

'Because lying means naughty.'

The authorities cited by the 22 heteronomous responses are, as with the boys, mainly parents. But they may be divine:

'God wouldn't love you if you told lies.'

Legal:

'It's against the law' (2 subjects).

'If people find out, they could tell the police.'

Parental:

'My parents have told me it's wrong' (2 subjects).

'It's naughty. Mummy says so.'

Parental, with social implications – and here we see the roots of that subsequent realisation that truthfulness is necessary to personal relationships which, for Piaget, is the precursor of autonomy:

'My Mummy says that if you tell lies no one will believe you.'

'No one will believe you in future. My Mum tells me.'

Educational:

'Teacher doesn't like it.'

Even friendship is cited:

'It's naughty. Margaret, my friend, told me.'

Of the three responses suggesting elements of socionomy, two still hold that lying is all right if undetected.

Total scores are similar in this age-group: boys 58·0 and girls 55·0.

Once again we find lower responses deriving mainly from the top infants' class, and higher responses from the first-year primary class. The latter have a higher mean age of 11 months and a higher mean socio-economic class of 0·7. Either, or both, factors may be significant here.

9-YEAR AGE-GROUP: BOYS

Heteronomy is still predominant, with 19 responses. Anomy is suggested by

'You always get found out in the end. (Q. 2) 'Yes.' (Q. 3) 'Yes. I'd just forgot about it.'

From mixed lower responses we may quote:

'It's not the rules to tell lies. It's naughty. You're not supposed to. It's God's rules.' (Q. 2) 'Yes.'

'You get into trouble.' (Q. 2) 'Yes.' (Q. 3) 'No. You *should* get punished.'

'You get found out in the end. Teacher doesn't like it.' (Q. 2) 'Yes. Because nobody would know.'

Piaget would be delighted by the strict heteronomy of

'I know it's wrong because I've been told by Mum.' (Q. 3) 'No. Because it's wicked to tell lies. I would go to bed early to punish myself.'

Religion is invoked in

'You get into trouble.' (Q. 3) 'It would still be wrong. God knows about it. When you go to Heaven, He'll say, "You can't come in".'

'It would be working on the Devil's side.'

Piaget's immanent justice appears as an 'act of God' in

'It's evil. The Devil tells lies, and God and Jesus doesn't. God might punish you. He might give you chicken-pox and make you stay in bed.' (Q. 2) 'Yes, But you *can* be caught, because God knows and He might put it into somebody else's mind.'

Progress towards socionomy appears in such responses as

'It's wrong. You hurt people.' (Q. 2) 'No. It's not fair on your friends.'

'You get a bad name with your friends. You get called a liar.'

The highest response is

(Q. 2) 'No. Because you would know yourself that you'd done wrong.'

9-YEAR AGE-GROUP: GIRLS

The 2 mixed low-level responses may be illustrated by

'You get found out and punished.' (Q. 2) 'Yes. No one would know.'

Pure heteronomy remains strong, as in

'It's awful wicked.' (Does not know why.) (Q. 2) 'No They *should* punish me.'

'It's being sinful and you're mocking God.' (Q. 2) 'No. It leads to more lies and you'll get caught.'

'You get punished.' (Q. 2) 'No. It wouldn't be nice. You might hurt yourself by it. It makes some people sulky.' (Q. 3) 'No. Your parents might be just letting you off this time. They'll watch to see if you do it again, and then they'll punish you.'

Heteronomy merges with socionomy in such responses as

'You get found out and punished.' (Q. 2) 'No. Her friends will call her a liar.'

'Your friends don't believe you.' (Q. 2) 'No. Lies are nasty and someone is sure to find out.'

The process of interiorisation is evidenced in

(Q. 3) 'Yes and no. It would be O.K. if my Mum and Dad said so. They always know best. It's wrong in another way, because I know you shouldn't tell lies.'

Again we see the seed of autonomy in

'You should always tell the truth, because Mother and Father don't trust you else.'

Reciprocity makes its first appearance in

'You wouldn't like it if anyone told a lie on you.'

The value of additional questions for probing in depth is clearly illustrated by

'You get found out and punished.' (Q. 2) 'No. It's forbidden.' (Q. 3)

'No. You'd *know* yourself.'

Dawning autonomy is seen in

'You hurt others by being deceitful.' (Q. 2) 'No. It's not nice to tell lies.' (Q. 3) 'No. It starts bothering you after a while.'

'You get found out.' (Q. 2) 'No. It's wrong to tell lies and it will be on your mind.'

The boys in this age-group remain broadly as at 7 years, with a small increase in total score of 3·0. Girls, with a sharp decline in anomy and rise in socionomy, increase by 12·5, and now already lead boys by 6·5 in total score. This early development in girls of 9 years parallels their lower mean intelligence, as compared with boys of this age, of 3·0. This development cannot therefore be attributed to intelligence. Moreover, it is only in this Lying Test that girls make such marked progress at 9 years; in the three other tests their development begins at 11 years. Responses suggest that this progress is due to the greater sensitivity of girls to personal relationships. Thus, whereas Piaget holds that development comes through the interaction of co-operation and reason, such evidence suggests that reason is not a key factor, at least at this age.

11-YEAR AGE-GROUP: BOYS

Even at this next age-group, boys show little change, with a minimal increase in total score of 1·5. Anomy is evident in

'You get found out. You get into trouble.' (Q. 2) 'Yes. Because no one would know about it.'

Typical of mixed lower responses is

'You get found out.' (Q. 2) 'Yes. Sometimes. But you're bound to get found out in the end.' (Q. 3) 'No. You still get found out, because they would keep on doing it till they were punished; then they would stop.'

Strong heteronomy may be illustrated from religion:

'It's a sin against God; it would be on your mind. He would ***not*** punish, though, but forgive you.' (Q. 2) 'No. You're bound to get found out in the end.'

'It's wrong because it's in the Ten Commandments.' (Q. 3) 'No. You still told a lie, so you should be punished. It's wrong in any case.'

'It's wrong because God knows. It says so in the Bible. We were taught about it in Sunday School.'

Suggestions of socionomy appear in such responses as

'It's not being honest with people – not telling them the truth.'

'Nobody will believe you. You'll be called a liar.' (Q. 3) 'No. Lying is naughty. You tell somebody and he thinks it's true, and passes it on as true.'

'You might cause trouble to other people and hurt them.'

Conscience makes its first appearance in

'You're getting away with something you shouldn't be.' (Q. 3) 'No. Conscience would make you own up in the end.'

'It gets on your conscience: you know you shouldn't do it. It comes from God.'

A comprehensive response is

'You get into trouble. It's better to be straight out and truthful, because you won't half feel a coward. You'll have a guilty conscience and blush.' (Q. 2) 'No. It's still a lie even if you're not found out. You keep thinking about it and want to get it off your chest.' (Q. 3) 'No. You'll think you can keep on getting away with it and suddenly you'll get a new teacher. Then you've had it.'

11-YEAR AGE-GROUP: GIRLS

Heteronomy is found in half the responses. To illustrate again from religion, we have:

'It's in the Ten Commandments, in Messiah's Law. Those who worship the Messiah must obey his laws.'

'The lie often comes back and tells on you.' (Q. 2) 'No. The Ten Commandments say you should not tell lies at all. It's one of God's rules.'

The agony of regret is prudentially expressed in

'It makes you miserable. It's better to own up – it makes you happier. You're afraid someone will find out, and then there'll be more trouble.'

Socionomy emerges in such responses as

'If your parents found out there'd be serious trouble.' (Q. 3) 'No. It would be on your mind. Your friends would call you a liar.'

'Other people will think what a horrible person you are.' (Q. 2) 'No. You'd know yourself, and Jesus would know. He doesn't like it – nor would anybody if they *did* find out.'

'You could get others into trouble. It's not fair to do this by telling lies.'

Autonomy appears in 13 responses. For example:

(Q. 2) 'No. Your conscience would worry you.'

'You're not being honest.' (Q. 2) 'No. You might cause trouble to somebody else.' (Q. 3) 'It's still wrong, whether others think so or not.'

'People will put trust in you and they'll be let down and hurt badly.'

(Q. 3) 'No. It's just the same as if you were.'

The girls' development towards socionomy and autonomy increases their total score by 11·5. The boys remaining static, the girls now lead boys by 16·5 in total score, and this parallels their lead in mean intelligence, at this age, of 8·9.

13-YEAR AGE-GROUP: BOYS

Again there is little development in boys' responses. There are 7 lower mixed responses. A verbose example is:

'It's wrong, I've always been told so. But it's very handy in time of need. Telling somebody false does you no good. It only leads to worse punishment.' (Q. 2) 'It's O.K.' (Q. 3) 'Yes. There are no consequences – you haven't offended anyone.'

A brief and blunt example is

'I don't think it's wrong – not if you can get away with it.'

From the 13 strongly heteronomous responses we may quote:

'You get into more trouble by lying.' (Q. 2) 'No. But I would.' (Q. 3) 'No. Teacher would be wrong not to punish.'

'You get punished. You cop out from Dad.'

Conscience is little more than a verbalism in

'It's not truthful. They usually catch up with you in the end – teachers or the police.' (Q. 2) 'No. It would still be on your conscience. You'd be worried in case you were found out.' (Q. 3) 'No. Teacher *should* tell you off.'

An interesting response is

'You're letting the Devil in, letting the bad part of you govern and rule. You get into the habit of lying, so that you don't know you're doing it.' (Q. 3) 'No. They would increase in you if not punished.'

Socionomy appears in 5 responses, such as:

'You might get somebody else into trouble who's got nothing to do with it.'

'It's not fair to the other person.'

'No one will believe you any more.'

6 responses show dawning autonomy. Thus:

'You get a bad reputation and lose your friends. You grow up lying all your life.' (Q. 2) 'No. Not a really bad lie. It would be on your conscience.'

'A lie told to a person might be an important matter. It might harm others and yourself too. I'd be ashamed.' (Q. 2) 'No. I'd have a guilty conscience. Truth is really the best.'

'It's just something I feel – that it's wrong. If people found out they wouldn't trust you. I like having responsibility. When I grow up it will help me to stand on my own feet.'

13-YEAR AGE-GROUP: GIRLS

Among the girls of this age-group anomy disappears, heteronomy decreases, socionomy remains constant, and autonomy increases out-outstandingly. From the 5 cases of full heteronomy we may quote:

'It says in the Commandments we shouldn't. Our parents tell us we shouldn't.'

Heteronomy merges into socionomy in such responses as:

'You get into trouble. My friends would think I'm a liar.' (Q. 2) 'No. You can never be sure.' (Q. 3) 'No. Lying is classed as wrongdoing. My mother told me when I was young, and I would wonder why I wasn't punished.'

'You don't get anywhere. People won't believe you in future.'

'It doesn't give you a good name.'

From 14 responses suggesting autonomy we may cite:

'You wouldn't be trusted afterwards. Adults wouldn't respect you if they found out.'

'It leads to more lies.' (Q. 3) 'No. I'd have a guilty conscience.'

'You should always tell the truth. If you lie, you get found out.' (Q. 3) 'No. *You'd* know you told it.'

Stronger autonomy is evidenced in 6 further responses, such as:

'You lead people to believe things that aren't true, and probably get others into trouble.' (Q. 3) 'No. You might still have done harm to somebody. And people won't trust you afterwards.'

'It's making people believe something that isn't true. A lie very often is something you wish to be. Instead of lying, you should try to fulfil that wish.'

'It's just a feeling inside me. If I lied I would have to tell someone in the end.'

Sex differences, as seen in total scores, are now at their highest. While boys show a minimal increase of 4·0, girls increase by 12·5. They now lead boys by a massive 25·0. At 9, 11 and 13 years the girls' score had increased by 12·5, 11·5 and 12·5. But while their mean intelligence was markedly higher than that of boys at 11 and 13 years, it was actually lower at 9 years, when development was broadly similar. Intelligence, therefore, is not the key factor.

15-YEAR AGE-GROUP: BOYS

Heteronomy is still strong. From 11 lower and mixed responses we may quote:

'It's not being honest. My parents told me.' (Q. 2) 'Yes.'

'You get found out, anyway. And the consequences would be worse.'

'Mum told me it was wrong. It's O.K. to tell lies to avoid being shown up.' (Q. 3) 'No. They deserve to be punished.'

In 3 responses heteronomy merges with socionomy. Thus:

'It's deceiving. You lose your friends.' (Q. 2) 'Big lies mean trouble in the end.'

'People don't like you. Your friends won't believe you in future.'

At last, in this age-group, boys show development. 16 responses show at least some evidence of autonomy. Thus:

'It is untruthful, and shows you can't be trusted.' (Q. 3) 'No. You're letting yourself down, undermining yourself.'

'Lying leads to more lies. You're found out and you get a bad name. You're not trusted.'

'It means trouble for others and for yourself equally.' (Q. 2) 'No. You'd feel guilty, especially if it caused trouble for another.'

'You're not being honest to others.' (Q. 3) 'No. Your own sense of values would judge.'

15-YEAR AGE-GROUP: GIRLS

Given the massive advance of the girls in the three previous age-groups, no such dramatic development can be expected. With small transfer from heteronomy to socionomy, the total score increases by a mere 2·0. 2 responses still judge that lying is all right if undetected. A feminine expression of heteronomy includes

'You'd be under suspicion for a long time.'

Socionomy is seen in such responses as:

'You will be an adult yourself, and you don't want people telling you lies.'

'If everyone told lies you wouldn't know who to believe or who not to believe.'

'You get others into trouble.'

Among the 17 responses showing partial or full autonomy we have:

'If I told a big lie I would punish myself, through my conscience, and that would make me think twice before telling lies in future.'

'You have been taught it. It becomes part of your personality that lying is wrong.'

'You're deceiving others as well as yourself. You're trying to make yourself believe one thing when it's another. You corrupt yourself as well as anyone else.'

The development of the boys, at this age, increases their total score by 16·0, as compared with the girls' 2·0. The girls, however, still lead in mean I.Q. by 3·0, so that once again intelligence is not the key factor.

17-YEAR AGE-GROUP: BOYS

3 subjects still judge that lying is all right if undetected. Heteronomy is mostly partial, as in

'You get into trouble and punished. It's not Christian to tell lies – it's a kind of sin. You may get someone else into trouble.'

Socionomy receives such familiar expressions as 'It's not fair'; 'People don't like you'; 'Your friends won't believe you'.

From the 19 responses revealing autonomy we may quote:

'It's deceitful to yourself, as well as to others.' (Q. 2) 'Yes. If you could live with your conscience. But in the end conscience catches up with you.'

'It shows a flaw in your character if you must lie to gain your own ends.'

'Lying is a sin, not a crime. There is no more trust between you and others. Trust is gone.'

'No. You punish yourself by spoiling relationships. It preys on your mind and you feel guilty.'

17-YEAR AGE-GROUP: GIRLS

Anomy has now wholly disappeared, and heteronomy reduced. 26 of the 30 responses are on the levels of socionomy and autonomy. Socionomy is strong, with 14 responses, such as:

'It ruins friendships. You wouldn't like a person who keeps lying.'

'You're not gaining anything and not helping others.' (Q. 3) (All right if unpunished?) 'Yes. Because wrong is what society punishes.'

'Society would be chaotic if everybody lied.' (Q. 2) 'No. Lying is wrong in itself – how wrong depends on the person and the pressures being put upon them.'

9 responses show partial, and 7 show full, autonomy. Typical are:

'It disturbs your conscience and makes you feel dishonest.'

'It doesn't get you anywhere. It gives you a conscience. It makes people distrust you in future.'

'Nobody would trust you if you're found out.' (Q. 2) 'No. Finally you wouldn't be able to trust yourself.' (Q. 3) 'No. A lie is a lie whether you're punished or not.'

Finally, we may quote a fulsome and trenchant criticism of the projective approach:

'It depends on what you lie about. It depends on the personality, doesn't it. *She* might do it. But if that's supposed to be *me* doing it, then it's silly, because that means I'd have to change my personality, and then it wouldn't be me, would it?'

The pattern of development

The total scores of the sex groups, at each age level, together with the girls' lead in both total score and mean I.Q., provide a comparative picture of development.

The Lying Test

Age-group	*Boys' Total Score N-30*	*Girls' Total Score N-30*	*Girls' Lead in Score*	*Girls' Lead in Mean I.Q.*
7-year	58·0	55·0	− 3·0	+ ·6
9-year	61·0	67·5	+ 6·5	−3·0
11-year	62·5	79·0	+16·5	+8·9
13-year	66·5	91·5	+25·0	+7·8
15-year	82·5	93·5	+11·0	+3·9
17-year	94·5	98·0	+ 3·5	+1·8

Since these figures show a different pattern from that derived from other tests, we may, in addition, observe the increases in sex-group scores at each age.

Increase in Total Score

Age-group	*Boys' Increase in Total Score*	*Girls' Increase in Total Score*
9-year	3·0	12·5
11-year	1·5	11·5
13-year	4·0	12·5
15-year	16·0	2·0
17-year	12·0	4·5

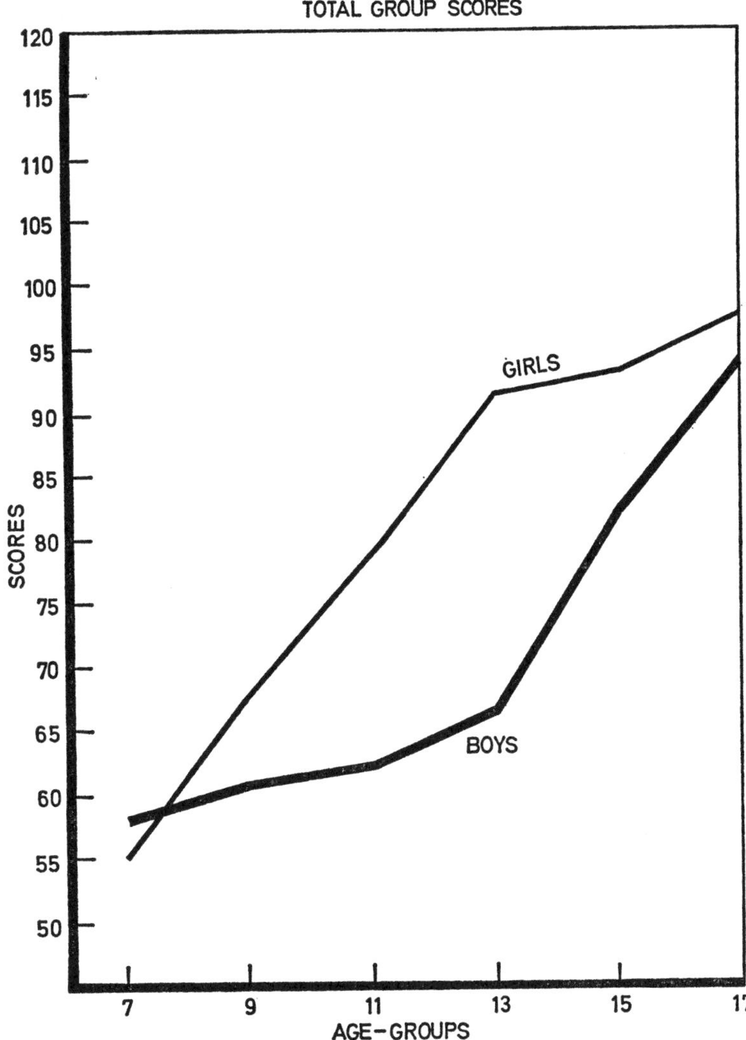
TOTAL GROUP SCORES
120
115
110
105
100
95
90
85
80
75
70
65
60
55
50
SCORES
GIRLS
BOYS
7
9
11
13
15
17
AGE-GROUPS

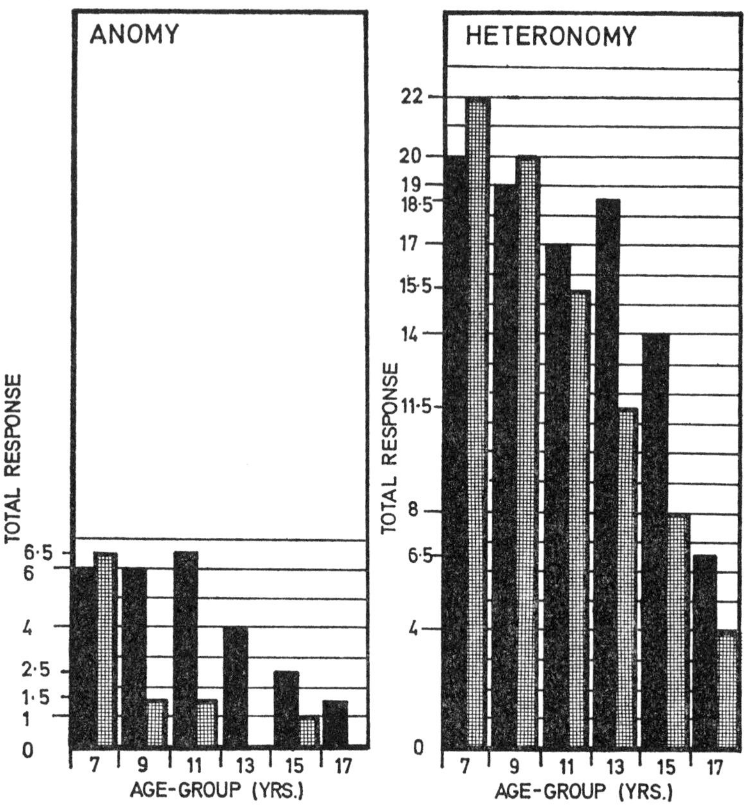

TABLE OF I.Q. VALUES

AGE-GROUP		7	9	11	13	15	17
MEAN I.Q.	BOYS	108·2	110·8	96·9	98·5	104·6	106·4
	GIRLS	108·8	107·8	105·8	106·3	108·5	108·2

SEX DIFFERENCES

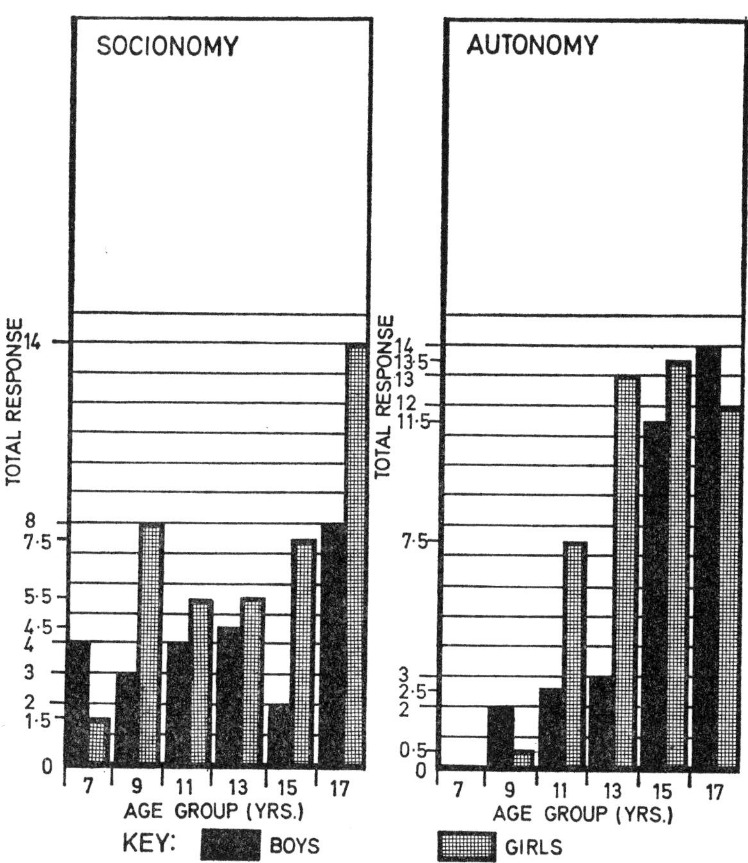

NOTE: N = 60 PER AGE-GROUP (30 BOYS + 30 GIRLS)

The first striking difference in this test pattern is that girls show a solid advance at 9 years, an age-group *earlier* than in the other tests, where development appears first at 11 years. This cannot be associated with intelligence, since the girls' mean I.Q. is lower than that of boys of this age, who, in fact, make a minimal advance. Our responses, we have deduced, suggest that this early development in girls derives from their greater sensitivity to personal relationships. This advantage parallels the advantage of the girls of the youngest age-groups in the Value of Life Test, where we found them to have stronger initial sympathy, merging into awareness of reciprocity. Both the sympathy found there and the interpersonal sentivity found here must clearly be innate; and we might see such innate factors in girls as supporting the view of McDougall that 'all altruistic conduct has its root and origin in the maternal instinct' (McDougall, 1960, 175). It is striking, too, that both these tests – Value of Life and Lying – are concerned intrinsically with persons. While both the other tests, Cheating and Stealing, do, of course, involve persons, they are not so directly centred upon them. Here, then, we may see the essence of the sex difference in moral judgement.

The second striking difference is that boys, in sharp contrast, begin their development at 15 years, an age-group *later* than in the other tests, where maturation first becomes apparent at 13 years. The only exception is the Value of Life Test, where boys do show a development at 11 years. But that is due to decrease in both anomy and heteronomy, replaced by partial glimmerings of socionomy and autonomy, and we might well expect this in a matter of life and death; and, even so, their total score at 11 years is only 3·0 above that of the girls of 7 years in the Value of Life Test. Thus the fact remains that boys atypically begin to develop an age-group later in judgements on lying. We can only see here further evidence of the far greater feminine sensitivity to and awareness of personal relationships, and the corresponding lack of it in boys.

We observe, thirdly, that intelligence is not the key factor in development, despite the fact that the girls' greatest lead in scores is shown at 11, 13 and 15 years – the very ages when their mean I.Q. exceeds that of the boys. For, first, girls show a strong advance at 9 years, when their mean I.Q. is lower than that of boys; and, secondly, boys make their strongest developmental surge at 15 years, when their mean I.Q. is lower than that of the girls. Intelligence is patently of no mean significance where moral judgement is concerned. We have found it to be associated with higher judgements, but decreasingly so with increasing age. Yet we have already observed such orectic factors as innate sympathy and sensitive awareness of persons to be strong influences upon the development of moral judgement. Hence our rejection of the Piagetian theory that autonomy is born of the interaction of intelligence and co-operation through a quasi-mechanical process. The unique early development in girls and the unique late development in boys, in the intensely personal area of truth-telling, clearly indicate that much more than reason is involved in the maturation of interiorised morality.

Lying to children and adults

Piaget's next concern – for him a minor one – is to contrast developing attitudes towards lying to children and lying to adults. We followed Piaget in asking whether it was judged worse to lie to children or to adults, or whether lying was the same to both.

Piaget used this aspect of lying to corroborate his thesis that 'the consciousness of lying gradually becomes interiorised and the hypothesis may be hazarded that it does so under the influence of co-operation . . . Intelligence animates co-operation' in a 'circular relation'. It follows that lies between children should be at first regarded as legitimate and later as illegitimate. Piaget found that, while younger children held that children might lie to each other, older children think it as bad, or worse, to lie to children as to lie to adults (op. cit., 168ff.). The figures quoted by Piaget are: '81% between 6 and 9 think it worse to lie to adults; 51% between 10 and 13 think it equally bad to lie to children, and of these, 17% are even of opinion that it is worse to lie to a companion than to an adult' (op. cit., 308).

1. THE 6-TO-9-YEAR AGE-GROUPING

We may reasonably equate our 7-to-9-year age-groups, 120 subjects in all, with Piaget's 6-to-9-year grouping. He finds 81% who think it worse to lie to an adult. Our figure is certainly 71·7%. But an additional 10% think it *equally* bad to lie to adult or child, and on a similar heteronomous basis. Such subjects, while rooted in heteronomy, do *not* hold that lies between children are allowed. Indeed, we found no evidence for this idea at all. Moreover, 9·2% thought it wrong to lie to either adult or child, both on grounds of untruthfulness; and 7·5% judged it *worse* to lie to children, on the ground that either they will believe, and thereby be deceived, or that it will set them a bad example.

We can then broadly agree with Piaget that the majority do think it worse to lie to an adult, adults being 'more important' or 'more respectable'. But we find no evidence that lies between children are allowed; 16·7% of our subjects hold it equally bad to lie to children; and 7·5% held it worse to lie to children.

If we may 'hazard' an alternative 'hypothesis', it is that lies are proscribed by adults; they are therefore wrong, particularly to adults; they are wrong, by extension, to children too; and especially wrong to children as deceiving or setting a bad example. This pattern, found at 7 years in embryo, steadily develops thereafter with maturation. The key factor in this progression is adult proscription, not, as with Piaget, peer co-operation.

2. THE 10-TO-13-YEAR AGE-GROUPING

We may reasonably equate our 11-to-13-year age-groups, 120 subjects in all, with Piaget's 10-to-13-year grouping. He finds that 51% think it equally bad to lie to children; we find 24·2%. We find 37·5% who still think it worse to lie to an adult, and a further 16·7% who think it as bad to lie to either, on heteronomous grounds. We also find 10% who think it worse to lie to an adult, not on grounds of heteronomy, but of breaking adult trust – a category quite unknown to Piaget. Piaget further finds that 17% of his 51% think it worse to lie to a child. Our figure is 11·7%, but 11 out of the 14 responses in this category judge thus, *not* on grounds of 'deceiving one's comrades', but because it is setting children a bad example – another category quite unknown to Piaget.

We thus find no evidence for Piaget's thesis that the key factor is peer co-operation. Moreover, and yet again, we find such a simplification of categories in Piaget's analysis as to produce, in effect, a blurred, if not false, picture. Thus, in the 10-to-13-year grouping we find 10% of subjects condemning lying as breaking adult trust; and this category, unknown to Piaget, is manifest at 11, 13 and 15 years – the very ages when we find climacteric development in moral judgement. Here we may see the process of interiorisation at work.

3. THE PATTERN OF DEVELOPMENT

We may now tabulate our responses, including those categories not found in Piaget, to illustrate the developmental pattern. (See opposite page.)

Lying to children and to adults

We recall Piaget's dictum that the dawn of autonomy appears when the child realises that 'truthfulness is necessary to the relations of sympathy

Age-group N-60	*Adult: Heteronomy*	*Adult: Trust*	*Same: Heteronomy*	*Same: Trust*	*Children: Bad Example*	*Children: Punish*
7-year	49	—	5	4	2	—
9-year	37	—	7	7	7	2
11-year	25	5	13	15	2	—
13-year	20	7	7	14	12	—
15-year	17	6	2	10	25	—
17-year	13	—	—	20	27	—

and mutual respect', and that reciprocity seems to be the 'determining factor of autonomy' (op. cit., 195). Only 2 out of all our responses specifically cited reciprocity in the strict sense. Interpreting reciprocity in its widest sense, as Piaget does, to embrace the whole sphere of interpersonal relationships, we can, of course, agree. Thus, when development really commences in the 11-year age-group we find 20, or 33%, of our total responses have come to realise that trust is essential to personal relationships. But 5 of these responses regard lying as breaking adult trust, and 15 regard it as breaking trust with both child and adult on exactly the same level. Only 2 responses regard lying as being worse to a child, and both on the ground of setting a bad example – a category that grows through adolescence and particularly in girls' responses. We find *no* evidence whatever that this realisation of lying as breaking trust is on grounds of 'deceiving one's comrades'.

We cannot therefore accept Piaget's theory that the autonomous conviction of the necessity of truth-telling grows out of mutual, reciprocal co-operation among peers. We observe, on the contrary, the extension and universalisation of the original adult proscription of lying. The majority of subjects at every age quote parental influence as shaping their increasingly autonomous conviction against lying – although, we observe, some subjects at all ages, and even 22% at 17 years, remain dependent upon heteronomy. Identification and introjection are clearly factors in the process of interiorisation. And once the interdiction of lying becomes interiorised, it applies to any human being, regardless of age or status. As so many of our responses put it: 'It's just the same. There's no difference between lying to adults and lying to children. Both are persons.'

4. TYPICAL RESPONSES

Quotations of responses at all ages will best serve to illustrate the pattern that we find in the responses from both boys and girls.

(a) The 7-year Age-group

For both boys and girls of 7 years, adults are typically 'more important' than children, so that lying to them is worse.

(b) The 9-year Age-group

For 1 subject it is worse to lie to children, since 'it might be you' – clear reciprocity. Another subject thinks it worse on the grounds that

> 'They'd tell the girl's parents, and they'd tell the child she'd lied about, and she'd hit the girl who told the lies.'

One boy also thinks it worse to lie to a peer on the ground that 'He'd get a gang who'd duff you up.' Another thinks it worse on the ground that children 'upset easier'; and another because 'they believe more, and might come to more harm.'

(c) The 11-year Age-group

2 responses hold it equally bad to lie to adult or child:

> 'You're letting an adult down; you're setting a bad example to children.'
>
> 'They're both your friends.' (If an enemy?) 'That would be just as bad.'

5 responses hold it worse to lie to adults, not on grounds of authority, but because they believe more, since they trust more. Hence trust is broken with adults.

(d) The 13-year Age-group

7 responses judge it worse to lie to adults, since

> 'You respect them more; they are older and wiser; they own you, kind of.'
>
> 'You respect them more; they expect they can trust you.'
>
> 'You lose their trust.'
>
> 'You lose their respect.'
>
> 'It's disloyal, impolite.'
>
> 'They'll think, "She tells lies." '

Typical of responses holding lying equally bad to adult or child are:

> 'You feel equally sorry.'
>
> 'Both believe you.'

'It's deceiving both of them.'
'You lose the trust of either.'
'A lie is a lie whoever you tell it to.'
'They're all people.'

Of the 12 responses judging it worse to lie to children, 9 are on the ground of setting a bad example; 3 on the ground that 'they believe you more', so that the deceit common to all lying is that much more heinous. Children are 'taken in more easily.'

(e) The 15-year Age-group

6 responses hold it worse to lie to adults, all citing respect or trust. One refers to reciprocity:

'You'll be an adult yourself one day, and you wouldn't like to be lied to.'

Another says:

'Adults are wiser. They can help if you've done wrong.'

Typical of responses holding it worse to lie to children are:

'Children take things as gospel. They might lie themselves.'
'It would do more harm. They are taken in more easily.'
'They'd grow up to think lies O.K.'
'They'd get a wrong idea of things.'
'They'd think they can tell lies as well.'
'He'd grow up suspicious of everything he was told.'

(f) The 17-year Age-group

Similar responses came from our 17-year subjects, of whom 21% are still dependent upon heteronomy; 33% cite breaking trust with either adult or child; and 46%, mainly girls, assume autonomy in concentrating on the bad example set in lying to children. A reasonable sophistication found in the older age-groups is that 'you have to lie to children sometimes', instancing 'Father Christmas'.

Lying to parents

Such evidence provides no confirmation whatever of Piaget's thesis. We leave his theory there for the present. We shall, however, in the next chapter, analyse in greater depth his assertion that, in this area of truth-telling, the development of autonomy is born of peer reciprocity.

For Piaget, of course, the influence of parents is substantially reprehensible. He therefore has no interest in child-parent relationships. But, since all our evidence points to development in moral judgement as being the progressive interiorisation of adult, and mainly parental, precepts, we thought it valuable to seek at least some evidence for the influence of parents. The limitations imposed on this research prevented us going as far as we would have wished into the influence of the home upon moral judgement. But at least in the lying situation, involving intimate personal relationships, we could seek some evidence.

We were not therefore content simply with Piaget's question on lying to adults and children. Later in the test we added an additional question: 'Is it worse to lie to father or mother, or is it just the same?'

1. HETERONOMOUS RESPONSES

We found three clear categories of responses. The first was clearly heteronomous, the authority being that of either father or of mother, or of both ('one would tell the other, anyway'). The heteronomy imposed by father was overwhelming:

Lying to Parents: – Heteronomy

Age-group N-60	*Father*	*Mother*	*Same*
7-year	32	5	5
9-year	27	5	12
11-year	19	—	14
13-year	11	2	7
15-year	7	1	3
17-year	5	2	2
Totals	101	15	43

Thus heteronomy wanes, and increasingly so as development in moral judgement proceeds through adolescence.

2. LEGALISTIC RESPONSES

A second category of responses asserted the interdiction of lying to both parents. The typical response was: 'They're both the same. You shouldn't lie to either.' Such responses could be distinguished from heteronomous responses. But they did not reveal a personal relationship with one or both parents. There may have been some slight development in such responses; but as it was not apparent, it seemed better to leave them as an isolated group in this 'legalistic' category.

Lying to Parents: 2. Legalistic

Age-group N-60	*Same to Both Parents*
7-year	15
9-year	12
11-year	15
13-year	15
15-year	11
17-year	14

The figures are broadly similar at all ages, suggesting a quasi-heteronomous type of response.

3. PERSONALISTIC RESPONSES

A third category of responses indicated a truly personal relationship with parents: either a common attitude to both parents, or a preference for one or other based upon liking or respect, or a sense of 'closeness'. Terms used were: 'liking', 'loving', 'respect', 'trust', 'closeness'.

Lying to Parents: 3. Personalistic

Age-group N-60	*Same to Both Parents*	*Father*	*Mother*
7-year	—	1	2
9-year	—	1	3
11-year	10	—	2
13-year	19	—	6
15-year	27	2	9
17-year	18	1	19
Totals	74	5	41

Development begins, yet again, at 11 years. Noteworthy is the minimal figure for a sense of closeness to father. Of the 5 citations of father, 4 are from girls—but only 3 of these from adolescent girls. Interesting, too, is the fact that of the 9 mother-relationships cited at 15 years 6 are from boys. Naturally, at 17 years, 14 of the 19 references to closeness with mother are from girls.

4. THE PATTERN OF DEVELOPMENT

Development may be best indicated by setting out these three response categories at all ages in terms of percentages:

Lying to Parents: 4. Categories as Percentages

Age-group N-60	*Heteronomous Category*	*Legalistic Category*	*Personal Relationship Category*
7-year	70·0%	25·0%	5·0%
9-year	73·3%	20·0%	6·7%
11-year	55·0%	25·0%	20·0%
13-year	33·3%	25·0%	41·7%
15-year	18·3%	18·3%	63·4%
17-year	15·0%	23·3%	61·7%

Development begins at 11 years, characterised by the decline of heteronomy and the growth of a sense of personal relationship with parents, and is broadly complete at 15 years. Responses suggest that the 38% of responses at 17 years which reveal no strong personal relationship with parents are by no means to be attributed to adolescent waywardness. The attitudes of some parents – rigidly authoritarian or humanly cold – simply make impossible the warm, affectionate relationships indicated in the majority of our responses.

5. TYPICAL RESPONSES

Quotations from responses best illustrate these three categories of judgements on lying to parents.

(*a*) *The 7-year Age-group*

Here we naturally find strong heteronomy, over half the responses citing Father. He is 'more important', he is 'the boss', he 'rules the house', he 'has a harder hand' and, of course, 'Daddies are bigger than Mummies.' 'Both are your parents' is typical of legalistic responses. One boy likes Father more; 2 responses think it worse to lie to Mother, since 'she would be more upset'.

(b) The 9-year Age-group

Heteronomy is still strongly imposed by Father. Punishment may still be physical: 'My Dad would take off his belt'; 'Father's more hasty.' But other punishments appear: stopping pocket-money; sending to bed without supper. Typical of legalistic responses are: 'It's just as bad to either'; 'It's still a lie.' 2 of the personalistic responses quote reciprocity;

'Mother bakes cakes for you, she washes and pays for your clothes, and she hasn't told you a lie, so you shouldn't lie to her.'

'Father pays for everything, and you should repay him by telling the truth.'

(c) The 11-year Age-group

Father's authority becomes less apparent, although he still 'has more temper', 'is more stern', 'more of a boss – more frightening'. And, as one maiden laments, 'Fathers *never* seem to understand.' Legalistic responses say: 'They're both parents'; 'They're both equal'; 'They're both grown-up.' Personalistic responses begin to grow:

'You're hurting both.'

'They're both kind.'

'They don't tell you lies.'

'You lose their trust. That would worry me.'

'They both love me, and I love them both.'

'They're both as close.'

'Father would be more hurt; Mother would take longer to forget.'

2 responses hold that 'Mother would be more hurt', one of them on the ground that 'Father can stand up to a lie more bravely than Mother.'

(d) The 13-year Age-group

Heteronomy is now much less apparent. Legalistic responses state that both parents are 'equal', so that lying to either is 'equally bad'. Personalistic responses increase:

'You would lose their trust.' (8 responses)

'They'd both be ashamed. It's worse lying to them than to anyone else.'

'They don't lie to you. They have faith in you – that you won't do bad things.'

'They both love me. I'm part of them both.'

'They love you and try to help. They can't help you if you lie.'

'I respect them both.'

'You'd lose their trust. They'd think they'd failed in bringing you up properly.'

2 boys hold it worse to lie to mother – one because 'she'd feel more ashamed'. The other is more subtle: 'Father would punish me more, so I'd feel more conscience about lying to my mother.' 3 girls hold that mother is 'closer', and another that 'she loves you more'.

(*e*) *The 15-year Age-group*

Heteronomy still further declines. Both parents are simply 'equal' in legalistic responses. All personalistic responses hold it worse to lie to parents than to others, and 11 speak of breaking trust. Other responses are:

'It would hurt them both. They'd think it was their fault.'

'If you can't tell the truth to them, who can you tell it to.'

'It's far worse to them than to teachers. They don't matter.'

'They're the closest people to you.'

'They're both hurt. They're like one person.'

'They trust and respect you. That's why it's worse to them.'

'I love them both equally.'

6 boys think it worse to lie to Mother, since 'She would be more upset'; 'She trusts you more, so she'd be hurt more'; 'I like her more'; 'I feel closer to her.' 2 girls name Father: 'He'd be more hurt'; 'I look up to him more.' 3 girls name Mother: 'I see her more'; 'We have more trust'; 'She's closer to me.'

(*f*) *The 17-year Age-group*

Heteronomy is still present, as in

'Mother would take it out on you more' (boy).

'Mother is more authoritarian' (boy).

'Father's the one I'd get the biggest walloping from' (girl).

And a maiden laments:

'Mother always believes me. Dad never does.'

The legalistic category is well illustrated by

'They're both people. Sex is irrelevant.'

'It doesn't matter who you are lying to. It's still a lie, whether it's to someone you hate or love.'

8 personalistic responses speak of 'breaking trust'. Other responses are:

'They trust you. They don't lie to you.'

'They're both hurt just as much.'

'It would show lack of trust and faith in both them and me.'

'It would hurt them both. They'd feel they'd brought you up wrongly.'

'They're the best friends you've got. You know you can trust them.'

'They're both as close.'

One girl judges it worse to lie to Father: 'But I couldn't lie to him anyway. He's too sweet.' 4 boys think it worse to lie to Mother, since 'She'd be more upset'; 'She thinks more of you'; 'She means more to a boy.' All the 14 girls who hold it worse to lie to Mother do so on the ground of 'closeness' to her.

6. RECIPROCITY IN LYING

It is noteworthy, finally, that only 8, or 2% of the 360 responses are motivated by reciprocity, in the exact meaning of the term. Nowhere in analysis of this Lying Test do we find it of any significance. Using the term, however, in the broad, almost blanket sense that Piaget gives it, we can certainly agree that the realisation of trust as the heart of all personal relationships is the essence of autonomy in this area.

But the development of this realisation is found, in our responses, to be within the context of child-parent relationships. It is because of – not as Piaget holds, in spite of – parents that children develop such autonomy. Nowhere do we find evidence that it develops within the context of mutual co-operation with peers, as Piaget claims. Moreover, heteronomy persists, even at 17 years, whereas Piaget's theory would assume its withering away. Such heteronomy, of course, prevents that personalistic relationship with parents which breeds a realisation of the necessity of mutual trust, and therefore of truth-telling. But where parents permit and promote a warm and human, rather than cold and authoritarian, relationship they give the child an experience that shapes and patterns his moral judgement on the vital place of truth-telling in personal relationships.

Chapter 9
Specificity and generality in lying

Piaget and telling tales

Piaget has one further, if minor, concern with lying – that of telling tales. He uses this as a subordinate illustration of 'the conflict between adult authority and equality or solidarity between children.' The significant terms used in judgement by the child – 'tell-tales' or 'sneaks' – are sufficient to show that this is a fundamental point in the ethics of childhood. Is it right to break the solidarity that holds between children in favour of adult authority?' (op. cit., 288ff.).

Piaget used a test story of a father who set one son to watch the other during his absence, and asked for a full report on his return. What should the boy do? Nearly 90% of children aged 6 to 7 years held that 'the father should be told everything. The majority of the older ones (over 8) think that nothing should be told, and some even go so far as to prefer a lie to the betrayal of a brother . . . a clear case of a lie being evaluated as a function of the motive that inspires it' (op. cit., 289ff.).

Such evidence buttressed Piaget's thesis of 'the contrast of the two moralities – that of authority and that of equalitarian solidarity.' The devotee of the former is the '*petit* saint' – 'goody-goody', suggests the translator; while the latter is represented by the 'chic type' – 'good sport' – who is 'the incarnation of solidarity'. Piaget, in a rare excursion into the specifically moral, is in no doubt as to which will make the better citizen (op. cit., 293).

Piaget's conclusion is foregone. 'Equalitarian justice develops with age at the expense of submission to adult authority, and in correlation with solidarity between children. Equalitarianism would therefore seem to come from the habits of reciprocity peculiar to mutual respect rather than from the mechanism of duties that is founded upon unilateral respect' (op. cit., 293f.).

Specificity

We were not simply concerned to test Piaget's conclusion on tale-telling. We incorporated, in fact, a section of four questions, of which that on tale-telling was but one. Our first question was: (1) Is it always wrong to tell lies? The responses to this would give us a clear-cut judgement to compare for consistency with our three further questions: (2) Is it all right to lie to help a friend? (3) Is it all right to lie to save him/her getting into trouble? (4) Is it all right to lie by not telling on him/her – for example, to the teacher? It was this final question, of course, that involved tale-telling. But whereas Piaget asks his question in the familiar form of what 'ought' the boy to do, we set ours in everyday actuality.

From this section we certainly hoped to secure responses shedding light on the influence of peer solidarity. But our wider concern was with the place of specificity in moral judgement; and no area, we conceived, could be more revealing for evidence of specificity than so intimate and constant a concern as lying. We have already examined the relative places of specificity and generality in moral judgement, particularly in the light of the claims made in the Character Education Enquiry (Chapter 1). 'Both theories are right in what they assert, and wrong in what they deny' (Eysenck, 1964, 18). Conduct is therefore never wholly and infallibly predictable; it exhibits both specificity and generality. But, as Allport concludes: 'Generality seems to be a matter of degree . . .. If there are no . . . strong general attitudes available, the individual will be more influenced by the stimulus situation and by such segmental habits as he may have' (Allport, 1935). Specificity is, therefore, the more likely in the person who is morally immature or psychologically weak. We recall, moreover, the illuminating findings, in the University of Chicago Studies of Values, that individual character – 'a persisting pattern of attitudes and motives which produce a rather predictable kind and quality of moral behaviour' – is a reality; and that even inconsistent individuals show 'an enduring, predictable kind of pattern' that has its own kind of "consistency"' (Peck & Havighurst, 1949).

Consistency

We begin with analysis of responses to our first question, Is it always wrong to tell lies?, to observe the general pattern that emerged in terms of consistency. We find two obvious categories, asserting that (1) lying is always wrong; (2) lying is not always wrong; but in addition we tabulate (3) responses which are consistent in answer to all four questions.

We observe, yet again, climacteric development at 13 years; but also, in this area, and even stronger, at 15 years, with deepening conviction at 17 years.

Age-group N-60	*Lying is always wrong*	*Lying is not always wrong*	*Consistency in all four responses*
7-year	55	5 (anomy)	39
9-year	50	10	25
11-year	46	14	23
13-year	37	23	11
15-year	19	41	3
17-year	11	49	2

But our main concern is with consistency; and here we observe a first development as early as 9 years, and others more normally at 13 and 15 years. Such inconsistency might, superficially, appear to provide strong evidence for specificity. But this would be a complete misreading of the situation. Heteronomy is naturally strong in younger subjects; and one of its virtues, if such it be, is consistency. It is precisely as the individual develops in moral judgement that he no longer finds himself content with a blanket rule that takes no account of persons, situations and motives.

Nor, on the other hand, do we find evidence here for the Piagetian thesis. All our subjects – save for 5 probably anomous responses at 7 years – hold that lying is wrong, a conviction that must be heteronomous in origin. The initial premise throughout is the wrongfulness of lying. Then comes the practical application in terms of situations involving relationships with peers *vis-à-vis* authority. Again and again subjects affirm that they would lie – mainly for the sake of friendship, sometimes for group solidarity. But the qualifications are almost universal:

'Yes. But I'd try not to.'

'Yes. But it's not right.'

'Yes. Unless it's serious trouble.'

'No. It's a lie. But I might.'

'It's wrong; but I would.'

Such responses are found throughout the age-groups, once heteronomy begins to lose its hold. The most common is: 'No. But I would' – to be translated, of course, as 'Yes. But it's really wrong.'

Here is a pattern giving no support whatever to Piaget's conclusion that higher moral judgement is fired in the kiln of inter-peer relations. Even the increasing number of 'it all depends' responses start from the premise that lying is wrong. Judgement 'depends' on the situation, the relationship involved, the circumstances, and the obligations felt. The almost universal qualifications are:

1. No one else must be involved or hurt.
2. The trouble must not be serious.
3. There must be a real obligation of friendship or loyalty.
4. The friend is not really deserving of just punishment.

Here we see the application of a known and accepted principle – that lying is wrong – to situations. We do *not* see the discovery of a principle in the situation. This rules out both Piaget's theory and also the situationism inherent in specificity. The individual does not come to the situation morally immature, there to intuit higher moral judgement. Nor, for that matter, does he come to the situation armed only with the abstract principle of agapeistic love, the sole weapon of situation ethics, to be somehow applied. He comes with the conviction, originally heteronomous but increasingly autonomous, that lying is wrong *per se.* It is this conviction that he applies to the situation – a conviction derived from heteronomy, not generated by mutual co-operation with peers; and it is a conviction that progressively deepens, with development, in the autonomy of conscience. The principle that lying is wrong is adapted to take into account obligations both of personal friendship and of group loyalty. Hence the many definitions of 'white lies' that will be our later concern. But, of course, 'white lies' presuppose 'black lies'.

What we observe, therefore, is the increasing subordination of a moral principle to persons, though not its abandonment; and this is a profoundly Christian insight, not a developing immorality. As 'the Sabbath was made for man, not man for the Sabbath', so 'truth-telling was made for man, not man for truth-telling'. Truth-telling remains the principle. It may be overridden, say our responses, for the sake of kindness, friendship, loyalty, love. But it may *not* be overridden for the benefit of self, or to save another from the deserts of serious wrongdoing, or if, in helping one, one hurts another.

Minor characteristics of our responses are also encouraging. Only one subject, after the anomous responses of 7 years, holds that lying is acceptable. Very few wash their hands in the safe water of indifference, responding, as one does: 'No. I wouldn't like to get involved' (15-year boy). Some certainly struggle with the fear of being caught themselves; others comfort themselves with the casuistry of 'Saying nothing is not lying'. But the heart of the dilemma, where it occurs, is the desire to adhere both to the principle of truth-telling and also to the obligations of friendship or loyalty.

Lying for a friend

We now turn to the three subordinate questions: whether it is legitimate to lie for a friend to help him, to save him from trouble, and by not telling on him. The three obvious categories of responses were – 'Yes', 'No', and 'It depends'. In the third question, on tale-telling, there was a minor category of responses holding it right to tell on the ground that it would be unfair to the rest of the class to remain silent.

The legitimacy of lying for a friend

Age-group N-60	*1. To help*			*2. To save trouble*			*3. Not to tell*			
	Yes	*No*	*Depends*	*Yes*	*No*	*Depends*	*Yes*	*No*	*Depends*	*Not fair*
7-year	12	48	—	12	48	—	22	37	—	1
9-year	19	39	2	21	38	1	23	36	—	1
11-year	21	32	7	20	37	3	17	39	2	2
13-year	37	18	5	35	23	2	32	28	—	—
15-year	30	9	21	23	16	20	39	14	5	2
17-year	28	6	26	17	9	34	31	9	20	—

1. CONTRAST WITH PIAGET

The third question, on tale-telling, stands somewhat apart. We may therefore deal with it in isolation, comparing our results with those of Piaget. English children share, of course, with his Geneva subjects a detestation of the 'goody-goody tell-tale', breaking group loyalty in heteronomous devotion to adult authority. Here the issue is clear-cut between subservience to authority and peer loyalty, save for the interesting development in 'it all depends' responses at 17 years – an age when, we might posit, the growth of individuality weakens a sense of group loyalty, and when, in any case, the heteronomous school situation is largely a thing of the past.

Piaget found that nearly 90% of his subjects aged 6 to 7 years approved of tale-telling; in our comparable age-group of 7 years we find 61·7%. It is still 60·0% at 9 years and 67·0% at 11 years, whereas Piaget found that 'the majority of the older ones [over 8] think that nothing should be told'. Once again we find it impossible to agree with Piaget's results. The contrast is the more striking in that far greater heteronomy appears in our subjects.

2. THE PATTERN OF DEVELOPMENT

Such a finding is congruous with our evidence from all other areas, confirming our conclusion that autonomy grows out of heteronomy. Moreover, while there is a small development before adolescence, we observe yet again the climacteric development at 13 years which continues thereafter; and in responses to all three questions.

Since the issue was simply between heteronomy and group loyalty in the third question on telling tales, we can trace development far more subtly in responses to our first two questions. Here again, therefore, we may see the weakness inherent in Piaget's limitation of his enquiry to one type of situation, as observed by Durkin in seeking to replicate Piaget's work on concepts of punishment (Durkin, 1959*a*, 1959*b*, 1961).

We find three broad types of response to the first two questions. First is the heteronomous 'No', which, though decreasing, is strong up to 11 years. At 13 years, with the waning of heteronomy, the response is a strong 'Yes' as the obligations of friendship and loyalty become felt. But at 15 years, and again at 17 years, there is a strong development in 'it all depends' responses; and this, at 17 years, is seen even in the tale-telling situation. Here we see greater subtlety in moral judgement. A blanket 'Yes' in defiance of the principle of truth-telling is now no more acceptable than the earlier blanket 'No' in subservience to authority. At 17 years, in answer to the first two questions, we find percentages of 43·3% and 56·5% of responses holding that 'it all depends' – on, that is, the situation, circumstances, relationship and motive. Though 'Yes' responses remain strong, there is much more subtlety and finesse in the application of the principle of truth-telling to these situations.

3. SEX DIFFERENCES

Yet again it is girls who excel in this subtlety of discrimination in moral judgement. At 7 years the sexes are almost exactly identical. At 9 years the girls are somewhat stronger in universalised heteronomy. At 11 years, however, the boys show greater heteronomy, substantiating the advance of the girls at this age found elsewhere. At 13 years it is the girls who give substantially more 'No' responses than boys – a distinction that might be attributed to greater feminine passivity as contrasted with masculine self-assertion. But at 15 years, and again at 17 years, it is girls who show greater subtlety in judgement. Thus, in the 17-year girls' group we find 4 responses holding that, in the tale-telling situation, it is legitimate to say nothing, since 'to say nothing is not lying'.

Typical responses

We may now cite significant responses to our three questions, deriving therefrom conclusions on the relevance of reciprocity and the significance of white lies.

1. LYING TO HELP A FRIEND

(a) 7-year Age-group
Boys and girls are identical, with 24 responding 'No' and 6 responding 'Yes' in each sex group. Typical 'No' responses are:

'It's naughty.'
'It's not nice.'
'No. Someone else might get into trouble.'
'No. Teacher will find out.'
'No. Then my friend will learn better.'

'Yes' responses show willingness to lie provided that 'I'm not found out'. As Durkin pointed out, apparent altruism may, in fact, be covert egoism, as in the response: 'Yes. I'll lose my friend if I don't.'

(b) 9-year Age-group
Here 16 boys and 23 girls give firm 'No' responses; 13 boys and 6 girls give 'Yes' responses; 1 of each sex judges, thus early, that 'it all depends'. 'No' responses are motivated by:

(i) Self-concern: 'I'd get found out' and so 'in trouble'.
(ii) Strict heteronomy: 'Lying is wrong' or 'you should always tell the truth', and so 'he should get punished'.
(iii) Negative reciprocity: 'They wouldn't help me.'

'Yes' responses are typified by:

'Yes. If it was a very best friend.'
'Yes. To help her.'
'Yes. If I wasn't caught.'

(c) 11-year Age-group
18 boys and 14 girls give 'No' responses; 8 boys and 13 girls give 'Yes' responses; 4 boys and 3 girls now hold that 'it all depends'. We may now see the pusillanimity, self-interest and consequent rationalisations in the 'No' responses. Thus:

'No. He should stick up for himself.'
'No. My friend should tell the truth.'

'No. It's his fault.'

'No. It's not really your business.'

Typical of the more attractive 'Yes' responses are:

'It's wrong, but I'd do it.'

'Yes. But I'd try not to.'

'Yes. But the right thing is to be true.'

'Yes. It's wrong but I would.'

Conditional responses now begin to appear:

'It depends. If it was a little lie, yes.'

'It depends on how serious the trouble is.'

'It depends whether she's guilty or not.'

'Yes. If it got no one else into trouble.'

(*d*) *13-year Age-group*

'No' responses now sharply decrease to 5 from boys and 13 from girls; 'Yes' responses rise to 23 from boys and 14 from girls; 2 boys and 3 girls give conditional answers. 'No' responses have little more to say than

'No. We'd both get into trouble.'

'No. My friend might still be caught.'

'Yes' responses include the 'No. But I would' response. Self-interest appears in:

'Yes. To keep my friend.'

'Yes. Or I'd have no friends.'

The typical conditions now appear:

'Yes. If no one else was blamed.'

'Yes. If it was not really bad trouble.'

Simple and direct is

'Yes. But it's wrong.'

Conditional responses include–

'Yes. If it was in a good cause.'

(*e*) *15-year Age-group*

Only 5 boys and 4 girls give 'No' responses; 17 boys and 13 girls give 'Yes' responses; 8 boys and 13 girls hold that 'it all depends'. Negative responses are drably self-interested:

'No. I wouldn't want to get involved.'

'No. I'd get into trouble myself.'

But one enlightened negative response is

'No. I wouldn't be helping my friend really.'

Positive responses include:

'No. But I might.'
'No. But everyone does.'
'Yes. If my friend needed help.'
'Yes. Friendship is everything.'
'Yes. If it wasn't serious.'
'Yes. If he'd helped me before' (reciprocity).

Situational responses now become familiar:

'It depends. If it involved the police, no.'
'It depends. It would be wrong if he was in real trouble.'
'It depends on the size of the lie.'
'It depends on the circumstances.'
'It depends – not if it harms someone else.'

(*f*) *17-year Age-group*

Only 1 boy and 5 girls give 'No' responses, while 20 boys and 8 girls give 'Yes' responses. 9 boys and 17 girls give conditional responses. Negative responses include:

'No. It's best to be silent.'
'No. It might be worse for her.'

Positive responses may be indicated by

'No. But I'd do it and live with my conscience.'
'Yes. If I could do it by keeping quiet.'
'Yes. But it probably wouldn't do much good.'
'Yes. For friendship' and 'Yes. To help.'
'Yes. But it's wrong.'

43% of this mature age-group hold that 'it all depends' on the familiar circumstances already noted, chiefly that the matter should not be 'too big', 'too important' or 'too serious'. One boy does show something of the subtlety of the girls:

'I would not deliberately volunteer a lie, but I'd be prepared to lie by keeping quiet.'

Yet even he misses the subtlety of the 4 girls who hold that 'keeping quiet' is definitely *not* 'lying'.

2. LYING TO SAVE A FRIEND FROM TROUBLE

The responses to our second situational question follow a similar pattern, but with some circumstantial variations.

(*a*) *7-year Age-group*

Again boys and girls are identical with 24 'No' responses and 6 'Yes' responses from each sex group. The heteronomous 'No' answers hold that lying is 'naughty' or 'rude', that 'teacher might find out', and that 'it might get someone else into trouble'. 'Yes' responses are motivated by friendship, though as a selfish rather than selfless concern, and with the condition that there is minimal chance of detection.

(b) 9-year Age-group

18 boys and 20 girls give negative responses, holding heteronomously that lying is 'naughty' and 'wrong'; that 'It's his fault' and therefore 'He should get punished'; or, self-interestedly, that 'I'd get into trouble', or 'I'd get put in a home.'

Self-interest appears in such 'Yes' responses as

'Yes. Or I'd lose my friend.'

'Yes. Or he'd fight me.'

It also appears in the hopeful reciprocity of

'Yes. And she should do the same for me.'

Conditional responses appear thus early in

'Yes. Unless she was bad.'

'It depends. If it's bad trouble, no.'

(c) 11-year Age-group

'No' responses from boys actually increase to 23, while those of girls decrease markedly from 20 to 14. Basic motives are:

'No. He deserves punishment' (6 responses).

'No. I'd get into trouble myself' (6 responses).

6 boys and 14 girls give such 'Yes' responses as

'No. But I would.'

'No. But I might.'

'It's wrong, but I would.'

Conditional responses hold that 'it depends on the trouble' or 'on my friend'; 1 will 'help if possible'.

(d) 13-year Age-group

While heteronomous 'No' responses from boys decrease dramatically from 23 to 7, those from girls rise slightly from 14 to 16. 'No' type responses are now familiar:

'No. Not if he deserved punishment.'

'No. We'd both be in trouble.'

'No. It's her problem.'

But 2 negative responses do at least suggest higher concern:

'No. She might repeat it.'

'No. She'd go on doing wrong.'

'Yes' responses from 22 boys and 13 girls are variously motivated by self-interest, as in 'to keep my friend' and 'Yes. Or I'd have no friends'; and by the obligations of friendship, as in 'to protect my friend', and 'for my best friend'. One moral optimist says:

'Yes. My friend would be grateful and try to improve.'

Friendship is so strong at this age that only 1 subject of each sex holds that 'it all depends'. Its strength is indicated by

'No. But I would.'

'Yes. At least, I would.'

'Yes. But it's wrong.'

(e) 15-year Age-group

The 8 negative responses from each sex have nothing new to add, save 'That's his affair.' 'Yes' responses decrease to 15 from boys and 8 from girls. We find the familiar 'No. But I would'. Outstanding as being a unique response is 'Yes. If it was bad trouble.'

Situational responses grow to 6 from boys and 14 from girls, the girls showing increased subtlety. The most common condition, again, is 'It depends on the trouble' (6 responses). Similar too are

'If it was small it would be O.K.'

'It depends. Yes. If it was trivial.'

(f) 17-year Age-group

Only 3 boys and 6 girls give 'No' responses. From the 13 boys and 4 girls who are willing to lie come the familiar

'No. But I would.'

'Yes. But it's wrong.'

One positive response of interest is

'Yes. If I loved the person.'

'It all depends' responses are given by 14 boys and 20 girls. The most common conditional criterion is, as one puts it, 'the gravity of the trouble'. Others make their situational judgement depend, more generally, 'on the circumstances'. Many, of course, are concerned with the closeness of the relationship.

3. LYING BY NOT TELLING ON A FRIEND

Our third situational question has already been considered as paralleling Piaget's single investigation in this whole area. Since it raised a categorical and specific situation, we find more definite responses, clear-cut between positive and negative. It is not until the final age-group that we meet more than minimal conditional responses.

(*a*) *7-year Age-group*

Negative, heteronomous responses are given by 19 boys and 18 girls. Lying is, typically, 'naughty'. More interesting are

'No. It might get someone else into trouble.'

'No. Or he might do it again.'

'No. My friend will learn better then.'

An additional girl holds it wrong not to speak up, since it would not be fair to the rest of the class to remain silent. 'Yes' responses – 11 from each sex – again show covert self-interest in apparently altruistic concern for friends. Typical responses are

'Yes. Or he'd get punished.'

'Yes. Because he's my friend' (5 responses).

'Yes. Or I'd lose my friend (4 responses).

'Yes. If I wasn't caught' or 'told on.'

'Yes. She would cry if she was sent into the corner.'

(*b*) *9-year Age-group*

16 boys and 20 girls judge it right to tell, with an additional girl judging thus on grounds of fairness to others. 14 boys and 9 girls refuse to tell. Typical of negative answers are

'No. I'd get told on' (3 responses).

'No. It's his fault.'

'No. Lies are wrong.'

'No. Your friends would call you a liar.'

'No. A lie is a lie.'

Positive answers are more mixed in motivation. Thus:

'No. But I would not tell.'

'Yes. Or I'd lose my friends' (4 responses).

'Yes. To help my friend.'

'Yes. Depending on the teacher.'

Self-interested responses cite such unacceptable penalties as 'I'd get thrown out of the gang and called a traitor'; 'I'd lose my friend and be called a meanie'; 'Her friend might kick or bite her else.' Quite unique is the response:

'Yes. It would be wrong, but I'd do it if he gave me some money.'

Truly Piagetian, in its delightful definition of the conflict between adult heteronomy and peer loyalty, is the response:

'Yes. It's right in my own way, but wrong in Teacher's way.'

(c) 11-year Age-group

Heteronomous 'No' responses are slightly increased, with 21 from boys and 18 from girls. 1 response from each sex holds it unfair to the rest of the class not to tell. 1 response from each sex thinks that 'it all depends'.

Negative responses are familiar: 'You should never tell lies'; 'It's his/her own fault'; 'I'd get told on.' Certainly no peer loyalty appears in such responses as

'No. I'd tell on my best friend.'

'No. I'd tell on a friend who'd done something wrong.'

'No. Even if it means losing my friend. Everyone's got to suffer punishment sometime.'

Subtly feminine is the response:

'No. Because she'd be taking me for granted – that I wouldn't tell on her.'

The strong heteronomy of this age-group, so un-Piagetian at this age, is evidenced also by the 'Yes' responses. In addition to the familiar self-interest, 'Yes. Or I'd lose my friend' in 3 responses, the difficulty of development out of heteronomy is suggested by

'Yes. It's wrong, but I would.'

'No. But I wouldn't split' (4 responses).

'Not really. But I wouldn't tell.'

(d) 13-year Age-group

'No' responses drop to 8 from boys, but actually increase to 20 from girls. Thus, while 22 boys boldly assert their loyalty to friends, 20 girls hold strictly to the principle of truth-telling.

Self-interest is not strong in negative responses. Typical are 'It's wrong to lie'; 'He/she deserves to be punished.' But 5 responses, naturally female, do at least suggest some subtlety:

'No. I'd be very unpopular in class if I told tales, but it's wrong really to tell a lie.'

'No. It might slip out one day.'

'No. She might repeat it.'

'No. I'd encourage her to own up' (2 responses).

'Yes' responses tend to be more fulsome in their self-justification. Self-interest is seen in the desire to keep the friend, to avoid 'being hit' or 'being called a spoil-sport', and to avoid simultaneous trouble. Reciprocity, rarely cited, motivates

'Yes. She may have stopped me getting into trouble.'

'Yes. For my friend, or he'd tell on you next time.'

'Yes. But it's wrong' appears in 5 responses. The most striking development in this age-group is the replacement in the motivation of boys of subservience to adult heteronomy by obligations of friendship. Thus:

'Yes. To protect my friend.'

'Yes. It's not right, but I'd do it for my best friend.'

'Yes. To save my friend and keep my friend. But it's wrong really.'

And from a girl:

'Yes. It's wrong, but I'd do it for my friend – because of the fact that she *is* my friend.'

3 responses, all from boys, hold that to say nothing is not lying:

'Yes. It's not a lie, keeping it back.'

We meet this sophistication again in girls of 17 years.

(*e*) *15-year Age-group*

Only 5 boys and 9 girls now make 'No' judgements, with 2 additional boys who insist on telling on the ground of unfairness to the rest of the class. 21 boys and 18 girls now judge it right not to tell on a friend, while 2 boys and 3 girls hold that 'it all depends'. 'No' answers are no less drab:

'No. It's nothing to do with me.'

'No. She's put it on herself.'

'No. Not to Teacher. I'd get found out.'

'No. She should own up.'

Self-righteousness is suggested by:

'No. I'd be failing in my responsibility.'

Some 22 of the responses indicating willingness to lie are of the 'No. But I would' variety. Such subjects would not 'creep', 'sneak', 'tell tales' and, most commonly, 'split'. A definitive response is

'No. But I wouldn't betray my friend. I can't say "trust" because you are breaking someone's trust in lying. Friendship is sticking by someone.'

The 5 situational responses would judge by the strength of the relationship, the seriousness of the offence, and, more generally, the circumstances. Even responses holding it unfair to the rest of the class not to tell may differ in motivation. Thus, 2 boys respond:

No. It's unfair to others. They'd tell on me, and then the teacher wouldn't trust me.'

'It would be unfair, in justice to the rest of the class.'

(*f*) *17-year Age-group*

Only 5 boys and 4 girls now insist on tale-telling. 18 boys and 9 girls judge it right not to tell. The main development is in the 7 boys and 13 girls who give conditional responses. The 'No' responses offer nothing new, save for the exceptional:

'No. It would play on my conscience.'

Typical 'Yes' responses are

'Yes. But it's deceitful.'

'Yes. Classmates should stand together.'

'Yes. I shouldn't, but I probably would.'

4 such responses from girls show the subtlety of

'Not saying anything isn't lying.'

Our main interest here is in the 20 situational responses. Most are concerned with the gravity of the offence. Judgement would depend on 'the seriousness', 'the gravity of what he'd done', 'the size', and, generally, 'the circumstances'.

Reciprocity in lying for a friend

Piaget, we recall, held that 'Equalitarian justice develops with age at the expense of submission to adult authority, and in correlation with solidarity between children. Equalitarianism would therefore seem to come from the habits of reciprocity peculiar to mutual respect rather than from the mechanism of duties that is founded upon unilateral respect' (op. cit., 293f.). Our responses give no support to such a theory. On the contrary, they evidence throughout the strength, and the progressive interiorisation, of the 'mechanism of duties'. External duties become internal duties. Autonomy grows out of heteronomy.

To support his theory, Piaget found the 'majority' of subjects over 8 years refusing to tell tales. We find the following percentages in our age-groups:

Approval of telling tales

Age-group *N-60*	
7-year	62%
9-year	60%
11-year	67%
13-year	47%
15-year	23%
17-year	15%

Here again, in a specific, parallel situation, we cannot agree with Piaget. The defects of his simple analysis are various. His misses the complexity of motivation, the manifest sex differences in judgement, and the development that can only be adequately seen in a wider age range than his. Above all, and as always, he minimises the strength, the perpetuation, and, of course, the progressive interiorisation of heteronomy. Thus Piaget is simply unaware of the moral dilemma, in this situation, between the obligation of truth-telling and the obligation of friendship.

It is certainly true that our responses reveal the progressive subordination of the principle of truth-telling to persons. But the principle stands firm, and may only be broken for strictly circumscribed reasons. One of these, certainly, is self-interest, but only for the sake of keeping one's friends; and even that becomes progressively weaker with age.

Piaget ascribes development to 'the habits of reciprocity'. If the term be understood in his broad, almost blanket, interpretation, it can be applied to this development descriptively, but not, we hold, definitively. For we observe the adaptation of an existing principle, not the discovery of it, in mutual relations. Reciprocity, in the strict sense of the term, has but a small part to play. The strength of personal relationships – both with respected adults, from whom the heteronomous principle derives, and with peers, for whose sake it is adapted – leaves small room for the mechanics of reciprocity. It is therefore rarely cited as a motivating factor:

Reciprocity responses in 3 lying situations

Age-group	*Boys N-30*	*Girls N-30*	*Total N-60*
7-year	—	—	—
9-year	5	5	10
11-year	2	—	2
13-year	1	1	2
15-year	—	—	—
17-year	—	—	—
Totals	8	6	14

Thus only 3·9% of our total sample invoke considerations of reciprocity in the lying situations used. They were concerned with peer relations *vis-à-vis* authority, situations surely the more calculated to evoke that sense of reciprocity to which Piaget attaches such vast significance in the development of moral judgement.

It is in the 9-year age-group that reciprocity is most pronounced. The 5 boys' responses are:

'My friend would help me, so I must help him.'

'If you help him, he'll help you later on.'

'We'd do it to help each other.'

'He'd do the same for you.'

'Yes. If your friend has helped you.'

The girls also provide 5 such responses:

'She'd do the same for me.'

There is also the negative reciprocity of

'No. They wouldn't help me.'

In the 11-year boys' group we find 2 such responses, though less explicit:

'He might do something for you.'

'If it was a good friend, and I owed him a favour.'

Finally, in the 13-year age-group there is a single reciprocity response from each sex:

'Yes. For my friend, or he'd tell on you another time.'

'Yes. She may have stopped me getting into trouble.'

It is significant that it is precisely in the 13-year age-group, as reciprocity dwindles away, that we observe strong development towards willingness to lie to authority – though reluctantly, conditionally, and with need of self-justification – for the sake of peers. Strict reciprocity certainly has no place in the motivation of such lying. And while, in the earlier stages of development, loyalty to friends is stronger, in the later stages the greater concern with lying is clearly evidenced by the stronger concern with the gravity of the offence. Moreover, the very fact that the main consideration is the nature of the offence, and not the relationship with the offender, shows that moral judgement is founded upon the principle that lying is wrong rather than upon obligations of mutuality. This principle is derived from heteronomy, not developed from insights born of mutual co-operation. Nor is the situation the dominant factor in determining moral judgement, although it is naturally and increasingly taken into account. The process we observe is dominated throughout by the principle of truth-telling derived from respected adults, and progressively interiorised. The heteronomous principle becomes an autonomous principle.

White lies

The conditions under which concessions may be made are clearly evidenced by the definitions of 'white lies' in our responses. The term itself first appears at 9 years, and is used thereafter with increasing frequency. But all conditional responses are involved here; for the common response, 'It all depends', is asserting, as one subject puts it, that there are 'good lies' as opposed to 'bad lies'. Such responses may therefore be included under the general category of 'white lies', even if the term itself is unknown or unused.

White lies responses in 3 lying situations

Age-group N-60	*White Lies Responses*	*Conditional Responses*
7-year	—	—
9-year	1	3
11-year	3	12
13-year	5	7
15-year	12	46
17-year	11	80
Totals	32	148

These figures are for all responses to all three questions and therefore include duplications. Quotations will best evidence the concepts held.

(a) 9-year Age-group

The 7-year age-group is naturally dominated by heteronomy, with its typical expressions: 'Teacher must know the truth'; 'It's naughty. Mum and Dad say so'; 'Mummy wouldn't like it'; 'Teacher will find out.' With the 9-year age-group the term appears in

'White lies might be all right.'

And the concept in

'Not if it's little fibs which don't hurt.'

It is in this age-group that we get the illuminating reponse:

'It's right in my own way, but not in Teacher's way.'

(b) 11-year Age-group

The term appears thus:

'It's wrong, except for white lies.'

'It all depends. White lies are all right.'

'White lies are O.K. – to small children who don't understand.'

The concept, without the term, appears in

'It's not always wrong. It would be all right for a prisoner-of-war who was escaping.'

'Not if it's helping to prevent crime, or if someone's trying to defend himself.'

(*c*) *13-year Age-group*

The term is found in 5 responses with such definitions as

'A white lie is all right – a bit of truth and a bit of lie.'

'Little white lies are all right – very small ones that don't really hurt anyone.'

'White lies are all right – like a story, not to mean any harm.'

The concept without the term may be illustrated by

'No. Like in giving Mum a present. It's not wrong then.'

'It's not always wrong – if you keep a promise not to tell.'

'Not if you're defending a close friend or parent.'

'With young children you sometimes have to cover up.'

'It's all right if someone you loved and trusted was in trouble.'

'It's all right when paying back a lie told to you.'

'It's sometimes necessary. In a case of illness if would be all right.'

(*d*) *15-year Age-group*

The term 'white lies' now becomes more familiar. 6 responses illustrated their legitimacy from the relationship between doctor and patient. Other interesting responses are:

'You don't tell the whole truth, because you don't want to hurt someone's feelings.'

'White lies are all right – when you lie to help someone else.'

'White lies are not so bad. They're a kind of fib.'

'There are true lies and white lies. A white lie is almost a lie in joke. You don't get anyone else into trouble.'

'White lies that don't have a serious consequence are O.K., but not if it becomes a habit.'

'White lies are O.K. for the good of someone else.'

2 responses are notable for rejecting white lies:

'It's all right to lie if it's for another's good. But there's no such thing as white lies.'

'Lying is wrong. I don't agree with white lies.'

Conditional responses now become substantial. The doctor lying to a patient is again cited, as well as lying to conceal birthday presents. Conditions become explicit:

'Lies are O.K. if it's to help someone.'

'Lying sometimes does good. I value his friendship more highly than Teacher's trust.'

'A small lie is O.K. Lies are wrong if they're associated with something else that's wrong.'

'It's all right to lie if you feel you'd hurt someone if you did not' (3 responses).

'Small lies are O.K. – for example, to get out of something like gym.'

'It's not that wrong if you're covering up for someone' (2 responses).

(*e*) *17-year Age-group*

The number of responses using the term remains much the same. But conditional responses increase strikingly from 46 to 80: 'White lies are O.K.', whereas 'Big lies are bad – they end in trouble.' Noteworthy responses are:

'Hurting people is more serious than telling white lies.'

'White lies are all right, protecting people from harmful truth.'

And the typically feminine:

'White lies are O.K. – like undeserved compliments, nice remarks about clothes. Lies are wrong. Only white lies are allowed.'

Responses not using the term give similar definitions. Thus:

'Lies are O.K. if it's to help someone else.'

'Lying is all right for reasons of love.'

'No. It's not wrong when the truth might break friendship.'

'No. It's not wrong if it's a good lie – like paying false compliments.'

'It's O.K. to save hurting a person's feelings.'

The conditional legitimacy of lying

The striking characteristic of these definitions of white lies, whether the term is used or not, is their humanistic concern for others. Anomy is conspicuous by its absence, and so, of course, is heteronomy. They indicate warm humanity that contrasts with the chilly rectitude of those who hold lying wrong in any and every situation. We can certainly agree with Piaget's strictures on the '*petit saint*', whose 'principles will always predominate over his common humanity'. But the '*chic*' type, the 'good sport', is not the only alternative. There is the humanistic – indeed, Christian – judgement that holds, with a 17-year boy, that 'Lying is O.K. for reasons of love.'

It is of interest that Piaget, in a footnote, observes: 'The children who think it sporting to tell a lie to protect a brother told us very definitely that the same lie would be "naughty" if told in self-protection' (op. cit., 292). We find exactly the same judgement common to the majority of our responses, and at all ages. Lying is only permissible for altruistic reasons – never for self-interest. But, of course, there are more subtle motivations, beyond the limits of Piaget's investigations. Lying is legitimate for the sake of others–to save them from 'harmful truth', from 'being hurt', 'to help', 'to avoid upsetting', and to pay those small compliments that, if not strictly true, mean so much. A bad lie is by definition 'a big lie', involving a serious offence, involving trouble for others, doing harm to others and hurting others. Such lies are never permissible.

We can agree with Piaget, too, that a lie is increasingly 'evaluated as a function of the motive that inspires it' (op. cit., 292 footnote). But where we must fundamentally differ from him is in finding clear and consistent evidence that lying is held to be always wrong in principle, even when it is permissible for altruistic reasons; and that the autonomous rejection of lying can be traced back – and is consciously traced back by many subjects – to the original heteronomous interdiction of lying. Yet again we conclude that the 'must' conscience precedes the 'ought' conscience. Autonomy is born of heteronomy.

Lying is in principle always wrong. It is only conditionally permissible, and only for altruistic reasons. It is 'all right for reasons of love', for 'hurting people is more serious than telling white lies'.

Chapter 10
Written tests

The purpose of written tests

This research into the development of moral judgement was based essentially upon the use of visual projection devices, in individual interviews, in preference to the use of written tests. Judgements could thereby be plumbed in depth. It was, however, decided to use written tests, in addition to the main investigation, so as to obtain ancillary evidence that could not have been derived from individual interviews without making them both exhaustive and exhausting.

A number of written tests were devised, based in the main on tests used in previous studies, but with substantial adaptation. Two Piagetian type tests were tried, but rejected in the light of pre-testing experience–one, incidentally, demonstrating the *naïveté* of some of his stories. The 6 remaining tests were tried out on a large scale, in 2 primary schools, 1 boys' secondary modern school and a parallel girls' school, and 1 mixed grammar school. In all, 637 pupils completed these tests. In the light of experience gained, the tests were revised where necessary. 24 subjects were used in the pilot-testing, derived from 5 primary schools, 3 secondary schools, and 2 colleges.

The futility of using written tests with the 7-year age-group became early apparent. Even when responses were written down for them, they were unable effectively to choose between alternatives, usually repeating the last one mentioned. We did, however, record their responses to the Ideal Person Test, requiring simply the name of the ideal chosen and the reason for choice.

The written tests were administered to all the other five age-groups. They were given to complete groups, normally classes, corporately and as a preliminary to the individual interviews. The value of this, in introducing the whole project and its purpose, in creating a friendly relationship, and in establishing good rapport, has already been noted. Reasons for answers were required throughout; simple 'Yes' or 'No' answers were neither required nor accepted, and, where the reason given differed from the answer, the former was used in assessment. Since the six written tests were each quite separate and different from each other, they could be administered singly or in sequence, according to convenience, while their variety limited monotony or boredom. Anonymity was, of course, insisted on throughout.

The value of these additional tests will be seen from a summary of their more significant findings.

(A) **The ideal person test**

The person I would most like to be

What person would you most like to be? Who is the person you admire most of all – the person you most wish to be like?

On the other side of this paper there is space for you to write your answer. Write, first of all, the *name* of the person you would most like to be. Then say *why* you have chosen that person. Give as many reasons as you can for your choice.

The person you choose may be a man, or a woman, or a boy, or a girl. It may be someone you know, or it may be someone you have never met. It may be someone from history, or it may be someone who is alive today. It may be you yourself. It can be *anyone*. The important thing is that it is the person you would *most* like to be.

There is no 'right' or wrong' answer to this question. It has nothing to do with school work or examinations. It is for someone who just wants to know the person you would most like to be, and why you have chosen that person. Your answers will be sent on to him and not seen in school.

There is no need to hurry in writing your answer. You can have as much time as you need. Spelling does not matter, and you need not worry about your writing. You can use pen or pencil, just as you please.

When you turn over this paper you will find a space to fill in your number. This is instead of your name. We do *not* want to know your name, so that you can write quite freely just what you think.

If you find there is not enough space for your answer on this paper, ask for another one. But make sure your number is on that paper too. Use this number on the other papers you are doing, too, so that we know they are from the same person.

Now you can turn over this paper and begin.

The significance of the concept of the ego-ideal has already been our concern in the context of conscience. Such ideals are derived not least from identification with people who are loved, respected, and admired. Hence the value and significance of the ideals chosen by children, and the long history of the Ideal Person Test, asking subjects to nominate 'The Person I would Most Like to Be'. At least six studies using this test are found between 1898 and 1911. Subsequent studies are those of Macaulay and Watkins (1926), Hill (1929), Phelan (1936), Havighurst, Robinson and Dorr (1946), Bray (1962), Pringle and Edwards (1964), Edwards (1965), and the study of adolescents made by E. M. and M. Eppel (1966). Such a sequence, over nearly seventy years, provides valuable evidence of developments relevant to our own findings.

The titles used in these studies have varied, as have their methodologies. We asked for a concrete nomination – who could be literally anyone – rather than for an imaginary figure, since to have requested a fictitious person might have inhibited less able and younger subjects, and produced flights of fancy from the more able. We also asked for reasons for the choice made, making the test doubly valuable.

1. MYSELF CHOICES

The most striking result of this test was that the numerically highest single category of responses was of subjects who preferred to remain themselves. 73 of our 360 subjects – this test including the 7-year age-group – or 20·3%, chose thus, forming 18·9% of the boys and 21·7% of the girls, indicating no marked sex difference. Even at 7 years, 5 subjects responded thus. But 48, or 65·7%, of these responses came from the 15- and 17-year age-groups. Thus 40·0% of our two mature age-groups, 38·3% of the boys and 41·6% of the girls, chose to remain themselves.

These responses at 15 and 17 years broadly approximate to those of the Eppels (1966), who, from a sample of 250 young London workers between 15 and 18 years of age, found that 52% of the girls and 37% of the boys – 44·5% for both sexes – chose to remain themselves. This was an urban sample, as compared with our sample from the South-west, which, despite the towns from which our subjects came, remains predominantly rural. It might have been thought that the 'Myself' choices of our subjects represented lethargic content with a sleepy, country way of life. But the findings of the Eppels explicitly contradict any such assumption. 44·5% of their young workers from the country's largest conurbation chose to remain themselves – 4·5% *more* than our corresponding figure.

The development in 'Myself' choices over the years is striking. Hill

(1929), with 8,813 responses from white American children, included among his mere 4% of 'miscellaneous' responses those who 'reply that they would like to be themselves'. Havighurst, Robinson and Dorr (1946), considering possible limitations of the test, commented on those who 'defensively insist on being like themselves and no one else'. But our responses are far from being 'defensive' in tone.

Could such responses derive from less able subjects? We compared the mean I.Q. of subjects nominating themselves in each sex and age-group, save the 9-year groups, which gave no such responses, with that of the whole group. In all the boys' groups the mean I.Q. of such subjects was consistently above that of the group, the increase ranging from 0·1 to 3·4. Only one girls' group, however, shows such an increase, that being a strong 6·7 at 13 years. But the lower mean I.Q. of girls making 'Myself' choices in the other age-groups is not markedly lower, varying only between 0·3 and 2·6. Such evidence indicated that lower intelligence is not a significant factor in subjects nominating themselves.

To what, then, may we ascribe such self-content? A brief selection of responses can best point to the answers:

'I like myself. I've got a nice Mum and Dad' (7-year boy).

'I'm glad I'm myself. I've got two nice cousins' (7-year boy).

'I like myself. Life is O.K. for me. If I want to be great, I'll make myself famous' (11-year boy).

'I'm quite satisfied with myself. I could be a bit better, but I'd like to see how I turn out' (11-year girl).

'I'm quite happy as I am. I've got a good home. I love my family. I'm happy at school' (11-year girl).

'There is no one I admire or envy' (13-year boy).

'I don't think there's anyone in the world as lucky as me, having my parents and my brothers and sisters' (13-year boy).

'I'm quite content as I am. I'm happy. I like my parents. I don't want to be famous – just to drift along in my own way without changing' (13-year girl).

'I'm young. I've got life in front of me. I'm not perfect, but I'm quite happy. I've got good parents, relations and friends' (15-year boy).

'I don't want to be famous. I enjoy living a natural life' (15-year boy).

'God created me as He wanted me to be. Your life is what you make it. I'm glad not to be others; they've always got something wrong' (15-year girl).

'I'm quite happy. I try to please people – that is all that matters' (15-year girl).

'We're all human. I could do what anyone else has done' (17-year boy).

'I do not covet. I have all I need – health, happiness and my own wealth' (17-year boy).

'I'm happy as myself and content. Better the devil I know than the one I don't' (17-year boy).

'I'm happy. I'm quite willing to face what is to happen to me' (17-year girl).

'I'm an individual. I'm content to be myself. I don't want to be a carbon copy of someone' (17-year girl).

'I'm content. There's good and bad in everyone. I'll remain as I am' (17-year girl).

We can agree with the Eppels (1966) that contentment is attributed mainly to 'a happy family life'; that 'a minority talk also of good friends, of both sexes'; and that 'some, especially the boys discuss their enjoyment of work and leisure' (E. M. & M. Eppel op. cit., 126). There is ample evidence of psychological health in these responses – if, as Hadfield puts it, 'To know oneself, to accept oneself, to be oneself is the first rule of mental hygiene'. Contentment is not necessarily complacency nor self-satisfaction in the responses of our adolescent subjects nominating themselves. Edwards aptly describes such adolescents as 'entering Winnicott's adolescent morality of "to thine own self be true" and the adolescent trying to find a self to be true to' (D. W. Winnicott, 'Adolescent Morals', *New Society*, No. 30, 1963, 8-11, Edwards, 1965).

Such contentment contrasts with the 'envy' that some specifically repudiate. Sturdy common sense sees that 'all is not gold that glitters'; that 'a natural life' is better than fame; and that, in any case, fame can be sought after if it is the chosen goal. These responses are wholly autonomous, dictated neither by authority nor convention. Self-fulfilment is the goal; it is based on self-acceptance; and the way to it is seen primarily in terms of happy social life, of satisfactory personal relationships. The tone of these responses is essentially humanistic; few think specifically in religious terms. Minimal altruistic aspirations are revealed; but the achievement of selfhood is the indispensable prerequisite of self-giving, and it is the proper goal of adolescence.

The remarkable development of such self-contentment, evidenced by the use of this test over the years, may be attributed to various factors: to the changing ethos in education, away from the authoritarian and heteronomous and towards the child-centred and democratic; to socio-economic changes, such as the rise in the general standard of living, resulting in a diminishing preoccupation with material necessities and, perhaps, a weakening of the hard thrust of ambition; to religious factors, such as the decay in a predominantly transcendental faith and a consequently increasingly humanistic outlook; to the decline in the Puritan tradition, with its typical fostering of guilt that must militate against self-acceptance and contentment. Whatever the factors involved, it is hard to deny that such a development is infinitely for the better.

2. CHOICES FROM THE IMMEDIATE CIRCLE

The second largest category of responses consists of choices taken from immediate circle. 19·2% of all subjects – 14·4% of the boys and 23·9% of the girls – make such choices, but 76·8% of all such responses come from the 7- and 9-year age-groups. From 11 years on, only 6·7% of subjects choose their ideal from the immediate circle. At 9 years, far more girls than boys choose thus; but since most nominate friends, rather than relations, we may see here, yet again, the greater feeling of girls for personal relationships.

Macaulay and Watkins (1926) found most ideals taken from the child's own circle, whereas Bray (1962) and Pringle and Edwards (1964) found most ideals taken from remote figures from radio, television and films. Of our own subjects of 7 and 9 years, 41 nominated friends, whilst only 8 nominated members of the family, and a further 4 other relatives. For all such responses from all age-groups, 72·5% nominated friends, 14·5% named members of the family, and 5·8% chose other relatives. Only 3 subjects named teachers as ideals, and one of them was ironic. 2 subjects of 15 years named an admired adult in the local community.

Pringle and Edwards concluded that 'The younger or less able the child, the more likely it is that his ideal person will be chosen from relatives or friends' (Pringle & Edwards, 1964). We have already confirmed the youthfulness of subjects choosing thus. The mean of the I.Q.s of these subjects was found to be almost consistently lower than that of their sex- and age-groups; and we can therefore confirm the lower ability of subjects choosing from the immediate circle.

3. GLAMOROUS ADULTS

The third highest category of responses consisted of 42 nominations of television stars, followed by film stars (27), pop stars (26) and sportsmen and sportswomen (26). These four categories represent fame, success, wealth, glamour. Together, these four categories total 121 responses, or 33·3% of our total sample, the highest grouped category.

Here again the use of this test shows a development over the years. In sum, glamorous adults have replaced heroes from history or literature. Macaulay and Watkins (1926) found three main sources of ideals – the immediate circle, fiction, and adventure stories, in that order. Hill (1929) and Phelan (1936) both found over 60% of ideals deriving from history and literature. Havinghurst, Robinson and Dorr (1946) found less than 10%; 'heroes' had yielded place to 'glamorous adults' and 'attractive visible young adults'. In 1963 Bray, from the essays of an 11-plus selection test, found a predominance of remote choices, indicating such basic needs as 'recognition and success', leading constituents of 'glamour'. In 1964 Pringle and Edwards found predominant choice of ideals, as we do, from radio, television and films. In short, the visualised fiction, as well as the glamorous adults, of television and film have replaced the verbal fiction of the book and live heroes of history.

Our responses show the almost total eclipse of ideals taken from literature, with only 3 such choices being made by 360 subjects. Heroes taken from history totalled 18, or 5% of our sample, the choice mainly of boys.

4. OTHER CATEGORIES

Ideals taken from royalty have also diminished over the years, as Pringle and Edwards (1964) note. 5% of our sample cited royal figures, mainly at 9 and 11 years.

Religious and moral ideals were chosen by 12 subjects, or 3·3% of our sample. Here there is no development. Hill (1929) found that only 'about 2% of the pupils selected ideals from among religious personages', such as 'God, Jesus, characters from the Bible, ministers.' Both Bray (1962) and Pringle and Edwards (1964) found junior girls making more choices in this category than boys. Edwards (1965) found 2·4% of secondary modern boys choosing thus. We found 6 subjects of each sex choosing ideals in this category.

The occurrence of the Miss World Contest during the period of testing fired 12 girls in all (3·3%) to choose beauties as their ideals. The masculine urge for adventure was focused in the main upon James Bond, 11 boys nominating thus. The combined categories of space, flying, science, and exploration produced only 8 responses from boys. Only 3 subjects, and one of them a girl of 7 years, saw wealth as their *summum bonum* in nominating a 'rich person'. The arts fared badly, with 4 nominations – 2 girls choosing musicians and 2 boys at Art College citing Picasso.

5. SEX DIFFERENCES

Each sex predominantly chose ideals from the same sex – 97·7% of boys choosing a male, and 86·6% of girls choosing a female. Only 4 boys nominated females, 3 of them from the 7- and 9-year age-groups, of whom 2 chose friends. 24 girls, 13·4% of their sex sample, chose males, predominantly stars of entertainment, and mainly at 13 years.

Hill (1929) found 'about one-third' of girls choosing male ideals. Bray (1962) found that only 48·3% of girls chose remote – as distinct from the immediate circle – female ideals, compared with the boys' 91%. Pringle and Edwards (1964), also testing juniors of 11 years, noted that 'male ideals are much more named by girls than female ideals by boys'. Hill's 'about one-third' becomes 13·4% in our sample; Bray's 51·7% of 11-year girls becomes 23·3% of our parallel sex and age group four years later. Only 3·3% of our combined 15- and 17-year age-group of girls nominate male ideals. We thus observe a development towards girls choosing ideals from their own sex, and an increasing one. E. M. & M. Eppel (1966) confirm this, finding that all the males among their workers of 15 to 18 years chose male ideals, and that only 7 girls, some 6% of their female sample, chose males – 4 of these in wishing that they had been born boys.

Such a development may be variously attributed to increasing sex equality; to the presence of a Queen on the throne; and not least to glamorous young females, known intimately through film and television, who have reached coveted pinnacles of success and glamour from the kind of modest background of most of our subjects. But we still need to bear in mind the 41·7% of our 15- and 17-year female subjects who are content to remain themselves, and who need no external ideal.

6. VALUES EMBODIED IN IDEALS

Subjects were asked to give as many reasons as possible for their choice of ideal. Younger and less able subjects inevitably gave a limited number, and the older and more able a plenitude. Reasons were many and mixed, and justice could only be done to them by allotting two reasons to each subject. Where one value was dominant it was counted as two. Where many reasons were given, the two leading values were taken. Classification was not easy, but 31 values were eventually isolated.

Age differences were of interest. Apart from the immature values of 7-year subjects, we find, for example, a strong urge for freedom at 15 years, and a desire for power that is strongest at 7 years (15·0%), strong at 9 years (8·3), but thereafter minimal (1·7%). Others will be observed.

In both sexes the main category was efficiency – the 'good (efficient)' as contrasted with the 'good (kind)'. In the boys' order it stands first, in girls' order second. Such personal fulfilment may be admired in any walk of life, but not least in glamorous young adults. Efficiency is most strongly admired by both sexes at 11 years (18·3%) and 13 years (19·2%). At 17 years it decreases to 7·5%, yielding place to the category of self-achievement (9·2%) as well as to 'contentment'.

Contentment and happiness describe subjects who nominate themselves. This is both a personal and social category, since they see themselves as individual persons in a happy social context. For all subjects of both sexes it develops from 12·5% at 11 years to 18·3% at 15 years, and 30·0% at 17 years. For all girls it is the leading value; for all boys it is subordinate to efficiency, adventure and fame.

Adventure, the second value for boys (10·5%) is of course, minimal for girls (1·1%). Contrariwise, dominant girls' values are physical looks (10·5%) and 'attractiveness' (8·6%) – the latter a quality of personality rather than a purely physical characteristic. The desire for fame – third for boys (10·0%) and eighth for girls (5·8%) – is another aspect of self-fulfilment.

The attraction of wealth is similar and by no means strong for either sex (boys 7·8%, girls 7·5%). But altruism – a leading value for 6·1% of all boys and 10·0% for all girls – shows a characteristic sex difference, as naturally does home-life (girls 7·2% and boys 1·9%), including for girls the home they look forward to creating as well as that already experienced.

Outstanding in both sexes, and increasingly so with age, is the desire for travel, to which success and wealth, for example, are seen as means, rather than as ends *per se*. Fondness for animals is unique to girls, with the familiar predilection for horses and riding at 13 years.

Grouped values of the total sample

Boys (N-180)	%	*Girls (N-180)*	%
1. Self-fulfilment	34·6	1. Contentment	27·2
2. Adventure	18·8	2. Self-fulfilment	21·1
3. Contentment	17·2	3. Personality	13·0
4. Material	8·1	4. Physical	10·5
5. Altruistic	6·1	5. Altruistic	10·0
6. Personality	5·8	6. Material	9·8
7. Physical	2·5	7. Adventure	4·7
(Immature	6·9)	(Immature	3·7)

Immature: values of the 7-year age-group that do not appear at any later age.

Total Sample: Both Sexes (*N*-360)

1. Self-fulfilment	27·8
2. Contentment	22·2
3. Adventure	11·7
4. Personality	9·4
5. Material	9·0
6. Altruistic	8·1
7. Physical	6·5
8. (Immature	5·3)

Grouped Values

Self-fulfilment: efficiency, self-achievement, fame, power, leadership, freedom.

Contentment: contentment, happiness, home, life, country life, sea life, security, love of animals.

Adventure: adventure, courage, travel.

Personality: attractive, popular, friendship, character.

Material: wealth, clothes, jewellery.

Altruistic: good (kind), service to God.

Physical: physical strength, physical looks, sex.

Immature: pleasure (play), name, older in age.

Thus, all in all, we observe the dynamic masculine urge for adventure, fame, self-fulfilment contrasting with the feminine values of physical looks, attractiveness of personality, altruistic kindness, and of happy personal relationships typically realised in home-life. Combining both sexes, we find contentment to be a supreme value, closely followed by efficiency as the expression of self-fulfilment. Fame and wealth follow, with altruism close behind them. Given the background of a competitive society, putting a premium on efficiency and success, together with the adolescent goal of achieving individuality and self-fulfilment, the pattern is not unexpected.

7. GROUPED VALUES

Edwards (1965) noted the contrast between junior and secondary pupils in their leading values. The junior scale of efficiency, adventurousness and goodness was replaced, in his secondary modern boys, by efficiency, fame and wealth. He concluded that it is 'largely during adolescence that the material values of the affluent society become a strong influence'.

The Eppels, testing a sample far more homogeneous than our own in age, education and interests, were able to make two classifications of the values of young workers aged 15 to 18 years. The fuller table of values, in descending order, was: 'physical appearance and popular personality; material (e.g. money, possessions, clothes); personality traits; leisure interests; social values; religious interests'. The authors concluded: 'The picture that emerges underlines once again the fact that the predominant concern of these young people is for personal adjustment and good human relationships often linked with an attractive appearance' (E. M. & M. Eppel, op. cit., 146f.).

A similar classification may be made from our findings, in a far broader sample, by grouping values. Eight groups of values emerge. For our whole sample of both sexes we find self-fulfilment predominant, followed by contentment, with adventure a poor third. Then come personal qualities, and thereafter material, altruistic and physical values. A combined grouping of personal and physical would be second only to self-fulfilment and contentment. If altruism is not striking, with a mere 8·1% of the total, neither is materialism with 9·0%. From the familiar sex differences, we may observe that, while altruism is fifth in order for both sexes, it makes up to 10·0% of girls' values as compared with 6·1% of the boys'. Every research using this test has shown girls consistently to excel boys in this value.

The Eppels found that 'only 1 in 8 subjects are dominantly materialistic, and among these, the boys significantly outnumber the girls 4 to 1'. While we do not find so striking a sex difference, we can agree with the conclusion drawn: 'It is perhaps surprising that so small a proportion (12½%) give evidence of embracing predominantly materialistic values, given the images of "success" purveyed by the popular Press and the pressures of commercial advertising' (E. M. & M. Eppel, op. cit., 147f.).

While each stage of development has its own basic needs, they amount in sum to self-fulfilment, taking its different forms at each age. Thus, the 7- and 9-year-olds long for power, the 11-year-old for wealth and fame, the 15-year-old for freedom. The urge to grow, explicit at 7 years, is implicit throughout. To find oneself, to be oneself, to fulfil oneself – these are the dominant themes; and when these urges are, in some conscious sense, being achieved, there is contentment. There are no signs of moral decadence in this broad picture. The leading values are self-fulfilment and contentment – the one primarily individualistic, the other primarily social. After the glittering dreams of fame and wealth of middle childhood comes the growing realisation that the heart of life is being a person with other persons. Hence the prevailing ethos of a humanism that sees the stuff of life in good personal relationships. There is no point in crying for the moon, in fixing envious gaze on remote and impossible goals. 'There's good and bad in all of us'; even idols have feet of clay. 'I enjoy life. I like it as I am', say many subjects. 'I would like earned wealth and a happy family', says one 17-year-boy. If complacency seems to tinge such realism, it yet embraces the urge to both self-fulfilment and contentment; and these are at the heart of human life and happiness.

The development of grouped values

Age-group (*N-60*)	*7-year* %	*9-year* %	*11-year* %	*13-year* %	*15-year* %	*17-year* %
1. Self-fulfilment	23·4	26·6	34·2	33·6	20·8	29·3
2. Contentment	15·1	5·9	25·0	12·4	38·4	35·8
3. Adventure	3·3	20·0	9·9	19·1	8·3	9·9
4. Personality	5·0	10·8	11·7	9·1	15·8	4·1
5. Material	3·3	9·2	11·7	13·3	5·0	10·9
6. Altruistic	10·0	17·5	1·7	9·2	6·7	3·3
7. Physical	8·3	10·0	5·8	3·3	5·0	6·7
(Immature	31·6)	—	—	—	—	—

Immature: values of the 7-year age-group that do not appear at any later age.

Grouped values

Self-fulfilment: efficiency, self-achievement, fame, power, leadership, freedom.

Contentment: contentment, happiness, home life, country life, sea life, security, love of animals.

Adventure: adventure, courage, travel.

Personality: attractive, popular, friendship, character.

Material: wealth, clothes, jewellery.

Altruistic: good (kind), service of God.

Physical: physical strength, physical looks, sex.

Immature: pleasure (play), name, older in age.

(B) **Virtues and Vices**

We recall that the choice of themes for our visual projection tests, used in individual interviews, was substantiated by the studies of Pringle and Edwards (1964), and Edwards (1965), using a 'Moral Wickedness Test' derived from the work of Macaulay and Watkins (1952). Subjects were asked to 'describe the most wicked deeds or actions in descending order'. We used this as one of our written tests, making a number of adaptations.

It seemed valuable, first, to enlarge the test to include not only wicked deeds, but also virtuous actions. It thus became, in the simplest nomenclature, the Good Deeds and Bad Deeds Test – though the word 'test' was, of course, never used throughout this whole research. Our purpose was, *inter alia*, to seek evidence for positive, as distinct from purely negative, knowledge of moral codes, thus seeking evidence for the suggestion of Durkin that 'the path of goodness is left highly undefined for the child' (Durkin, 1959).

The test form provided for only 10 items, under each of the two categories, with space for an additional 4, and only a brief space for each item. We therefore sought to rule out long and turgid, if not imaginary, vices and virtues.

Again, in classifying responses, we found that many subjects gave personal qualities, rather than concrete actions. We therefore use the broad terms 'virtues' and 'vices' rather than the narrower 'good deeds' and 'bad deeds' in analysis.

Good deeds and bad deeds

What do you think are the *best* deeds that anyone can do? What do you think are the *worst* deeds that anyone can do?

On the other side of this paper there are spaces for you to make two lists. In the first list, write down what you think are the best things that people can do. Begin with what you think is the finest deed of all. Then write the next best, and so on. There are ten spaces for you to fill up. You can write more than ten if you wish.

Next make a list of what you think are the worst things that people can do. Begin with what you think is the worst deed of all. Then write the next most wicked deed, and so on. There are ten spaces for you to fill up. You can write more than ten if you wish.

There are no 'right' or 'wrong' answers. This has nothing to do with school work or examinations. It is for someone who just wants to know what you think, and your answers will be sent on to him, and not seen in school.

There is no need to hurry in making your lists. You can have as much time as you need. Spelling does not matter. You can use either pen or pencil, just as you please.

When you turn over this paper, you will find a space to fill in your number. This is instead of your name. We do not want to know your name, so that you can write quite freely just what you think. Use this number on the other papers too, so that we will know that they are from the same person.

Now you can turn over this paper and begin.

The test was administered, with the other written tests, to whole groups, preceding the individual interviews. Given the simplicity and immaturity of the responses of the 9-year age-group, there seemed no value in recording responses from 7-year subjects to this test. It was therefore administered to the five age-groups from 9 to 17 years inclusive, giving a total sample of 300 subjects, with, of course, equal numbers of boys and girls.

I. OVERALL ANALYSIS

A norm of 10 items from each subject gave a possible maximum total of 3,000 responses, under each category. In the event, the virtue category produced 2,144 items and the vices category yielded 2,211 – the average number of items per subject thus being 7·1 for virtues and 7·4 for vices. Here was a first slight indication of stronger awareness of negative morality.

The outstanding category under virtues is helpfulness, with 47·5% of the total of items. It broadly parallels, under vices, offences against the person which made up 27% of the total, although the parallel between a general personal quality and concrete offences is by no means exact.

Items citing personal virtues total 459, or 21·4%. The parallel figure for personal vices, including a 'self-indulgence' category from older subjects, is 990, or 44·8%. Here is far stronger awareness of negative vices rather than of positive virtues.

The third category is that of altruistic qualities, wholly concerned with relationships with others, and thus distinguished – if, perhaps, subtly – from personal virtues. The 452 items make up 21·1% of the total of virtues. Personal and altruistic virtues combined total 911, or 42·5% of responses, second only to helpfulness.

On the negative side, the next category is that of offences against property, naturally a stronger concern of younger subjects, and less significant with age. By contrast, offences against the person are not only more strongly, but also consistently, condemned throughout our age-range.

Items extolling the virtues of kindness to animals, totalling 114, or 5·3%, are broadly similar to the 138, or 6·3%, condemning cruelty to animals. The latter is again more significant to younger subjects, while positive kindness to animals remains significant at all ages.

The final and smallest category is that of specifically religious actions and qualities. Such items total 4·7% of virtues and 1·5% of vices. Here the emphasis, such as it is, is positive, and indicates that failure to observe religious practices is no longer seen as wrong in itself.

2. OUTSTANDING VIRTUES AND VICES

Pringle and Edwards (1964), testing boys and girls of 11 years, found 'considerable unanimity over the six most wicked actions' and also 'in their respective degrees of wickedness'. Edwards (1965), testing secondary modern boys of 11 years and 14 to 15 years found the first four evils identical with those of the junior. We may now compare the three results, listing in descending order.

The most wicked actions

Pringle & Edwards *Boys and Girls,* *11-years* *N-226*	*Edwards* *Boys* *11, 14-15 years,* *N-234*	*This Research* *Boys and Girls,* *9-17 years* *N-300*
1. Murder.	1. Murder.	1. Stealing.
2. Physical cruelty.	2. Physical cruelty.	2. Murder.
3. Stealing.	3. Stealing.	3. Physical cruelty.
4. Cruelty to animals.	4. Cruelty to animals.	4. Cruelty to animals.
5. Lying.	5. Blackmail.	5. Lying.

Here we observe remarkable unanimity in definition of the four 'universal' evils. The only real difference is in the secondary modern boys, for whom lying comes but tenth, and with only 1·02% of responses. We also have confirmation here that our visual-testing devices were emphatically based on the most heinous offences in the judgement of children and adolescents. In our sample the leading seven vices were stealing, murder, cruelty, cruelty to animals, lying, not helping, cheating. Taking the vice of 'not helping' to be involved in our drowning scene, all these vices were used in our visual tests.

Stealing, third in the two researches quoted, is first in ours. But it is not that our sample shows a massive concern with stealing. A revealing contrast with the results of Edwards (1965) indicates this.

The Four Universal Vices

Edwards (1965)		*This Research (1966)*	
1. Murder	32·8%	1. Stealing	10·1%
2. Physical cruelty	18·4%	2. Murder	7·4%
3. Stealing	15·2%	3. Physical cruelty	7·2%
4. Cruelty to animals	11·2%	4. Cruelty to animals	6·2%
Total	77·6%	Total	30·9%

Edwards's sample of secondary modern boys was thus overwhelmingly concerned with these four universal vices. Our subjects – of both sexes, from a wider age-range, and with a full range of intelligence – are concerned with a far wider range of evils, are far more sophisticated in their choice, and, particularly girls, far more concerned with offences between persons than with concrete crimes *per se*.

The first four major virtues are aspects of helpfulness. If the fifth, kindness to animals, be included, 45·9% of the total items come under this head. Active benevolence thus dominates children's ideas of virtue, just as active malevolence is the essence of vice.

Some virtues and vices are inevitably positive and negative parallel forms of the same item. Thus, kindness to animals (5·3%) parallels cruelty to animals (6·2%); honesty (4·01%) parallels dishonesty (2·1%); obedience (3·9%) parallels disobedience (3·1%); truthfulness (2·4%) parallels lying (5·4%); and kindness (4·2%) parallels cruelty (7·2%). Yet again we observe a virtue to be best known by its negative vice.

The broad picture revealed is a healthy one. But it is realistic to recognise that these are moral judgements – that they do not necessarily represent moral behaviour. The virtues affirmed may perhaps be better understood as ideals, and the vices as temptations. Hadfield observes that 'It is a well-known fact that preachers are always preaching against the sins to which they are, unconsciously, most prone (and usually rigidly avoid those to which they are consciously addicted)' (Hadfield, 1923, 37). Similarly, we find that boys condemn cruelty to animals far more than girls; and that girls deplore meanness, cattiness and jealousy while boys seem scarcely aware of such failings.

Yet it remains true that there can be no moral progress without ideals: nor avoidance of wrongdoing if it is not recognised as such. Moral knowledge is an essential prerequisite of moral behaviour.

3. VIRTUES

Helpfulness, the largest single category (47·5%), is naturally expressed most strongly in the home, with the major contributions from younger subjects. Helpfulness to the aged is, by contrast, broadly consistent at all ages. It is, in the main, only in the 15- and 17-year age-groups that the necessity is recognised to help the poor, the needy, the police, the local community, and world peace. These combined heads produce only 3·7% of virtues cited. If the picture is again healthy, it is circumscribed; our subjects are far more concerned with the personal and local than with the impersonal and remote. The Eppels record that 'Reference to world insecurity and the atom bomb are made gratuitously by 40 per cent. of these adolescents, often several times each' (E. M. & M. Eppel, op. cit., 220). Only 0·5% of our responses made any such reference. The contrast may, of course, be related to different testing devices.

Among the personal virtues (21·4%) honesty is outstanding, and regard for it grows steadily, if unspectacularly, over the years. Obedience, strongest at 9 and 13 years, follows closely, and, thereafter, truthfulness. The combined citations of honesty and truthfulness, representing 6·4% of virtues, parallel the combined figure of 7·5% of the opposite vices of lying and deceit. In terms of age-groups, we observe a falling-away at 15 years in the recognition of personal virtues, suggesting a lack of definitive moral values at this betwixt-and-between age. There is more certainty at 17 years, particularly in girls. Girls, in fact, provide 55·3% of all personal values, as compared with 44·7% from boys – yet further evidence of the substantial sex difference in sensitivity to personal relationships.

Altruistic virtues provide 21·1% of the total, so that personal and altruistic virtues combined make up 42·5%, second only to the 47·5% for the practical category of helpfulness. Kindness (4·2%), and the more formal 'giving to charities' (3·5%) are the outstanding altruistic qualities. A further 9·2% represent a group of related qualities – saving life, generosity, sharing, neighbourly love, considerateness. Such specifically Christian virtues as self-sacrifice, forgiveness and love of enemies are rarely mentioned. But the sophisticated categorisation of virtues – the only method of doing justice to the diffuseness and subtlety of our responses – conceals the fact that, for example, unselfishness, which in isolation is poorly represented, is in fact implicit in many other applauded qualities. A falling off at 15 years is again apparent in this category, the 68 responses contrasting with 137 at 17 years. At 17 years there is a substantial increase in regard for kindness, considerateness, unselfishness and friendliness. Girls (54·4%) again provide more responses than boys (45·6%). For personal and altruistic items combined, girls account for 54·8% of the total and boys for 45·2%. Here is emphatic evidence of the sex differential.

Girls, too, provide 57·1% of responses praising kindness to animals, compared with the boys' 42·9%. This category provides 5·3% of all quoted virtues.

Specifically religious 'good deeds' make up 4·7% of the total. Almost half the citations are concerned with church-going. While the 9-year age-group is strongest, there is a curious rise in regard for church-going in 17-year boys, among whom only 2 showed strong religious views in overall testing. Here, too, we may see recognition of an ideal, rather than of a practice, with, perhaps, overtones of guilt feelings. Hence the rare and untypical result that boys excel girls in this category with 54·4% of responses. We must recognise that this category, in isolation, does scant justice to the many profoundly religious virtues recognised by our subjects and included under other categories.

4. VICES

Personal vices made up 42·0% of the total of 'bad deeds'. Lying was outstanding with 13·0% of responses in this category, followed by 'not helping' with 9·3%. Thereafter came the strong condemnation of cheating and swearing. But while cheating was most strongly condemned at 11 and 13 years – a characteristic reminiscent of Piaget's 'equality', in which to be good is to be fair – the denunciation of swearing was broadly consistent throughout. So was that of disobedience. Thereafter followed a number of 'vicious' attitudes – deceit, unkindness, making trouble, rudeness, greed, selfishness, hurting others, and a few more precisely defined. The characteristic falling-off at 15 years is again apparent; and at 17 years a unique emphasis, chiefly in girls' responses, upon the evils of deceit, selfishness, ill-temper, and despising others. The sex difference is, indeed, even stronger in this category, girls providing 64·2% of the citations. They lead boys at every age, and increasingly, save for the 15-year decline. Significantly, the only categories in which boys lead girls are cheating, swearing, blackmail, using others, and cowardice, although the lead is minimal.

Offences against the person make up 27·0% of evils quoted, with murder (7·4%) and physical cruelty (7·2%) expectedly outstanding. Younger age-groups are more concerned with assault, fighting, and bullying: and the older with sexual offences, racial discrimination, and dangerous driving. The characteristic decline at 15 years might, in this category, be partly attributed to physical development bringing relief from fear of physical assault; yet even in the outstanding category of murder there are fewer condemnations than at any other age. The sex difference is minimal; for boys are in their element when it comes to the physical, as distinct from the psychological, aspects of personal relationships, and so produce 49·4% of the total. At 17 years girls lead boys only in their condemnation of cruelty to children, of dangerous driving and, minimally, of causing war, while boys lead girls in terms of murder, sex offences, and racial discrimination.

Offences against property provide 20·4% of evils itemised. This contrasts with 27·0% for offences against the person and 42·0% for personal vices – a healthy sign of far stronger respect for the person than for property, in terms of a Christian scale of values. But there is no lack of respect for the property of others – which is, in that scale, an extension of the person. Stealing is the pre-eminent offence, with 10·1% of the total of quoted vices. Responses make the usual subtle distinctions. There is general 'destructiveness', just as there is general 'helpfulness'. More specifically, there are offences against private property, vandalism against public property, robbing and swindling, starting fires, keeping others' property, trespassing, damaging plants and gardens, and the more contemporary shoplifting. The progressive decline with age, in such citations, results uncharacteristically in no observable decline at 15 years. While the 9-year age-group provides a third of all such responses, necessarily heteronomous, stealing is uniformly condemned at all ages. Boys are again in their element, providing 58·2% of responses. While this may be strongly attributed to the peccadilloes of 9-year boys, males do have a stronger concern with offences against property than females.

Cruelty to animals provides 6·2% of vices quoted. Of these condemnations, 65·2% are concerned with hurting animals and the remaining 34·8% with killing animals. The 9-year boys provide almost half of the latter. The totals decline consistently with age, save for a slightly larger decline at 15 years. Boys contribute 60·9% of such condemnations, thus showing themselves far more aware of, and concerned with, cruelty to animals than girls. This is strikingly confirmed by the fact that, in recognising the parallel but positive virtue of kindness to animals, girls provide 57·0% of citations and the boys 43·0% – a reversal of the situation.

A separate category had to be made of responses from older subjects condemning smoking, drinking, extra-marital sexual intercourse, gambling, and drug-taking. This combined group made up 2·8% of all vices quoted. But 39·3% of these citations were concerned with smoking and drinking under age – the concern mainly of boys of 13 and 15 years. Omitting this concern, responses in this category derive in the main from 17-year subjects. Drunkenness and gambling are similarly condemned by both sexes, though not strongly. Sexual self-indulgence and drug-taking are, however, much more the concern of boys, if again not strongly so. In the result, boys provide 77·1% of these responses. We may attribute this to their greater general concern with physical evils, the assumed masculinity of drinking and smoking, and the stronger male sexual urge.

The 1·6% of items quoting specifically religious vices contrasts with the 4·7% quoting specifically religious virtues. We deduce that, while religious practices are to be admired, if minimally, even less condemnation attaches to failure to observe them. Boys provide 58·8% of the responses, a sex difference similar to that for positive religious practices. Yet of the 10 boys of 17 years extolling the virtue of church-going, only 1 condemns the corresponding vice of not attending. Of interest, too, is the fact that only 2 of the 90 girls in our 13-to-17-year age-groups inclusive find anything to condemn in the specifically religious sphere; and that only 11 of them quoted religious practices in their listed virtues.

5. VIRTUES AND VICES

The broad picture emerging from this test is of a practical and humanistic morality. The greatest virtue is to help others; the greatest vice is to harm others. Virtue does not go to the limit of self-sacrifice; nor is the concept of vice really aware of the mental, psychological and spiritual harm that can be done to others. The admired altruism is mild, rather than strong; its vision is limited to the personal and local in the main. Girls excel in the niceties and subtleties of personal relationships; boys come into their own in concrete, physical aspects of moral behaviour. Girls, in short, are concerned with being, boys with doing.

The virtues admired are those which promote, and the vices condemned those which mar, personal relationships. If there is no great idealism revealed, neither is hypocritical pretension evident. The ideal is personal integrity, and interpersonal amity. Whatever the code portrayed may lack, it is at least well supplied with the milk of human kindness.

(C) **Choosing reasons test**

Here is a story:

A girl named Joan lived on a farm. Her father had all sorts of animals on his farm. There were big animals, like horses and cows. There were small animals, liked geese and chickens. Joan was kind to them all. Why do you think that she was never cruel or unkind to the animals? Here are four different reasons for you to choose from:

1. They might attack her if she was cruel to them.
2. Everyone would call her a nasty, cruel girl.
3. She knew that her father would punish her.
4. She knew that animals can feel pain.

Which do you think was the real reason? Put a cross (×) in front of the one which you think explains why Joan was always kind to the animals.

Your cross will be in front of 1, or 2, or 3, or 4. It will show which you think was the true reason. Now write on these two lines why you think this was the real reason.

....

....

When you turn over this page you will find more stories, just like that one. Each story has four reasons for what the boy or girl did. Put a cross in front of what you think is the true reason. Then write why you think so.

There are no 'right' or 'wrong' answers. These stories have nothing to do with school work or examinations. They are from someone who just wants to know what you think. Your answers will be sent on to him and not seen in school. There is no need to hurry. You can have as much time as you need. You need not bother about writing and spelling. Use pen or pencil, just as you wish.

When you turn over this page, you find space to fill in your number. This is instead of your name. We do not want to know your name, so that you can write quite freely what you think.

Now you can turn over and begin.

This test, derived and adapted from the work of McKnight (1950), consisted of eight concrete moral situations. Four alternative reasons were given for the action of the boy or girl in each story, and these represented respectively the four levels of moral judgement used as the basis of our visual tests – anomy, heteronomy, socionomy, and autonomy. Subjects had to select the reason judged to be the real one, and to give the reason for the judgement made. Where the reason given contradicted the choice made, the reason was used in scoring. The test paper gave a specimen story for a trial run, so that subjects would be clear as to what was required. The four levels of judgement were, of course, permutated in the eight situations so as to avoid giving priority to any one. As a result of extensive pre-testing, some situations were rejected and replaced, and others amended. The test was administered to groups; and such was its attraction that we did, in fact, use it as the first of the six written tests. Since it proved quite beyond the capacity of 7-year subjects, it was administered to the remaining 300 subjects in the age-groups from 9 to 17 years inclusive.

No test exposed more clearly the limitations inherent in all written tests. The constricted nature of responses, particularly from less able pupils, was in complete contrast with the comprehensiveness and depth obtained from personal interviews. Every word mattered in framing the four reasons for each story, so that each might best express its own level of moral judgement without possibility of misunderstanding. Less able subjects tended simply to repeat the reason given as their own. Nor was it always easy to distinguish from a brief written statement between a heteronomous and an autonomous judgement.

The test had, however, a number of merits. Since scoring and analysis was on the same basis as those for the visual tests, a comparison of results might be of interest. More important, we wished to assess the value of concrete moral situations in moral judgement and, potentially, in moral education. Above all, thirdly, since all eight situations were different in their moral concern, we sought evidence from judgements upon them for the place and significance of the situational element in moral judgement; and it is on this valuable evidence that we concentrate in this summary of our findings. For the rest, we find familiar patterns. The most striking was the sex differential. Thus, in terms of total scores, girls lead boys in every age-group from 9 to 17 years by 48·5; 56·5; 54·0; 125·5; 29·0. The massive lead at 15 years was due to boys' total score falling back to a level below that achieved by boys of 11 years. Boys of 17 years recover to a figure a little above that of 13 years. Thus we observe yet again moral uncertainty at 15 years, particularly here among boys.

1. HONESTY WITH PROPERTY

Finding a purse in the road was, it will be recalled, the theme of one of our rejected visual tests. No situation produced a higher total of autonomous responses, although some may have been motivated by sympathy or reciprocity. The marked increase in autonomy at 11 years may have included disguised heteronomy; but there was little change in figures thereafter. In terms of responses to all eight situations, this story was first in autonomy, fifth in socionomy, fifth in anomy, and seventh in heteronomy. While sex differences were not outstanding, girls showed greater autonomy, and boys the familiar need, in dealing with property, for greater heteronomy.

2. SHARING SWEETS WITH FRIENDS

This situation, by contrast, produced the fewest autonomous responses, and almost the highest total of socionomous responses. It was second in socionomy, fourth in heteronomy, sixth in anomy, and eighth in autonomy. Sharing sweets is overwhelmingly motivated by social concern, rather than by moral conviction; and, in the younger age-groups, by heteronomy. But although autonomous responses are low, they still equal those for anomy and heteronomy combined. Girls lead in autonomy throughout; boys lead girls more strongly in anomy, and particularly at 15 years. But in the predominant socionomous motivation, there are only slight differences between the sexes.

3. BULLYING

While this situation was not expected to be strongly evocative, it deserved a place as an important aspect, for children, of one of their four universal evils – physical cruelty. Results by comparison with the other situations were undistinguished – third in heteronomy and fourth in anomy, socionomy and autonomy. The total of autonomous responses was, however, more than any two others combined, girls substantially leading boys – but, no doubt, motivated by strong sympathy, since they lead at all ages. Boys lead in heteronomy, particularly at 9 and 13 years: and in anomy, particularly at 15 and 17 years. Bullying is, as could be expected, the concern of boys, and particularly of younger boys. But the strength of autonomous responses shows yet again the universal detestation of physical cruelty.

4. CARE FOR PROPERTY OF OTHERS

This situation, involving the care of library books, produced results that were second in both anomy and autonomy, and eighth in both heteronomy and socionomy. Here, in an entirely different pattern, judgement is clear-cut between anomy and autonomy. Anomy responses were second only to a cheating situation, and autonomy second only to the 'finding a purse' situation. Boys provide more heteronomous responses, and girls far more socionomous responses. The sex difference is stronger in anomy than in autonomy, but in both cases in the familiar direction. Care for borrowed books is motivated primarily either by regard for the books themselves and for other borrowers: or by the prudential concern that carelessness may result in being refused further use of the library.

5. HONESTY IN THE CLASSROOM

Yet again we find a complete contrast in judgements as compared with the previous situation. Anomy and autonomy are negligible in this situation concerned with honesty over undeserved marks in the classroom situation. It is first in socionomy, fifth in heteronomy, and seventh in both anomy and autonomy, compared with the other situations. But the total figure for autonomy is still larger than the combined total for anomy and heteronomy. Anomy is low, and derived mainly from boys. Heteronomy shows little sex difference. Socionomy is strong for both sexes and in all ages from 9 to 15 years inclusive. At 17 years there is a dramatic transfer from socionomy to autonomy in both sexes, affected, no doubt, by the fact that, although engaged in further education, our 17-year subjects had left the classroom situation behind. In the result, therefore, the pattern of response to this situation shows socionomy to be outstanding, while autonomy, though much less evident, is far stronger than the other two levels of judgement.

6. TRUTHFULNESS IN THE CLASSROOM

This situation involved owning up to an accidental misdemeanour in the classroom. As compared with the other situations, the response pattern was second in heteronomy, third in anomy, fifth in autonomy and seventh in socionomy. Heteronomy, deriving substantially from the two youngest age-groups, is not significant. But over half the anomous responses come from the two oldest age-groups of 15 and 17 years; and, while autonomy appears at all ages from 11 years, it too is strongest at 15 and 17 years. Moreover, the total of autonomous responses is comparatively very high.

Thus, above all in older subjects, the picture is of a relatively clear choice between anomy and autonomy in truth-telling in the classroom situation. Girls characteristically lead boys in both higher autonomy and in lower anomy.

7. SWEARING

Here the response pattern showed judgements to be, comparatively, first in heteronomy, third in socionomy, sixth in autonomy, and eighth in anomy. Anomy is, in fact, negligible. While heteronomous responses are in fact, less than those for autonomy, and naturally strongest at 9 and 11 years, they are as many at 17 years as at 13 years, and that for both sexes. Socionomy is strong, even at 9 years, but decreases at 17 years, when the main choice is between heteronomy and autonomy. Girls lead in autonomy and socionomy, though not strongly; and boys in heteronomy, although at 15 and 17 years the sexes show similar heteronomy. The detestation of swearing as a 'bad habit' was evident at all ages, either as a socionomous concern or as an aspect of autonomous self-respect. Those who lacked either motivation were dependent upon heteronomy.

8. CHEATING

The response pattern to this situation was, comparatively, first in anomy, third in autonomy, and sixth in both heteronomy and socionomy, the two latter deriving mainly from the younger age-groups. Here, then, the issue is substantially between autonomy and anomy. That no other situation evoked so much prudential anomy is further evidence that cheating in the classroom is not a serious moral offence in child morality. Anomy is nearly as strong at 15 years as at 9 years. Autonomy, however, increases steadily with age, even including, rarely, the 15-year age-group. But such autonomy is, in effect, the realisation of the folly of cheating ('you only cheat yourself') that develops with normal maturation as a strongly cognitive judgement.

9. THE SITUATION ELEMENT IN MORAL JUDGEMENT

While the use of half-scores helped to mitigate the limitations of brief, written responses, a measure of inexactitude was inevitable in analysing the responses to this test. But the broad pattern gives overwhelming evidence of the place of the situational element in moral judgement. Each situation produces its own response pattern, as in the case of our visual tests. The situational element is a constituent factor in moral judgement.

This truth is clearly evidenced in the patterns of response to our eight different situations. Using the letter A (anomy), B (heteronomy), C (socionomy) and D (autonomy), they are:

Story 1	D	C	A	B
Story 2	C	D	B	A
Story 3	D	C	B	A
Story 4	D	A	C	B
Story 5	C	D	B	A
Story 6	D	B	A	C
Story 7	D	B	A	C
Story 8	D	A	C	B

While autonomy is predominant in the response patterns, we observe that in situations 2 and 5 the chief moral guide is socionomy. The only other observable similarity is in stories 4 and 8, where the identical pattern (D A C B) appears.

Another pattern may be derived from a comparison of the eight situations based on the order in which they come in terms of judgements produced at each level. The pattern is now:

Story 1	D	A/C		B
Story 2	C	B A		D
Story 3	B	A/C/D		
Story 4	A/D	B/C		
Story 5	C	B	A/D	
Story 6	B	A	D	C
Story 7	B	C	D	A
Story 8	A	D	B/C	

Here too we observe the similarity between responses to situations 2 and 5. Socionomy is predominant in these situations concerned with sharing sweets (2) and with honesty in pointing out unearned marks (5). Here the yardstick is mainly social prestige rather than autonomous conscience, although in the case of the latter situation the strong swing of responses at 17 years from socionomy to autonomy may indicate, subject to the proviso noted, that conscience is involved.

The other similarity is between the situations concerning borrowing books (4) and copying in the classroom (8). Here the decision is relatively clear-cut between autonomy and prudential anomy.

Heteronomy, on the other hand, is strong in response to the situations concerning bullying (3), owning up in the classroom (6) and swearing (7). In judgements on bullying and swearing in particular the issue is mainly between autonomy and heteronomy. Either a subject has an inner moral sanction or he needs the strong arm of heteronomy.

In short, we find that in two situations the issue is broadly between socionomy and autonomy; in two others between anomy and autonomy; and in three others between heteronomy and autonomy. The remaining situation, that concerned with finding a purse (1), produced overwhelmingly autonomous responses, the other three levels being far less significant. But, as suggested, sympathy and reciprocity may be concealed factors here.

The clear conclusion is that there is a strong situational element in all moral judgement. Each situation elicits its own appropriate judgement. Thus, as McPherson comments, 'The moral ideal implies not a single virtue but a system of virtues, regrouping according to the situation. Each situation has its pattern of goodness, dictated by reason. No two patterns are ever wholly identical' (McPherson, 1949).

Thus 'circumstances alter cases'. But we do not find here the situationism expounded, for example, by Fletcher (1966). Certainly the situation affects judgement; but it does not determine it. The situation is quite subordinate to the judge. He makes a moral judgement, not only in the light of the situation, but also within the limits of his moral development.

10. CONSISTENCY IN MORAL JUDGEMENT

This test, finally, threw some light on the possibility of consistency in moral judgement. Complete consistency would have meant 8 responses all on one judgement level. Given the situational factor, however, such consistency was not to be expected. The most consistency we found was 5 responses on one level – for example, heteronomy in younger subjects and socionomy in older subjects. But we could at least look for consistency in autonomy. Scoring this level at 4, such complete consistency would mean a score of 32. This was rare, particularly as many responses were mixed, this earning half-scores. We therefore note here subjects scoring 30 or over, thus approaching consistency in autonomy. We also repeat our caveat as to the difficulty of exactitude in analysing limited, written responses.

Subjects Approaching Consistency in Autonomy

Age-group	*Boys N-30*	*Girls N-30*	*Total N-60*	*% of Total Age-group*
9-year	—	—	—	—
11-year	3	6	9	15·0
13-year	3	10	13	21·7
15-year	1	6	7	11·7
17-year	11	7	18	30·0
Totals	18	29	47	

Comparison of the means of variables of these subjects with those of their separate age-groups show intelligence to be a significant factor. Girls, yet again, lead boys, save in the 17-year age-group. Here, however, while the mean score of boys is 24·9, that of the girls is 25·7, suggesting, as is indeed the case, that more girls than boys had total scores approaching the 30 taken as the minimum for this analysis. Yet even in the mature age-group of 17 years less than 1 subject in 3 even approaches consistency in autonomy. It is not only the situational element in moral judgement that limits consistency in evoking judgements at different levels; it is also limited by the individual's moral controls. As we have seen from the outset, by no means all individuals develop complete autonomy; and such conscience as is achieved may be limited in both quantity and quality. Some situations fall within the province of the individual conscience, and thus evoke it; others do not. Some individuals, therefore, need the solid, external control of heteronomy; others are controlled by social, rather than personal, sanctions. Moral judgement, in short, while related to the situation, is determined by the individual's moral understanding.

(D) **Vice and Virtue**

Right or wrong stories

Here is a story.

John loved cars. His father often parked his car in the street outside their house. One day he caught John playing about in the car, pretending to drive it. He warned John that he would be punished if he did it again. Peter, his elder brother, heard what Father said. The very next day he saw John in the car, playing with the controls, pretending to drive it. Should Peter tell Father?

What answer would you give – 'Yes' or 'No'? Write your answer here.

....

Now write why you think that is the right thing for Peter to do.

....

....

When you turn over this page, you will find other stories, just like that one. After you have read each story, you will find a space to write your answer. It will be 'Yes' or 'No'. Then you will find two lines to write the reason why you think that is the right answer.

These stories have nothing to do with school work or examinations. This is for someone who just wants to know what *you* think are the right answers to these stories. Your answers will be sent on to him.

There is no need to hurry in reading the stories, writing the answer, and giving the reasons for your answers. You can have as much time as you need to finish all the stories. You need not worry about spelling or writing. Use pen or pencil, just as you wish.

When you turn over this page, you will find a space to fill in your number. This is instead of your name. We do *not* want to know your name, so that you can write quite freely just what you think. Use this number on the other papers, too, so that we will know that they are all from the same person.

Now you can turn over this page and begin.

Moral judgement is not always between vice and virtue, between black and white. All too often the conflict is between virtue and virtue; and hence the dilemma implicit in the question, 'What shall I do?' Here, therefore, was another area of the moral field concerning which evidence might usefully be sought.

McPherson (1949), in a study concerned with moral education, used problem situations which formed the basis of our own test. He saw the 'problem of moral instruction' as 'the problem of conflicting values . . . The essence of morality is weighing values against each other in highly specific circumstances, deciding which values are of paramount importance in each instance and acting accordingly.'

Eight situations were used to make up this written test. Four were concerned with conflict between vice and virtue, and four with the conflict between virtue and virtue. Each situation required a specific 'Yes' or 'No' response, so as to rule out neutrality, together with the reason for the decision made. The outstanding impression made by the reasons given was the complexity of the motivation revealed. The permutations of child-thinking are infinitely diffuse and varied. We can fully agree with McPherson in finding 'exhaustive samples of the child's rationalisms, "conventionalisations", hypocrisies, moral realism, wishes, desires, and interests', thus affording 'vast psychological insight into, and induced sympathetic understanding of, the child's point of view' (McPherson, 1949).

The test was administered with the other written tests, and with a similar procedure, to the 300 subjects composing the 9-to-17-year age-groups inclusive, the sexes being equally represented as always. Such was the complexity of responses that scoring categories had to be devised for this test. The basic criterion was insight into the situation. The lowest level (A-1) indicated complete lack of insight due to irrelevance, anomy, heteronomy, and self-interest. A second level (B-2) indicated some insight, typically revealed by sympathy, by preventive action, or by highly prudential action. A third level (C-3) indicated social interaction, seen, for example, in reciprocity, in shaming, and in just – rather than vengeful – retaliation. The highest level (D-4) showed mature and insightful judgement upon the situation.

1. VICE *v.* VIRTUE

The four stories used as test situations under this category involved the conflict between greed, however rationalised, and generosity, allied with good example; between hearsay, gossip, prejudice, and open-minded fairness; between honesty and taking the opportunity for revenge; between self-control and angry retaliation.

Taking all four situations together, development in moral judgement is indicated by increase in total score from 605 at 9 years to 721 at 17 years. Total scores for each age-group, as percentages of potential scores, and from 9 to 17 years inclusive are 63·0%: 66·5%: 76·1%: 77·9%: 75·1% The greatest increase is thus, familiarly, between 11 and 13 years.

Sex differences are no less familiar. Girls lead boys in total score in the five age-groups by 2·5: 30·0: 31·5: 26·5: 13·0. Girls make a first solid advance at 11 years, an age-group before the boys, and repeat it at 13 years. Mean age-group scores for boys range from 2·50 at 9 years to 2·90 at 17 years, and for girls from 2·52 at 9 years to 3·03 at 17 years.

Evidence for the situational element may be sought by observing the total score for each situation as a percentage of the possible maximum: fairness *v.* prejudice, 76·1%; honesty *v.* revenge, 75·5%; greed *v.* generosity, 73·9%; self-control *v.* retaliatory anger, 61·4%. There is thus broad similarity, save for the striking difference in response to the fourth and difficult situation, concerning totally unjust defamation of character.

Evidence for the influence of the situation can also be traced from inconsistency in responses to the four varied situations. Only 12 subjects were completely consistent in their responses – 10 of these from the 15- and 17-year age-groups, representing 4% of the total sample. The influence of the situation is thus strong. Of the 12 consistent subjects, 9 were boys. Consistency is not a typically feminine trait. But complete consistency could only mean cold rigidity, subjecting persons to codes; and feminine sensitivity to the warm complexity of interpersonal relationships could scarcely stomach such intransigence.

2. VIRTUE *v.* VIRTUE

The four situations used under this category similarly involved diverse conflicts – between loyalty to a brother and public safety as well as the brother's ultimate well-being; between love of animals and public safety; between loyalty to a friend and honesty as well as the friend's ultimate well-being; between public health and public safety, on the one hand, and sympathy and kindness on the other.

Increase in total scores for all four stories was from 496·0 at 9 years to 791·5 at 17 years. Total scores for each age-group, as percentages of the possible maximum, and from 9 to 17 years inclusive, were 51·7%: 60·4%: 78·7%: 76·2%: 82·4%. Again we observe the climacteric increase between 11 and 13 years, the familiar lapse at 15 years, and a rise at 17 years derived entirely from girls' responses.

Girls lead boys in total score in all five age-groups by 14·0: 56·5: 37·5: 26·0: and a striking 68·5 at 17 years, when girls showed far greater insight into the overriding concerns of public health and safety, and no less into the ultimate well-being of individuals. The mean age-group scores for boys range from 2·0 at 9 years to 2·9 at 17 years, and for girls from 2·1 at 9 years to 3·6 at 17 years. Yet again girls lead boys throughout.

The total scores, as percentages of the possible maximum for each situation, are: love of animals *v.* public safety, 76·9%; sympathy and kindness *v.* public safety, 71·8%; loyalty *v.* public safety, 68·6%; honesty *v.* loyalty, 62·2%. Such evidence for the influence of the situational element is supplemented by inconsistency in individual responses. The total of 34 cases of complete consistency represent 11·3% of the total sample. In the category of vice *v.* virtue we found boys outnumbering girls in cases of consistency. Here, however, in the more subtle situations involving virtue *v.* virtue, we find markedly more cases of consistency among girls – a total of 26 as compared with 8 boys, and all, in the significant age-groups, at the highest level. Here, too, we find 34 cases of consistency as compared with 12 cases in the vice *v.* virtue category. Since the increase is due overwhelmingly to girls, and at the highest level, we observe their more mature insight in this more subtle area of moral judgement.

3. COMPARISON OF TWO CATEGORIES

We come, finally, to our leading concern in this test. Do children show greater facility in judging between vice and virtue than in making judgements in the potentially more complex situations where virtue conflicts with virtue?

First, we may contrast the total scores for the four situations in each category as percentages of the possible maximum and in descending order:

Vice *v.* Virtue	Virtue *v.* Virtue
76·1%	76·9%
75·5%	71·8%
73·9%	68·6%
61·4%	62·2%

The overall range is remarkably similar, the means of the percentage scores under the two categories being 71·7% and 69·9% respectively. Here is slight evidence that judgement is easier between vice and virtue. But the differences in percentage scores in the virtue *v.* virtue category are broadly regular, whereas in the vice *v.* virtue category there is a very marked difference in response to the fourth story – the complex situation involving defamation of character. If we exclude this – and particularly if we hypothesise a more straightforward situation similar to the other three – there is far firmer evidence that moral judgement is more easily made where the conflict is simply between vice and virtue. On the other hand, however, the four situations requiring judgement between virtue and virtue were all of greater complexity, and the similarity in responses to the two categories is far closer than had been hypothesised.

In short, we do not find strong evidence that our subjects find it easier to make judgements between vice and virtue. Those with insightful moral perception are just as adept at judging between opposing virtues; and, as we might expect, they are predominantly in the older age-group.

In terms of age-groups, there is far greater facility at 9 years in making judgements between the simple 'black and white' conflict of vice and virtue. It is still pronounced, though less so, at 11 years. But at 13 years, with the familiar climacteric development, there is markedly greater facility at judging between virtue and virtue. While this declines familiarly at 15 years, it becomes even more pronounced at 17 years, even if derived almost entirely from girls.

Sex differences may be observed simply in the lead of girls in total score at each age-level:

Age-group	*Vice* v. *Virtue*	*Virtue* v. *Virtue*
9-year	2·5	14·0
11-year	30·0	56·5
13-year	31·5	37·5
15-year	26·5	26·0
17-year	13·0	68·5

Nothing could better illustrate the far greater facility of girls in moral judgement than this evidence of their massive superiority in the more complex category of judging between opposing virtues. The contrast is between a mean superiority of 20·7 in the category of vice *v.* virtue, and of 40·5 in the category of virtue *v.* virtue. Here would appear to be the subtle area of feminine superiority *par excellence;* and the outstanding fact is the superiority of girls above all at 17 years when, we have found reason to conclude, development as such, in moral judgement, is complete.

(E) **Concepts of justice**

A further written test made opportunity for examining children's concepts of justice, an area to which Piaget devoted the longest chapter of his work. He found a 'law of evolution' and three 'broad stages' emerging from his investigations. Up to 7 to 8 years the child is dominated by the morality of constraint, with its ethic of heteronomy in which good is defined in terms of submission and obedience, rules are sacred, punishment related to the consequences of offence and not to intentions, and the letter rather than the spirit of the law is to be obeyed. The second stage, from 7 to 8 to 11 to 12 years, sees the development of the morality of co-operation, in which justice is defined in terms of progressive equalitarianism, its essence is reciprocity, punishment is related to restitution, rules are arrived at by agreement, and fairness is all. The third stage, emerging towards 11 to 12 years, sees the morality of equity, in which equality is sought in relativity rather than in identity, taking into account all such mitigating factors as motives, intentions, rights and duties and relationships. In short, reciprocity, becoming 'indefinitely sustained', 'tends of itself' to higher morality, guiding conduct to 'universality itself' (Piaget, op. cit., 323).

What would be fair?

Here is a story.

Dick was playing in his room when his mother called him. She asked him to go for a loaf of bread, as there was not enough bread for tea for the whole family. Dick said, 'I'll go in a minute'. But he never went. When his father came in for tea and heard about it, he was very angry. He wondered what would be the best way to punish Dick:

1. Stop him going out with his friends that evening.

2. Make him go without any tea, as he could not be bothered to get the bread.

3. Refuse to help Dick when he next wanted something done.

4 Give him a talking-to.

What do you think would be the best way for Father to punish Dick?

Write what you think here:

....

Now write why you think so:...

....

When you turn over this page you will find more stories like that one. Read each story, and then write what you think should be done, and why you think so. There are no 'right' or 'wrong' answers. These stories have nothing to do with school work or examination. They are from someone who just wants to know what *you* think would be the fair thing to do in each story, and why you think so. Your answers will be sent on to him and not seen in school.

There is no need to hurry. You can have as much time as you need.

Make sure that you answer all the stories. You need not bother about writing or spelling. Use pen or pencil, just as you wish.

When you turn over this page you will find a space to fill in your number. This is instead of your name. We do *not* want to know your name, so that you can write quite freely what you think.

Now you can turn over and begin.

This written test, entitled 'What would be Fair?' was made up of six story situations. Four were adapted from Piaget. The other two, while stemming from Piaget, were associated with the studies of Durkin in replicating Piaget's work.

1. EXPIATORY AND RECIPROCAL PUNISHMENTS

The first two stories examined Piaget's simple contrast between expiatory punishment, rooted in constraint and the rule of authority, and punishments by reciprocity. Piaget lists these latter, from the more to the less severe, as: social exclusion; suffering the natural consequences of the offence; deprivation of the object misused; doing to the child exactly what he has done; requiring restitution; and censure without punishment as such (op. cit., 205ff.).

Here we used Piaget's stories, suitably adapted. Testing 'about a hundred' subjects with them, he derived 'about 400' responses in all. He divided his subjects into three age-groups, 6-7 years, 8-10 years, 11-12 years, for which we had parallel age groups. Since he gives the percentages of responses indicating reciprocity punishments, we can parallel our results with his:

Age-group		*Expiatory Punishment*		*Punishment by Reciprocity*	
Piaget	*Us*	*Piaget*	*Us*	*Piaget*	*Us*
6- 7 year	—	72%	—	28%	—
8-10 year	9 -year	51%	38·3%	49%	61·2%
11-12 year	11-year	18%	16·7%	82%	83·3%
—	12 year	—	21·7%	—	78·3%
—	15-year	—	23·3%	—	76·7%
—	17-year	—	20·9	—	80·0%

While the results are dissimilar at 8-10 years, we observe strong similarity at 11-12 years. But expiatory punishments by no means wither away, as Piaget's striking decreases appear to suggest. Indeed, the strength of reciprocity at 11 years – its high-water mark, as we have found – leads to their diminution. But thereafter they rise to a fairly consistent level, recalling Piaget's conviction that 'some minds are irrevocably attached to the idea of expiation' (op. cit., 208). While we can broadly agree with Piaget's findings, we observe again the incompleteness, if not distortion, of the developmental picture he produces through not continuing testing into adolescence.

There is, too, a simplicity in Piaget's analysis that fails to see, or ignores, the subtlety of children's responses. For example, censure, the least severe of reciprocity punishments, is advocated in our age-groups from 9 to 17 years in the following percentages of responses: 16·1%; 10·0%; 12·5%; 17·5%; 20·8%. At 9 years censure is clearly preferred for its leniency. It is even more strongly preferred at 15 and 17 years, not on grounds of its leniency – 1 subject views it as the most severe of the suggested punishments – but as being the most appropriate and effective.

Again, even expiatory punishments are far from simple. Thus, being kept indoors is often recommended, not as a direct expiatory punishment, but to teach the offender a lesson, to teach him responsibility, to make him look silly to his friends – the most effective punishment, in some recommendations – while letting them down will be no less effective. Such punishments are not purely expiatory.

In general we can agree with Piaget that younger children favour expiatory punishments, and older children favour punishments by reciprocity. But the picture is nothing like so clear-cut and simple in our responses as he finds it.

2. HETERONOMY, EQUALITY, EQUITY

The third story in this test was taken directly from Piaget, elucidating his three stages. Since he quotes figures derived by his colleague, testing 167 subjects – ours, in the three parallel age-groups, totalling 180 subjects – we can make a direct comparison of results.

Age-group		*Punishment*		*Equality*		*Equity*	
Piaget	*Us*	*Piaget*	*Us*	*Piaget*	*Us*	*Piaget*	*Us*
6-9 yr	9 yr	48%	66·6%	35%	16·6%	17%	16·6%
10-12	11 yr	3%	60·0%	55%	10·8%	42%	29·2%
13-14	13 yr	0%	33·3%	5%	10·8%	95%	55·8%
—	15 yr	—	20·8%	—	3·3%	—	75·8%
—	17 yr	—	36·6%	—	5·0%	—	58·3%

Here again, while we can generally agree with the broad development, the pattern is nothing like so massively clear-cut as Piaget's figures show. His almost suspect figures of 0% and 95% at 13 to 14 years are never likely to be achieved, as the responses of older age-groups clearly indicate. Even if his colleague was testing girls – unlikely, no doubt, but Piaget does not say – we could certainly never equal such a classic result. Yet again, too, there are subtleties in responses that Piaget never seems to meet.

A second story, taken from Piaget, was also used in seeking evidence for his three stages. But as he interprets responses in terms only of constraint and equality, we cannot make a useful comparison.

From a comparison of our results thus far with those of Piaget, using his own stories, three points may be made. First, his failure to continue testing into adolescence produces a distorted picture of development. Secondly, his results ignore the finer subtleties of children's moral judgements. And thirdly, therefore, we find his categories to be strait-jackets in which it is difficult indeed to confine the range of complexity in our responses. In short, his categories do scant justice to the moral judgements of children. As with reciprocity, they become so broad as to conceal, rather than to expose, the comprehensiveness of the developmental pattern.

3. RECIPROCITY IN PHYSICAL AGGRESSION

We now turn to the first of the two final stories in this test. While both are Piagetian, we were concerned here with the replication of Piaget's work by Durkin (1959*a*, 1959*b*, 1961). The first of three studies was concerned with justice in a situation involving physical aggression. It was based on Piaget's simple question: 'If anyone punches you, what do you do?' (op. cit., 297). Durkin elaborated the question in two ways. First, if a subject gave a strict equalitarian 'eye for an eye' response, he was asked about the justice of giving back more than the exact aggression received, since Piaget found no evidence for such arbitrary punishment. Secondly, if a subject asked about circumstances or motives, he was asked if these would make a difference and, if so, why, thus yielding evidence of equity.

Durkin (1959*a*) tested 101 American boys and girls, aged 7, 10 and 13 years, these approximating to Piaget's 'three great periods' in the development of justice concepts – namely, 'up to the age of 7-8, approximately 8-11, and a period which sets in towards 11-12' (op. cit., 314). Durkin confirmed Piaget's broad thesis of development in moral judgement with age; his finding that reciprocity did not permit revenge; and his conclusion that equity increases with age. But no support was found for Piaget's assertion that reciprocity increases with age, save between 7 and 10 years. In general Durkin found great perplexity among children as to 'what constitutes rightful self-defence and what constitutes unlawful aggression' (Durkin, 1959*a*).

Piaget gives percentage figures under four categories derived from 167 subjects, tested by his colleague, aged 6 to 12 years inclusive. We can therefore only parallel our results – using Durkin's development of the situation, slightly elaborated – for the 9- and 11-year age-groups. Following Piaget, the figures for boys and girls are separated:

Age-group	*Sex B./G.*	*Naughty*		*Repay Same*		*Repay More*		*Repay Less*	
		Piaget %	*Us* %	*Piaget* %	*Us* %	*Piaget* %	*Us* %	*Piaget* %	*Us* %
6-year	B.	50	—	37·5	—	12·5	—	—	—
6-year	G.	82	—	18	—	—	—	—	—
7-year	B.	27	—	27	—	46	—	—	—
7-year	G.	45	—	45	—	10	—	—	—
8-year	B.	45	—	22	—	33	—	—	—
8-year	G.	25	—	42	—	8	—	25	—
9-year	B.	29	15	57	51·8	14	31·0	—	—
9-year	G.	14	10	29	73·3	—	16·7	57	—
10-year	B.	8	—	54	—	31	—	7	—
10-year	G.	—	—	20	—	—	—	80	—
11-year	B.	—	20	31	50·0	31	16·7	38	13·3
11-year	G.	—	13	33	73·0	—	—	67	13·3
12-year	B.	—	—	67	—	10	—	23	—
12-year	G.	—	—	22	—	—	—	78	—

Piaget's purpose here is to prove that reciprocity grows with age in both sexes and 'in spite of inevitable irregularities of detail'. But the 'irregularities' in his percentage figures for reciprocity ('repay same') are so large as to make the conclusion a very shaky one. Sex differences are so strong as to make even Piaget take notice of them – a situation of which only one other example can be recalled in his whole book (op. cit., 69). He observes that the heteronomous 'it is naughty' response 'almost completely disappears after the age of 9', while we find it stronger at 11 years than at 9 years. Again, Piaget ignores any concern with circumstances and motivation, whereas we find subjects thus concerned to number 7 at 9 years, 17 at 11 years, 37 at 13 years, and thereafter to be the overwhelming majority. Moreover, in complete contrast with both Piaget and Durkin, we find subjects at every age demanding revenge with both conviction and indignation.

In short, to do justice to our responses we found it essential to make an alternative analysis. Our five categories now became: revenge; heteronomy; reciprocity; concern for motives; full equity.

Age-group	*Revenge*	*Heteronomy*	*Reciprocity*	*Concern for Motives*	*Full Equity*
9-year	15·0%	14·1%	53·3%	15·9%	1·7%
11-year	7·6%	16·9%	44·9%	20·2%	10·2%
13-year	5·8%	5·8%	32·5%	35·0%	20·9%
15-year	8·5%	1·7%	41·5%	27·9%	20·4%
17-year	9·2%	3·3%	29·2%	35·0%	23·3%

Here, in more precise analysis, we observe an element of revenge throughout, overwhelmingly from boys. Piaget himself states that they are inclined to repay more, and girls less, than the blows received (op. cit., 301f.). Heteronomy, which Piaget finds almost non-existent after 9 years, is even stronger at 11 years. Reciprocity, far from increasing, is already decreasing at 11 years, Piaget's contrary conclusion being based on limited testing and imprecision in analysis. Concern for circumstances and motives grows with age, save the familiar decline at 15 years. Full equity grows, too, though not so strongly. Even at 17 years we find 29·2% of responses still rooted in reciprocity. Piaget's thesis that reciprocity 'tends of itself towards a morality of forgiveness and understanding' (op. cit., 231) finds no support in these figures – nor indeed, in any other evidence derived from this research.

We can, however, agree with Piaget that girls, after leaving heteronomy behind, think it better to repay less aggression than has been received. While feminine aversion to physical violence lies behind this judgement, the overall pattern of development shows girls in advance of boys at every stage, as in most other areas of this research.

4. RECIPROCITY IN LENDING PROPERTY

In a second study (1959*b*), Durkin made a further analysis of Piaget's thesis that reciprocity grows with age. Would his thesis hold good with subjects of different nationality and social class, and in other areas of justice violation? Durkin used stories concerned with justice in terms of property. Contrary to Piaget, reciprocity was found to decrease with age. Moreover, evidence of specificity – only 4 out of 101 subjects were completely consistent in recommending reciprocity in responses to all four stories used – showed clearly the flaw in any theory derived from judgements upon a single type of injustice.

In a third study (1961), Durkin analysed in further detail the evidence derived from the two previous studies. Two conclusions are of particular relevance and interest. First, the reasons given for some responses, superficially identical, showed them to be 'quite different in kind'. Sharing, for example, might be motivated by kindness or by hope of future advantage; and thus apparent altruism might, in fact, be covert egotism. Again, some responses not overtly advocating reciprocity could, in fact, 'actually represent indirect forms of reciprocity'. A glaring example was found in 'responses promoting the Bible ideal of turning one's cheek because it was "a way of getting even" '. Hence a second conclusion, for which we have already found evidence in this study – 'the possibility that a definition of reciprocity as being a return of identical behaviour is too narrow in that it fails to include the more subtle forms of reciprocity' (Durkin, 1961).

One of Durkin's five stories concerning property was used as the final situation in this test. It involved lending in the classroom. Durkin found two responses. The first 'reflected the acceptance of reciprocity' in that 'property should not be shared with a child who has previously refused to share his'. The second 'recommended sharing with another regardless of his past behaviour'. We too found these two categories of response. We also confirmed Durkin in finding the Piagetian concept of reciprocity to be far too narrow; and apparently identical responses to be essentially different. We also observe that this situation was solely concerned with the free interplay of practical justice between children. Hence the almost complete absence of heteronomous responses.

Lending property

Age-group	*N*	*Heteronomy*	*Reciprocity*	*Equity*
9-year	60	5·0%	89·2%	5·8%
11-year	58	—	91·4%	8·6%
13-year	60	—	69·2%	30·8%
15-year	59	—	65·2%	34·8%
17-year	58	—	62·9%	37·1%

Here we see clearly the grave limitation of Piaget's work in not continuing testing into adolescence; and hence the fallacy of his conviction that reciprocity increases with age. It is, as previously found, maximal at 11 years. Its decline is an aspect of the massive development between 11 and 13 years that is of a piece with the constantly recurring pattern of this research.

Such a broad picture conceals subtle distinctions. We may first note striking sex differences in responses:

Lending property: Sex differences

Age-group	*Heteronomy*		*Reciprocity*		*Equity (Altruism)*	
	B. %	*G.* %	*B.* %	*G.* %	*B.* %	*G.* %
9-year	10·0	—	85·0	93·3	5·0	6·7
11-year	—	—	82·1	100·0	17·9	—
13-year	—	—	81·7	56·7	18·3	43·3
15-year	—	—	65·0	65·5	35·0	34·5
17-year	—	—	75·8	50·0	24·2	50·0

Yet again we observe the climacteric advance of girls at 13 years, the familiar decline at 15 years, and further advance at 17 years, in terms of altruism. Boys' development in equity comes an age-group later, at 15 years. At 17 years girls' responses show 50% equity as compared with the boys' 24%, such is the sex difference; and since 75% of boys at this mature age are cemented in reciprocity, we find no evidence for Piaget's thesis that reciprocity 'tends of itself' towards higher moral judgement.

5. ANALYSIS OF RECIPROCITY

Subtle distinctions may also be seen in those responses falling within the broad category of reciprocity. Phrases used are:

Age-group	*Pay Back*		*Tit-for-tat*		*Teach Lesson*		*Indirect Reciprocity*	
	B. %	G. %	B. %	G. %	B. %	G. %	B. %	G. %
9-year	—	—	83·3	90·0	—	—	1·7	3·3
11-year	—	—	71·4	93·3	3·6	3·3	7·1	3·3
13-year	3·3	6·6	68·4	40·0	10·0	10·0	—	—
15-year	6·6	8·6	36·6	51·7	16·7	1·7	5·0	3·5
17-year	5·1	7·0	62·1	35·0	7·0	3·5	1·7	5·1

The 'tit-for-tat' category of exact return of injustice received naturally predominates, although within it we see the girls advance at 13 years, and boys at 15 years. Indirect reciprocity is seen in the typical response: 'Yes. She will lend it, so that she'll be able to borrow things back in return.' Subjects responding thus form but 3·1% of the total, but while few, they do exist.

Reciprocity ranges from the tit-for-tat of 'one bad turn deserves another' to the more enlightened 'two wrongs don't make a right'. Not lending may be motivated by the desire to 'pay him back', or by the insistence that 'it's only fair'. And this on the basis of the iron rule of 'an eye for an eye', which a number of responses cite as melancholy proof of Biblical knowledge. Some justify not lending as 'teaching a lesson', but others use exactly the same justification for lending.

If such an attempt to analyse reciprocity is unproductive, it does at least show the realm of reciprocity to be far broader than Piaget indicates. As a principle of moral behaviour, it is far more complex than a strict and unitary tit-for-tat. Such complexity may indicate a need for far deeper analysis of the nature of reciprocity. But, as previously suggested, the mechanics of reciprocity concern so vast an area of interpersonal relationships as to make the concept a generalisation rather than a precise definition of moral functioning.

6. ANALYSIS OF EQUITY

We turn, finally, to analysis of responses to this test revealing equity, to use Piaget's term. For him it is 'a higher form of reciprocity' which is 'justice itself extended along a purely autonomous line of development' (op. cit., 281f.). This higher mode of reciprocity moves of itself towards universality in Piaget's thesis.

Equity, too, has subtle differences in motivation. If we take responses indicating equity, and first abstract those which are, in effect, forms of indirect reciprocity, we find three types of response. The first and lowest category is one of self-interest. It is right to lend to one who has refused you in the past, but it is in order not to lose a friend; or not to be called mean; or not to lose social esteem; or to ensure being able to borrow back in the future. Secondly, it is thought right to lend in order 'to teach a lesson' – the same motive cited by some for refusing to lend. Such motivation is higher, if primly self-righteous: 'I will lend it to you, though you don't deserve it. And remember to lend your things in future.' Thirdly, there are responses indicating pure, disinterested altruism. They ignore self-interest in responding solely to the other's need. Piaget, in a key passage, used variously the terms 'forgiveness', 'generosity', and 'love' to define the highest level of moral judgement which – for him – comes about by the mechanics of linear development from reciprocity to equity to universality.

The figures for these categories of equity, as percentages of total responses, are:

Responses indicating equity

Age-group	*Self-interest*		*Teach Lesson*		*Pure Altruism*	
	B. %	*G.* %	*B.* %	*G.* %	*B.* %	*G.* %
9-year	3·3	—	—	—	1·7	6·7
11-year	3·3	—	—	—	14·3	—
13-year	5·0	11·7	3·3	15·0	10·0	16·7
15-year	1·7	8·6	16·7	7·0	16·7	18·9
17-year	—	3·5	7·0	15·5	17·1	31·0

The total number of responses, for all age-groups, in each of these three categories are: self-interest, 11; teach a lesson, 19; pure altruism, 39. Thus, of 69 responses superficially indicating equity, 30, or 43·5%, are *not* purely altruistic. If 'teaching a lesson' is shorn of self-interest, as the response pattern suggests, then 15·8% of apparently altruistic responses are, in fact, self-interested.

The 39 responses indicating pure altruism form 13·2% of our total sample. They naturally derive from older age-groups, forming 17·8% and 24·1% of the 15- and 17-year age-groups respectively. Thus in our maturest age-groups some 24% indicate unselfish altruism. If we include responses motivated by the desire to 'teach a lesson', the figure would be 35%.

Thus, as with the concepts of autonomy and reciprocity, equity requires subtler definition than Piaget gives it. His interest is so much in the process that goals are poorly defined. But we can find no evidence of his linear, automatic progression. That equity, as a higher mode of reciprocity, moves by its own inherent mechanics towards universality remains pure theorising.

Our evidence therefore compels us to reject both Piaget's theory of the process of development and his loose definitions of the staging-posts along the way in the growth of the idea of justice. We can fully concur with Durkin that 'the factors affecting a child's understanding of justice are sufficiently multiple, and that justice, operationally defined, is sufficiently complex that any theory which attempts to explain "The Development of the Idea of Justice in the Child" is from the start doomed to inevitable over-generalisation and consequent error' (Durkin, 1959*b*).

(F) **Sentence-completion**

Finishing Sentences

Here is a sentence that has not been finished—

WHAT I LIKE BEST IS____

It could have all kinds of endings. Here are some:

What I like best is when people say nice things about me.

What I like best is being with my friends.

What I like best is feeling happy.

How would you finish it? Write your ending here:

What I like best is____

When you turn over this page, you will find more sentences just like that one. They all need to be finished. Read each one, and finish it with the *first* thing you think of. Do them as *quickly* as you can. Do *not* stop to think of a 'clever' answer. Write in the very first thing that comes into your mind.

See how quickly you can finish these sentences. At the end of the sentences there is a place to write down how long you have taken. Make sure you finish *all* the sentences. But do them as quickly as you can.

As you can see, there are no 'right' or 'wrong' answers. This has nothing to do with school work or examinations. It is for someone who just wants to know what endings *you* give to these sentences. Your answers will be sent on to him, and *not* seen in school.

You can use pen or pencil, just as you wish. You need *not* worry about your spelling or writing, so long as your answers can be read. When you have finished all the sentences, write in the time you have taken.

When you turn over this page, you will find a space to write in your number. This is instead of your name. We do *not* want to know your name, so that you can write quite freely the first things that come into your mind. You will use this number on all your other papers, too, so that we shall know that they are from the same person.

When you have written your number, you can start timing yourself and start finishing the sentences.

Now you can turn over this page and begin.

A sentence-completion test was the last of our six written group tests. As a projective technique, exploring inner attitudes, the test has a history showing its attested values. It avoids the direct questioning that tends to produce self-consciousness and defensive attempts at concealment. Since the subject cannot know what is being sought, it is difficult for him to seek to disguise his real attitudes. Moreover, and especially with children, the essential need for spontaneity can be disguised by putting strong emphasis upon speed. In administering the test we therefore encouraged competition in completing it, and made provision on the *pro forma* for the time taken to be entered. Such emphasis upon competition and speed made this a complete contrast to the other tests, and a pleasurable conclusion to group testing.

1. THE TEST

Our test consisted of 60 items covering six areas: religious items, 14; moral items, 7; home relationships, 7; the environment, 9; personal attitudes, 16; open items, 7. Open items might fall into any category and be scored accordingly. Items under each category were, of course, distributed randomly. The areas of our concern, in using this test, are evident. But such were the limitations imposed upon this research that, in the event, we were unable to do more at this stage than to analyse the religious items.

While the religious and moral items were original, others were derived from a variety of previous forms of the test. They included the Sacks Test of 60 items, quoted by Abt and Bellak (1959); Forer's Structured Sentence-completion Test of 100 items, cited by Rabin and Haworth (1960); the test consisting of 17 items, partially derived from previous tests, used by Bene (1967); and the test of 15 items designed by E. M. & M. Eppel (1966).

Despite the attraction of Bene's double coding of responses, we had to rest content with a simple five-point and ascending scoring scale: very negative, 1; negative, 2; neutral, 3; positive, 4; very positive, 5. This scale has shown itself, in analysis of our large-scale pre-testing, to be quite adequate for our purpose.

2. RELIGIOUS ITEMS

Responses to this test were fascinating in the extreme, and that in all areas; but, as stated, we were limited to analysis of the religious items. These had to be original, since no previous test could be traced which concerned itself with religion in any way. Of our 14 items, 4 proved to be unsuitable for scoring analysis because of the diffuse responses made to them. The remaining 10 items were concerned with saying prayers; singing hymns; God; going to church; Jesus; seeing a church; reading the Bible; Heaven; school prayers; being in church.

These 10 items were scored on the five-point scale, and a mean score derived from each of the 300 subjects in our 9-to-17-year age-groups inclusive. This score for religious attitudes could be correlated with individual variables. In particular, we wished to find what relationship, if any, could be found between religious attitudes and religious class based upon Church affiliation.

3. RELIGIOUS ATTITUDES AND RELIGIOUS CLASS

Two statistical analyses were made from our research findings. We sought to ascertain if any relationship or association was indicated between pairs of measured variables, and to put quantitative measures on relationships. In the first analysis the formula used was the product-moment formula for the linear correlation coefficient. The significance of the correlation coefficient was tested by the Student's t-distribution, locating the value of t in the t-distribution table for the appropriate value of $n-2$; the null hypothesis being that the variables involved are uncorrelated, and that the value of p, corresponding to the tabled t, indicates the probability that the particular value of the correlation coefficient r could come from random sampling of the population from which it is drawn. A significance level of 5% was chosen for the purpose of hypothesis testing.

It was in this first analysis that we sought evidence for relationship between the derived measures of religious class and of religious attitudes. Positive correlations were found in 7 of the 10 sex age-groups.

Such evidence of relationship between Church affiliation on the one hand and religious attitudes on the other supported our use of religious class as a measure for statistical analysis. It at least suggested that church attendance is not so crude a yardstick of religious influence and conviction as might be supposed. The Sentence-completion Test – not, so far as we can ascertain, previously used in seeking evidence of interior religious attitudes – could clearly be of real value in this area.

A second statistical analysis of all our research findings was made, using the Goodman-Kruskal measure of association for ordered tables as a more appropriate method of analysing qualitative, rather than quantitative, material. We conclude with an account of this second analysis.

Religious class and religious attitudes: Correlations

9-year boys . . .	0·366
9-year girls . . .	—
11-year boys . . .	0·513
11-year girls . . .	—
13-year boys . . .	0·566
13-year girls . . .	0·547
15-year boys . . .	0·631
15-year girls . . .	0·593
17-year boys . . .	0·491
17-year girls . . .	—

Chapter 11
Statistical Analysis

Methodology

The aim of the statistical analysis was to seek to measure the levels of association between the results of the tests used, both verbal projection tests and written tests, and the three variables – I.Q., socio-economic class, religious class. Since the 360 subjects were divided, not only equally into six age-groups, but also equally between the sexes, the sex differentials could also be observed.

One possible method was to put the scored responses on a straightforward linear scale 1-4, and to calculate the standard product-moment correlation coefficient between the test scores and the variables. Such an approach was, as previously mentioned, originally made. It is open to criticism, however, on the ground that the use of this correlation coefficient is only really valid when various distributional assumptions can be made about the variables in whose association we were interested. In this particular study, where the observations were scaled in a somewhat arbitrary manner, the distributional assumptions were not likely to be fulfilled. Accordingly, we sought a distribution-free measure of association.

A more appropriate alternative was, therefore, a contingency-table approach to the problem, dividing the data up into two-way tables, classifying each subject by scored response and measured variable. The analysis was thereby reduced to that of measuring the level of association between the two classifications used in forming the table.

Many such measures have been proposed. They have been described and compared by various writers, including Kendall and Stuard (1961, *The Advanced Theory of Statistics*). One that seemed appropriate to the present analysis was the Goodman-Kruskal measure of association –G. Like the product-moment correlation coefficient, it can take values ranging from -1 to $+1$. It is $+1$ when the classifications are perfectly associated positively, indicating, for example, that a high test score would be associated with a high I.Q. Similarly, it is -1 when the classifications are perfectly associated negatively, indicating, to use the same example, that high score goes with low I.Q. G also has the property of being a distribution-free statistic based on a ranking procedure, there being a natural order, or rank, of the classifying variables and responses. One test result indicates a higher level of moral judgement than another, as one socio-economic class is higher than another; and knowledge of this ordering conveys statistical information that may be used to measure association.

The number G is such a rank measure of association, appropriate to our situation, in which we have a natural order associated with the classifying variables. Unlike the correlation coefficient, it is not derived from an artificial scaling of test results and classifying variables. Hence our use of G as the measure of association, in the form described by Kendall and Stuart (op. cit., Vol. II, ch. 33).

For an assessment of the statistical significance of the results embodied in the tables we need to know the sampling properties of the Goodman-Kruskal measure of association-G. These are less straightforward than those of the usual product-moment correlation coefficient. In particular, the standard error of G, with which the significance levels are intimately connected, is given by a cumbersome formula (op. cit.), and the sampling distribution of G is complicated. There exist, however, simple approximations developed by Goodman and Kruskal themselves. If these are used, we find that the 5% significance level of G is approximately 0·46, and the 10% level approximately 0·37, for a sample size of 30 and a contingency table with the structure of ours. This means that, on the hypothesis of no association between the attributes under study, a G-value of 0·46 or more is to be expected only 5% of the time, and is therefore by convention described as significant. Similarly, a G-value of 0·37 or more is to be expected only 10% of the time: and is, therefore, to be regarded as suggestive, although not necessarily significant.

In the resulting tables, 87% of the significant and suggestive G-values obtained are positive. Of the total of 312 G-values, calculated in the statistical analysis, 42 are significant at the conventional level of 5%, and 68 at the level of 10%. On the hypothesis of no association, the expected numbers of G-values 'significant' at 5% and 10% would, of course, be approximately 16 and 31 respectively. There are thus well over twice as many significant G-values as would be expected if there were no association. We can say, therefore, that there is convincing evidence of the existence of associations.

General Discussion

We have already observed that the significant associations found were far higher than would be expected if there were no association; and that the overwhelming majority were positive. We find, too, that the majority of associations form patterns, rather than being isolated and spasmodic in their appearance.

Statistical analysis was made of each sex-group within each age-group, and for each test separately. Hypothetically we might expect a particular variable to be more pronounced in one situation than in another. We might also conceive that one variable would appear more strongly than another for a particular sex- and age-group; and such is the case. Meantime, from the total picture of associations found for separate sex- and age-groups we can observe an overall pattern.

G-values were calculated for both the written tests, and also for the verbal projection tests administered in individual interviews. As we have observed, the individual interviews enabled us to probe in depth and so to analyse responses comprehensively. The resulting evidence is thereby more precise and exact than that from written tests. We may therefore give stronger weight to associations derived from verbal testing. Where, however, they are confirmed by the written tests, they have additional weight. Moreover, we must not lose sight of the fact that some written tests – for example, on justice concepts – provided evidence that could not be derived from the verbal tests, and that had a reasonable measure of precision.

G-values were calculated for each test separately; and, of course, for each sex in each age-group separately. Under each separate test we sought evidence of associations between moral judgements and the three variables – intelligence, socio-economic class, religious class. Sex differences could, of course, be observed from associations found for the separate sex-groups.

In the case of the verbal tests, calculations were made for each of the four situations – the value of life, cheating, stealing, lying. In addition, associations were sought between the three variables and the development of conscience, as derived from the four tests.

In the case of the written tests, calculations were also made under five heads – the Choosing Reasons Test; justice concepts as revealed by the test 'What would be Fair?'; justice concepts as derived from the Piagetian stories replicated by Durkin; moral situations involving judgements between vice and virtue; moral situations involving judgements between virtue and virtue.

In the event, 55 associations were derived from the verbal tests, including conscience development, from a potential 180; and an identical total of 55 associations from the written tests, from a potential 150.

1. THE BROAD PATTERN

Before making a detailed analysis, we may sum up the broad pattern of associations found, bearing in mind that this is a general, and therefore imprecise, picture. Intelligence appears as the most significant variable, socio-economic class as of less significance, and religious class as the least significant. In raw, total figures we find 42 positive and 3 negative associations with intelligence; 30 positive and 7 negative associations with socio-economic class; 24 positive and 4 negative associations with religious class.

Associations with intelligence appear more strongly in girls, and particularly so in the verbal tests. Associations with socio-economic class appear more strongly in boys, and again particularly so in the verbal tests. While associations with religious class are not impressive, they are stronger in girls, and yet again more so in the verbal tests.

Contrasting associations derived from the verbal tests with those from the written tests, intelligence is more clearly apparent in the verbal tests. Associations with socio-economic class are broadly similar in both groups of tests. Associations with religious class are more apparent in the written tests.

Such generalisations require much closer scrutiny if we are to derive a clearer picture of the influence of variables upon development in moral judgement as evidenced by statistical analysis.

2. CONSCIENCE DEVELOPMENT

We may clear the ground at the outset by observing our almost total failure to find association between the variables and the development of conscience. Out of a possible total of 36 associations, for all sex- and age-groups and for the three variables, we find but 5. One of these, a positive association with intelligence is part of a total pattern for 15-year girls. The remaining four are negative associations and at the 10% level. Of these, two negative associations with intelligence for both boys and girls of 17 years lose what little purport they might seem to have when we find only scattered associations in both sexes in this age-group and for all tests, both verbal and written.

Two reasons for this failure immediately suggest themselves. The first, and more obvious, is the imprecision of our instruments, whether conceptual or statistical or both. A second possible reason is that the roots of conscience are so intertwined, and its growth so complex, that no one variable can be so powerfully influential as to stand out in isolation.

In the event, we found no more evidence of associations in the earlier age-groups, when conscience develops through fear and guilt, than after the climacteric stage of 11 to 13 years, when conscience as such makes its appearance. The result of this failure is that, in analysing the verbal tests, we are in practice concerned simply with the four projection tests–the value of life, cheating, stealing, lying.

3. INTELLIGENCE

We recall that, despite every effort to achieve random selection of our sample at each age, we found the mean I.Q. of girls to exceed that of boys at every age save 9 years. The actual percentage figures for the girls' lead are: 0·6 at 7 years; −3·0 at 9 years; 8·9 at 11 years; 7·8 at 13 years; 3·9 at 15 years; 1·8 at 17 years. The girls' lead is therefore greatest at 11 years – when subjects of both sexes were taken from the same schools, classes, background, and, possibly, homes – and at 13 years. We could suggest no other reason for such a sex difference than innate factors, manifesting themselves with the onset of adolescence.

Similarly, we bear in mind that a raw measure of intelligence based on verbal reasoning might be assumed to give advantage to girls. Their more loquacious and fulsome verbal judgements might well give a superficial impression of greater development and subtlety in moral judgements as compared with the more typically stolid responses of boys. Despite the care taken to probe the judgements of boys from every possible angle, rather than to be content with terse definitions, girls may still have an advantage in verbal responses. We do observe, however, that when with girls of 11 years we get a complete pattern of associations with intelligence from all four verbal tests, we get a similar complete pattern from their written, and therefore much more limited, responses to the paper tests; and this when the girls' lead in mean intelligence is at its highest. A similar pattern of associations from 13-year girls, in response to all four verbal tests, is, however, only carried through to one of the five written tests; but their lead in mean intelligence at this age is reduced from 8·9 to 3·9. We might, therefore, suggest that here too we see some evidence of innate intelligence at work rather than mere verbal agility and fluency.

Evidence from the verbal tests shows intelligence to be already significant in girls of 7 years in responses to three of the four tests; and this contrasts with but one test association for boys, for whom socio-economic class is of equal significance to intelligence for girls. At 9 years, the only age when boys lead girls in mean intelligence, association appears in boys' responses to three of the four tests, as compared with two for girls; but boys still show the significance for them of socio-economic class.

It is at 11 years that we find in girls the strongest and most consistent pattern of association between moral judgements and intelligence. It is consistent in responses to all four verbal, and all five written, tests, being only absent from analysis of the development of conscience, where the G-value is 0·258. It is, of course, at this age that girls have their greatest advantage in mean intelligence. This lead is not due to a sudden upsurge of the girls in mean I.Q., for, from 7 to 17 years inclusive, it varies by only 3·0. It is due, rather, to a lowering of mean I.Q. in boys, whose overall figure varies by 13·9 between 7 and 17 years inclusive; and the same is true at 13 years, when again the girls' lead is strongest. We have already examined how far such differences may be attributed to sampling deficiencies.

By contrast, boys of 11 years show association with intelligence in responses to two of the four verbal tests and to two of the five written tests; while, yet again, socio-economic class is for them of significance in three of the four verbal tests.

At 13 years intelligence is much less apparent, despite the fact that the girls lead the boys in mean intelligence nearly as strongly as at 11 years. In responses to the four verbal tests, there is but one suggestion of association from each sex. In responses to the five written tests, there are two significant associations for each sex, with an additional, and rare, negative association for girls.

At 15 years there are two negative associations for boys from the verbal tests, but three positive associations from the written tests. We recall that the girls' lead in mean intelligence is now reduced to 3·9. Yet, once again, we observe a consistent pattern of strong association from girls in responses to the verbal tests: and it even includes a unique positive association in terms of conscience. Unlike findings from the 11-year girls, however, the pattern does not reveal itself in responses to the written tests, where there is but one positive association. Girls of 15 years also show rare suggestions of association between their judgements and socio-economic class in three of the four verbal tests, and in one of the written tests; and similar, but stronger, evidence of the significance of religious class. At this age, therefore, in strong contrast with the 11-year girls, while intelligence is still strongly significant for girls, the other two variables come clearly into the picture.

At 17 years there are no indications whatever of positive association between intelligence and moral judgement from either sex and from any of the nine tests. All we find are the two negative associations with conscience. At this age we have found evidence to suggest that development in moral judgement as such is complete – without, of course, implying in any way that there cannot be further advance in adulthood in both the quality and the span of moral judgement, and even less that experience of life cannot develop the concern for others and the wisdom that are the hallmarks of moral maturity. It is the 'formal operations', to use a Piagetian phrase, of the moral self that would now appear to have been realised. In the process of development towards it we find intelligence to be a strong factor, as indeed we might expect. In the more precise analysis of verbal tests, we find it only of suggested significance for boys at 9 and 11 years. In girls, however, it is of far greater significance, above all at 11 years, when girls make their first surge in development. It is not apparent in girls of 13 years, when their lead in mean intelligence is no less strong. While intelligence is of patterned significance at 15 years, both socio-economic background and religious class are now of real influence; and at 17 years intelligence has disappeared as a significant factor.

We might, therefore, conclude that intelligence is a leading constituent factor in moral judgement; and that, as such, it facilitates development in moral judgement. But it is not by any means the only factor. Intelligence *per se* does not guarantee higher levels of moral insight and action.

4. SOCIO-ECONOMIC CLASS

Already at 7 years we observe the significance of socio-economic class for boys in three of the four verbal tests – no written tests, it will be recalled, being administered to this age-group; while it appears significant for girls in two of the four tests. At 9 years, it is significant for boys in two verbal tests, but of no significance for girls. The evidence from the less precise written tests, at 9 years, is conflicting for both sexes, with both positive and negative associations. Again at 11 years we find evidence of suggested significance for boys in three of the verbal tests, and in one written test; while minimal significance is found from girls' responses. At 13 years there is suggested association from boys in responses to two of the verbal, and to two of the written, tests. But while, yet again, girls show no evidence of association in responses to the verbal tests, they show a quite rare pattern of positive association in four of the five written tests, and a negative association in the case of the fifth test. The only parallel to this finding is in the responses of the 15-year girls to the four verbal tests where we observed, not only a pattern of association with intelligence, but also strong patterns of association for both socio-economic class and religious class.

At 15 years, boys show no associations in responses to the verbal tests, and two in responses to the written tests. Girls, however, as noted, show a pattern of suggested association in three of the four verbal tests, and one significant association in the case of the written tests. At 17 years, girls show no associations whatsoever in responses to any of the nine tests. Boys show only one in responses to the verbal tests, and that, significantly enough, in the case of stealing, from our evidence a strongly masculine temptation; and two suggested associations, one positive and one negative, in responses to the written tests.

The broad picture that emerges is that socio-economic class has the significance in the judgements of boys that intelligence has in the judgements of girls; and indeed the numbers of associations revealed almost exactly indicate this. We have already observed, from our developmental study, that heteronomy is far more strongly apparent in the judgements of boys than in those of girls, indicating their far greater need of and reliance upon external controls. Such a finding is of a piece with the broad statistical finding that socio-economic class is in far closer association with the judgements of boys than of girls. Given the greater reliance of boys upon environmental influences, it follows that socio-economic class must inevitably be of greater significance for them. The one finding thus supports the other.

5. RELIGIOUS CLASS

Our measure of religious influence was Church affiliation. While this may be thought a crude yardstick, it may have added significance in times when church attendance is permissive; and, moreover, we found strong association between church attendance and positive religious attitudes. Yet such a raw measure may do scant justice to the intricate and subtle religious influences impinging upon the child in the home, in the school, in the local community, and, indeed, in the region of the country (see Alves, *Religion and the Secondary School*, S.C.M. Press, 1968).

Statistical evidence for association between moral judgements and religious class was not strong. Associations found were generally scattered, unpatterned, and inconsistent. In responses to the verbal tests, boys produced three positive and two negative associations. These were single, save for two suggested associations at 15 years in the stealing and lying situations. Girls' responses to the verbal tests produced seven positive and one negative associations. Of these, three strongly significant associations formed a pattern at 15 years. It is of interest that, for both sexes together, half of the positive associations found should derive from the 15-year age-group.

A different picture emerges from the written tests. Boys' responses produced eight positive and one negative associations; from girls' responses came seven positive associations. Here it was the 13-year age-group that yielded nearly half the positive associations found. It may be of interest to observe that the percentage figures for weekly church attendance of total age-groups were 60% at 7 years, 42% at 9 years, 50% at 11 years, 48% at 13 years, 23% at 15 years and 18% at 17 years. Including both weekly and monthly attendance together, there was an actual increase in attendance in the 13-year age-group. But such monthly attendance, however, may do no more than indicate the beginning of the steep decline in attendance so apparent at 15 years.

In analysis of the written tests we also find at least some slight patterning. Boys of 9 years show suggested association in response to three of the five tests. At 13 years, each sex group shows three significant associations. The strongest pattern of associations derives from the 15-year girls in two of the written tests, in addition to three of the four verbal tests. The one significant association for boys of 15 years, in the written tests, parallels two suggested associations in their responses to the verbal tests.

The evidence is not strong. But, such as it is, it suggests two points of interest. First, 63% of all positive associations between moral judgements and Church affiliation came from the 13-year and 15-year age-groups, and only slightly less from boys than from girls. These are at least significant ages, not only from the broad maturational point of view, but also in terms of development in moral judgement.

Secondly, the tests that elicited the strongest evidence of association are worthy of note. In the case of the verbal tests, it was the Lying situation, closely followed by the Value of Life Test, that gave the clearest evidence, even if it is not strong. Both tests involved respect and concern for others; so that religious influence may be seen as a factor in shaping such attitudes.

In the case of the written tests, one of the two tests concerned with justice concepts was outstanding in revealing evidence of positive association between moral judgements and religious background, showing it in 6 of the 10 sex- and age-groupings – both sex groups at 9 years, boys at 11 years, both sex-groups at 13 years, and boys at 15 years. The test consisted of two Piagetian type stories, replicated by Durkin, one concerned with physical aggression and the other with lending property to a classmate who had previously refused to lend. Higher judgement, in both these situations, would involve refusal to retaliate in tit-for-tat reciprocity, if not positive forgiveness. Since four of the six associations derived from boys, the aversion of girls for physical aggression is not involved. Here, then, we may see some evidence of religious influence upon higher moral judgements.

6. SEX DIFFERENCES

The foregoing discussion has suggested the differences between the sexes in statistical analysis of associations between our three variables and moral judgements. In the more precise evidence from the verbal tests, we observe strong associations between the judgements of girls and intelligence, and almost as strong associations between the judgements of boys and socio-economic class. Girls, too, show more evidence of association between moral judgements and religious background, if less strongly. The more diffuse evidence from the written tests gives a less clear picture and, we may suspect, a blurring of such sex differences. Evidence from both verbal and written tests combined shows the broad pattern, if, again, less clearly.

We thus find that verbal reasoning has a key place in moral judgements; and that where it is present, as it is generally in our female subjects, there is less need of and reliance upon environmental influences. Conversely, socio-economic class becomes far more significant for boys, and this is congruous with the far stronger element of heteronomy in their judgements.

A deeper spiritual sensitivity in the female is suggested by our evidence, if much less strongly than in the case of the other two variables. Our developmental study showed the moral judgements of maturing adolescents to be increasingly humanistic, in the true sense of the word, and with minimal specific religious reference. Statistical analysis of both verbal and written tests suggests that, at both 13 and 15 years, religious background is a factor of some positive significance.

7. THE TESTS

We have seen throughout this study the strength of the situational element in all moral judgements. Hypothetically, therefore, it might also be revealed as a factor in statistical analysis, such as to make variables of differing significance according to the test situation.

(*a*) *Verbal Tests*

Intelligence showed up most strongly in the Lying Test – slightly more so, in fact, than in the Cheating Test, where we had hypothesised that intelligence might be the cardinal variable. Socio-economic class was most significant in the cheating and stealing situations and predominantly for boys in both tests. Religious class was most significant in the Lying Test and for both sexes, followed by the Value of Life Test, where it was significant for girls only.

(*b*) *Written Tests*

Intelligence was most apparent as a significant variable in the test involving situations where virtue conflicted with virtue; and only slightly less so in the Choosing Reasons Test, and in the Piaget-Durkin test of justice concepts. It was the latter test that also gave the clearest evidence of both socio-economic class and religious class as being associated with moral judgements.

(*c*) *All Tests*

No test, however, in either group gives striking evidence of association with any one variable *per se*. It is, of course, the patterns of association, running through a number of tests, that are of real significance. As we might expect, where one variable is strongly at work, it is operative and therefore evident over a variety of situations.

8. CONCLUSION

Such is the evidence we find, from statistical analysis of this research, for association between moral judgements and our four key variables – intelligence, socio-economic class, religious class, and sex. It may be thought to be of some relevance to the current concern with moral development and with moral education, or, alternatively, singularly unimpressive. In either case a number of factors must be borne in mind.

First, the major purpose of this research was to make a developmental study of moral judgement. The attempt to find evidence of association between moral judgements and the key variables was a quite secondary concern. This aspect of the work may, therefore, not have been given the attention and concern that it deserved. Indeed, it may be thought to be over-ambitious to seek to achieve two such purposes in one and the same study, and therefore detrimental to one or other.

Secondly, the measures used for the three variables may be thought to be crude – no more, in fact, than umbrellas, covering a group of subtly intricate and interacting factors that influence and shape the development of moral judgement. Clearer, possibly different, patterns of association might be evidenced from studies that concerned themselves with a finer analysis of the variables at work.

Subjectivity, thirdly, may have affected the evidence found, and in at least two ways. The stage framework of development, used as the basis of analysing and scoring responses, might itself be regarded as a subjective criterion. A similar criticism might also be made of the actual scoring of responses, particularly since the limitations imposed on this research prevented the use of a larger panel of assessors in order to achieve objectivity in scoring – assuming, that is, that subjectivity can be completely eliminated from any analysis of so complex and value-ridden an area as that of moral judgement. Any such subjectivity must naturally affect evidence of association between judgements and variables.

Finally, all such evidence might be criticised as having been derived from a limited area of the country, and therefore questioned as being, at least potentially, unrepresentative of the country as a whole. Thus, for example, religious influence has been found to vary from one region of the country to another, and to be outstandingly strong in the South-West, where this study was made (Alves, op. cit.). That the evidence found for positive association between religious class and moral judgement was small may be no real answer. It may, rather, be the result of using a crude measure, a blunt instrument that bludgeoned the area covered by the variable rather than a fine instrument that might have probed its subtle ramifications.

Religious influence, while thus not strongly revealed, may, of course, be deep-rooted in upbringing and therefore influential in the shaping of attitudes; and consequently, as Hartshorne and May suggested, be an intrinsic part of a familial pattern of living, rather than an isolated and recognisable influence *per se*. The home in general, and family relationships in particular, must be of powerful significance in the shaping of moral attitudes, and not least in patterning the heteronomy that we have found to be the seed-bed of development in moral judgement. Native intelligence and the differences in moral equipment that we have found to be characteristic of the sexes are allied hereditary factors that interact with the environmental. Any study of so complex an area of child-development cannot hope to do justice to all its intricacies. This present study is offered as a broad, developmental picture in the hope that it may contribute to the current debate on so vital an area of education.

Bibliography

ABT and BELLAK, eds. (1959), *Projective Psychology*, New York: Grove Press Inc., John Calder.

ALEXANDER, A. B. D. (1914), *Christianity and Ethics*, London: Duckworth (3rd impress., 1931).

ALLINSMITH, W. (1957), 'Conscience and Conflict: The Moral Force in Personality', *Child Development*, 28.

—— (1960), 'Moral Standards. II: The Learning of Moral Standards', in *Inner Conflict and Defense*, Miller and Swanson, New York: Holt.

ALLPORT, G. W. (1937), *Personality*, London: Constable (6th reprint of English edn., 1962).

—— (1937), *Pattern and Growth in Personality*, London: Holt, Rinehart & Winston (1st English edn., 1963).

—— (1953), 'Attitudes', in *A Handbook of Social Psychology*, ed. Murchison, Worcester, Mass: Clark University Press.

—— (1955), *Becoming: Basic Considerations for a Psychology of Personality*, New Haven: Yale University Press.

ANASTASI, A. (1961), *Psychological Testing*, New York: The Macmillan Co., 2nd edn.

ANDERSON, A., and DVORAK, B. (1963), 'Differences between Three Generations in Standards of Conduct', in *Psychological Studies of Human Development*, ed. Kuhlen and Thompson, New York: Appleton-Century-Crofts.

ARGYLE, M. (1958), *Religious Behaviour*, London: Routledge & Kegan Paul.

ARISTOTLE, *The Nicomachean Ethics*, tr. J. A. K. Thompson, London: Penguin Books, 1955.

ARONFREED (1960), 'Internal and External Orientation in the Moral Behaviour of Children: the Relevance of the Child's Position in Society and of Maternal Disciplinary Measures', paper to Amer. Psych. Assoc., Ohio, 1960.

ASPECTS OF EDUCATION (1964) 'Morality and Education'. *J. of Instit. of Ed., University of Hull*, 1, July 1964.

AUSUBEL, D. P. (1951), *Prestige Motivation of Gifted Children*, Gen. Psych. Monographs, ed. Murchison, 43.

AYER, A. J. (1966), 'The Relevance of Humanism', in *An Inquiry into Humanism*, London: B.B.C. Publications.

BACKHOUSE, W. H. (1940), 'The Religious and Moral Training of the Adolescent', unpub. M.Ed. thesis, University of Leeds.

BANDURA, A. and MCDONALD, F. J. (1963), 'The Influence of Social Reinforcement and the Behaviour of Models in Shaping Children's Moral Judgements', *J. Abnor. and Soc. Psych.*, 67, 3, 274-81.

BARBU, Z. (1951), 'Studies in Children's Honesty', *Quart. Bull. Brit. Psych. Soc.*, 2, 53-7.

BARBU, Z. (1966), 'Social Psychology' in *A Guide to the Social Sciences*, ed. Mackenzie, London: Weidenfeld & Nicolson.

BARRY, F. R. (1966), *Christian Ethics and Secular Society*, London: Hodder & Stoughton.

BELL, J. E. (1948), *Projective Techniques*, New York: Longmans Green.

BENE, E. (1957), 'The Objective Use of a Projective Technique, illustrated by the Differences in Attitudes between Pupils of Grammar Schools and of Secondary Modern Schools', *Brit. J. Ed. Psych.*, XXVII, 89-100.

BERKOWITZ, L. (1964), *The Development of Motives and Values in the Child*, New York, London: Basic Books Inc.

BHASIN, P. (1959), 'An Investigation into the Stages of Moral Development of a Child's Judgement, with Special Reference to the Idea of Justice', unpub. thesis, Dept. Ed., University of Birmingham.

BLATT, J. (1952), 'Historical and Modern Aspects of Moral Education', unpub. B.Ed. thesis, University of St. Andrews.

BLOOM, L. (1959), 'Piaget's theory of the Development of Moral Judgements', *J. Genet. Psych.*, 95, 3-12.

BOEHM, L. (1957), 'The Development of Independence: a Comparative Study', *Child Development*, 28, 85-92.

—— (1962*a*), 'The Development of Conscience: a Comparison of American Children of Different Mental and Socio-economic Levels', *Child Development*, 33, 3.

—— (1962*b*), 'The Development of Conscience: a Comparison of Students in Catholic Parochial Schools and in Public Schools', *Child Development*, 33, 3.

—— and NASS, M. L. (1962), 'Social Class Differences in Conscience Development', *Child Development*, 33, 3.

BOTTOMORE, T. B. (1962), *Sociology*, London: Unwin University Books.

BOWDEN, J. S. (1952), 'An Enquiry in Religious Education in the West Midland Counties', unpub. Ph.D. thesis, University of Birmingham.

BOWLBY, J. (1953), *Child Care and the Growth of Love*, London: Penguin Books.

BRAHMACHARI, S. (1937), 'Moral Attitudes in Relation to Upbringing, Personal Adjustment, and Social Opinion', unpub. Ph.D. thesis, University of London.

BRAY, D. H. (1962), 'A Study of Children's Writing on an Admired Person', *Educ. Review, J. Instit Ed. University of Birmingham*, 15, 1.

BRICKMAN, W. W. (1963), 'On Shoben – Moral Behaviour and Moral Learning', *Rel. Ed.*, LVIII, 2.

BRONFENBRENNER, U. (1958), 'Socialisation and Social Class through Time and Space', in *Readings on Social Psychology*, New York: Henry Holt (3rd ed.).

—— (1962*a*), 'The Role of Age, Sex, Class and Culture in Studies of Moral Development', *Rel. Ed.*, July/Aug. 1962.

—— (1962*b*), 'Soviet Methods of Character Education: Some Implications for Research', Research Supp. to *Rel. Ed.*, July/Aug. 1962.

BROWN, A. W., MORRISON, J. and COUCH, G. B. (1947), 'The Influence of

Affectional Family Relationships on Character Development', *J. Abnor. and Soc. Psych.*, 42, 422-8.

BUBER, M. (1947), *Between Man and Man*, tr. R. Gregor Smith (4th impress, 1954), London: Routledge & Kegan Paul.

CASTLE, E. B. (1958), *Moral Education in Christian Times*, London: Allen & Unwin.

—— (1961), *Ancient Education and Today*, London: Penguin Books.

CATTELL, R. B. (1941), 'Sentiment or Attitude?' ,*Char. & Person.*, 1940-1, LX.

—— (1946), *Description and Measurement of Personality*, London: Murray.

—— (1950), 'The Integration of Psychology with Moral Values', *Brit. J. Ed. Psych.*, 41 Parts 1/2, September 1950.

CENSUS (1951, 1961), *England and Wales: Occupation Tables*, London: General Register Office.

CHARTERS, W. W. (1928), *The Teaching of Ideals*, New York: Macmillan.

CHEETHAM, D. (1965), 'Moral Education', unpub. Diploma Religious Education thesis, University of Nottingham.

Children and Their Primary Schools, 'A Report of the Central Advisory Council for Education (England)'. Vols. I and II, London: H.M.S.O. (1967).

COREY, S. M. (1937), 'Professed Attitudes and Actual Behaviour', *J. Ed. Psych.*, 28, 271-80.

CRANE, A. R. (1958), 'Pre-adolescent Gangs and the Moral Development of Children', *Brit. J. Ed. Psych.*, XXVIII, November 1958, Part III.

CREBER, J. W. P. (1965), *Sense and Sensitivity*, London: University of London Press.

CRISSMAN, P. (1942), 'Temporal Change and Sexual Difference in Moral Judgements'. *Jl Soc. Psych.*, 16.

CRONBACH, L. J. (1963), *Educational Psychology*. London: Rupert Hart-Davis.

DAVIS, A. (1962), *Social Class Influences upon Learning*, Cambridge, Mass.: Harvard University Press.

DAVIS, K. (1948), *Human Society*. New York: Macmillan.

DEWAR, L. (1964), *Moral Theology in the Modern World*, London: Mowbray.

DOLGER, L. and GINANDES, J. (1946), 'Children's Attitudes towards Discipline as related to Socio-economics Status', *J. Exper. Ed.*, 15, 2.

DOUVAN, E. and ADELSON, J. (1966), *The Adolescent Experience*. New York, London: John Wiley & Sons Inc.

DOWNES, D. M. (1966), *The Delinquent Solution: A Study in Subculture Theory*, London: Routledge & Kegan Paul.

DOYLE, T. (1955), 'The Influence of Conscience on Cheating Behaviour', Unpub. B.Ed. thesis, University of Aberdeen.

DUBOIS, F. S., 'The Security of Discipline', *Ment. Hyg.*, XXXVI, 3.

DUKES, W. F. (1955), 'Psychological Studies of Values', *Psych. Bull.* 52, 1.

DURKHEIM, E., (1925), *Moral Education*, ed. Wilson (Amer. edn., 1961). New York: Free Press of Glenco Inc.

DURKIN, D. (1959*a*), 'Children's Concepts of Justice: a Comparison with the Piaget Data', *Child Development.* 30, 59-67.

—— (1959*b*), 'Children's Acceptance of Reciprocity as a Justice Principle'. *Child Development*, 30, 289-96.

—— (1961), 'The Specificity of Children's Moral Judgements', *J. Genet. Psych.*, 98, 3-13.

EDWARDS, J. B. (1965), 'Some Moral Attitudes of Boys in a Secondary Modern School', *Ed. Review*, 17, 2.

—— (1965), 'Some Studies of the Moral Development of Children', *Ed. Research*, VII, 3.

ELVIN, L. (1964), 'Moral Values in a Mixed Society', in 'Morality and Education', *J. Instit. Ed.*, University of Hull, 1.

—— (1965), *Education and Contemporary Society*, London: Watts.

EMMET, D. (1966), *Rules, Roles and Relations*, London: Macmillan.

EPPEL, E. M. and M. (1966), *Adolescents and Morality*, London: Routledge & Kegan Paul.

EVANS, I., ed. (1965), *Light on the Natural Law*, London: Burns & Oates.

EYSENCK, H. J. (1960), 'The Contributions of Learning Theory', *Brit. J. Ed. Psych.*, XXX, part 1.

—— (1964), *Crime and Personality*, London: Routledge & Kegan Paul.

—— (1965), *Fact and Fiction in Psychology*, London: Penguin Books.

FLAVELL, J. H. (1963), *The Developmental Psychology of Jean Piaget*, Princeton, N.J.: D. Van Nostrand.

FLETCHER, J. (1966), *Situation Ethics*, London: S.C.M. Press.

FLETCHER, R. 'A Humanist's Decalogue', in *Youth in the New Society*, ed. Raison, London: Rupert Hart-Davis.

—— (1965), *Human Needs and Social Order*, London: Michael Joseph.

FLUGEL, J. C. (1945), *Man, Morals and Society*, Peregrine Books (1962), London: Penguin Books.

FOSHAY, A. W. and WANN, K. D. (1954), *Children's Social Values: an Action Research Study*, New York: Columbia University Bureau of Publications.

FRANKENA, W. K. (1963), *Ethics*, New York: Prentice-Hall.

FREEMAN, F. S. (1963), *The Theory and Practice of Psychological Testing*, New York: Holt, Rinehart & Winston (3rd edn.).

GIBSON, A. B. (1966), 'Discussion on 'Morality: Religious and Secular', in *Christian Ethics and Contemporary Philosophy*, ed. Ramsey, London: S.C.M. Press.

GINSBERG, M. (1956), *On the Diversity of Morals*, London: Mercury Books (1962).

—— (1965), 'Durkheim's Ethical Theory', in *Emile Durkheim*, ed. Nisbet, New Jersey: Prentice-Hall.

GOLDMAN, R. J. (1962), 'Some Aspects of the Development of Religious Thinking in Childhood and Adolescence', Ph.D. thesis, University of Birmingham.

—— (1966), 'The Reformation of Religious and Moral Education', *Learning for Living*, 5, 5.

GORHAM, D. R. (1956), 'A Proverbs Test for Clinical and Experimental Use', *Psych. Reports*, Mono. Supp. 1., Southern Universities Press.

GRAHAM, D., *et al.* (1966), 'Some Minor Findings of a Research in Moral Development'. *J. Inst. Ed.*, University of Newcastle, 87.

GRANT, D. G. (1959), 'An Investigation of the Moral Judgement of Children in Secondary Modern Schools', unpub. Dip. Child. Psych. thesis, University of Birmingham.

GREEN, P. (1932), *The Problem of Right Conduct.* London: Longmans, Green.

GREEN, T. (1966), 'Is Education Dependent on a Theory of Man?' *Learning for Living*, 5, 4.

HADFIELD, J. A. (1923), *Psychology and Morals*, London: Methuen University Paperbacks (1964).

—— (1962), *Childhood and Adolescence*, London: Penguin Books.

Half Our Future (1963), 'A Report of the Central Advisory Council for Education (England)', London: H.M.S.O.

HALL, C. S. and LINDZEY, G. (1957), *Theories of Personality*, New York: John Wiley & Sons Inc.

HALLORAN, J. D. and BROTHERS, J. eds. (1966), *The Uses of Sociology*, London: Sheed & Ward.

HARDING, D. W. (1953), *Social Psychology and Individual Values*, London: Hutchinson's University Library.

HARE, R. M. (1952), *The Language of Morals.* Oxford Paperbacks (1964), London: Oxford University Press.

HARROWER, M. R. (1934), 'Social Status and the Moral Development of the Child', *Brit. J. Ed. Psych.*, IV, Part I.

HARTSHORNE, H. and MAY, M. A. (1928-30), *Studies in the Nature of Character: Studies in Deceit* (Vol. I), *Studies in Service and Self-control* (Vol. II), *Studies in the Organisation of Character* (Vol. III), New York: Macmillan.

—— (1930), *Studies in the Organisation of Character*, Rel. Ed., Vol. 25.

—— (1963), 'Studies in the Organisation of Character', in *Psychological Studies of Human Development*, ed. Kuhlen and Thompson, New York: Appleton-Century-Crofts.

HAVIGHURST, R. J., ROBINSON, M.Z. and DORR, M. (1946), 'The Development of the Ideal Self in Childhood and Adolescence'. *J. Ed. Research*, XL, 4, December 1946.

—— and TABA, H. (1949), *Adolescent Character and Personality* (Science Edn., 1963), New York: John Wiley & Sons Inc.

—— and NEUGARTEN, B. L. (1955), *American Indian and White Children*, Chicago: University of Chicago Press.

HEMMING, J. (1957), 'Some Aspects of Moral Development in a Changing Society', *Brit. J. Ed. Psych.*, XXVII.

—— (1963), 'Moral Education in Chaos', in *Youth in the New Society*, ed. Raison, London: Rupert Hart-Davis.

—— (1966), 'Morals Without Religion', in *An Enquiry into Humanism*, London: B.B.C. Publications.

HEMMING, J. (1966), 'The Changing Foundations for Moral Values', *New Society*, 180, March 1966.

HERRICK, V. E. (1936), 'The Generality and Specificity of Attitudes', unpub. Ph.D. thesis, University of Wisconsin.

HIGHFIELD, M. E. and PINSENT, A. (1952), *A Survey of Rewards and Punishments in Schools*, Report by Nat. Found. for Ed. Research, London: Newnes.

HILL, D. S. (1929), 'Personification of Ideals by Urban Children', *J. Soc. Psych.*, I (1930), 379-92.

HILLIARD, F. H. (1959), 'The Influence of Religious Education upon the Development of Children's Moral Ideas', *Brit. J. Ed. Psych.*, XXIX, Part I.

HIRST, P. H. (1965), 'Morals, Religion and the Maintained School', *Brit. J. Ed. Studies*, XIV, I.

HOFFMAN, M. (1962), 'The Role of the Parent in the Child's Moral Growth', *Rel. Ed.*, July/August, 1962.

HOPKINSON, S. (1964), 'Modern Morality and Religion', *Learning for Living*, January 1964.

HOSPERS, J. (1961), *Human Conduct: an Introduction to the Problems of Ethics*, New York: Harcourt, Brace, & World Inc.

HURLOCK, E. B. (1942), *Child Development* (4th Edn. 1964), New York: McGraw-Hill.

HUXLEY, J. (1964), Essays of a Humanist, London: Chatto & Windus (Pelican Books, 1966).

ILG, F. L. and AMES, L. B. (1955), *Child Behaviour*, London: Hamish Hamilton.

INSTITUTE OF CHRISTIAN EDUCATION, *Evidence Submitted to the Plowden Committee*. London: Institute of Christian Education (1964).

JACQUES, J. H. (1965), *The Right and the Wrong*, London: S.P.C.K.

JAENSCH, E. R. (1930), *Eidetic Imagery*, New York: Harcourt, Brace.

JAHODA, G. (1958), 'Immanent Justice among West African Children', *J. Soc. Psych.*, 47, 241-8.

JAHODA, M. and WARREN, N. eds. (1966), *Attitudes*, London: Penguin Books.

JARRETT-KERR, M. (1964), *The Secular Promise*, London: S.C.M. Press.

JEFFREYS, M. V. C. (1962), *Personal Values in the Modern World*, London: Penguin Books.

—— (1966), *The Unity of Education*, Religious Education Press.

JERSILD, A. T. (1960), *Child Psychology*, 5th Edn., London: Staples Press.

JOHNSON, E. C. and JOSEY, C. C. (1931-2), 'A Note on the Development of the Thought Forms of Children as described by Piaget', *J. Abnor. and Soc. Psych.*, XXVI (1931-2).

JOHNSON, R. C. (1962*a*), 'Early Studies of Children's Moral Judgements', *Child Development*, 33, No. 3.

—— (1962*b*), 'A Study of Children's Moral Judgements', *Child Development*, 33, No. 2.

JONES, V. (1946), 'Character Development in Children: an Objective Approach', in *Manual of Child Psychology*, ed. Carmichael (2nd edn. 1963), New York: John Wiley.

KENNEDY-FRASER, D. (1923), *The Psychology of Education*, London. Methuen.

KENWRICK, G. J. (1950), 'The Training of the Religious Sentiment', unpub. Ph.D. thesis, University of London.

KNIGHT, M. (1955), *Morals without Religion*, London: Dennis Dobson.

KOHLBERG, L. 'The Development of Children's Orientations towards a Moral Order: I. Sequence in the Development of Moral Thought; II. Social Experience, Social Conduct, and the Development of Moral Thought'. *Vita Humana*, Basel, 1963, 1964.

KROUT, M. H. (1931), 'The Psychology of Children's Lies', *J. Abnor. and Soc. Psych.*, XXVI, No. 1, 1-27.

LEE, R. (1966), 'Contemporary Movements in Psychology and Their Bearings on Religious Education', in *Religious Education*, 1944-1948, ed. Wedderspoon, London: Allen & Unwin.

LEEDHAM, L. R. (1956), 'An Empirical Investigation into Areas of Moral Awareness and the Formulation of Principles basic to the Construction of a Scale to measure Conscience', unpub. M.A. thesis in Psych., University of British Columbia.

LERNER, E. (1937*a*), *Constraint Areas and the Moral Judgement of Children*, Menasha, Wis.: Banta.

—— (1937*b*), 'The Problem of Perspective in Moral Reasoning', *Amer. J. Sociol.*, 43, 259-69.

LINCOLN, E. A. and SHIELDS, F. J. (1931), 'An Age-scale for the Measurement of Moral Judgement', *J. Ed. Research*, XXIII, No. 3., March 1931.

LIU, C. H. (1950), 'The Influence of Cultural Background on the Moral Judgement of the Child, Ph.D. thesis, Columbia University.

LOUGHRAN, R. (1964), 'A Search for a Pattern of Development in the Moral Judgements made by Adolescents', unpub. M.Ed. thesis, University of Birmingham.

LOUKES, H. (1961), *Teenage Religion*, London: S.C.M. Press.

—— (1965), *New Ground in Christian Education*, London: S.C.M. Press.

LUCAS, J. R. (1966), 'Discussion on "Morality: Religious and Secular" ', in *Christian Ethics and Contemporary Philosophy*, ed. Ramsey, London: S.C.M. Press.

MACDONALD, J. (1924), 'The Education of the Ethical Consciousness', unpub. D.Litt. thesis, University of Edinburgh.

MCDOUGALL, W. (1908), *An Introduction to Social Psychology*, London: Methuen University Paperbacks, 1960.

MACIVER, R. M. and PAGE, C. H. (1950), *Society*, London: Macmillan.

MCKNIGHT, R. K. (1950), 'The Moral Sanctions of the Child', unpub. B.Ed. thesis, University of Glasgow.

MACPHERSON, D. (1949), 'An Investigation into the Effectiveness of a Particular System of Moral Instruction', unpub. B.Ed. thesis, University of Glasgow.

MACRAE, D., Jr. (1950), 'The Development of Moral Judgement in Children', unpub. Ph.D. thesis, Harvard University.

—— (1954), 'A Test of Piaget's Theories of Moral Development', *J. Abnor. and Soc. Psych.*, 49.

MALLINSON, V. (1966), 'Morals without Religion in Continental Western Europe', in *World Year Book of Education*, 1966, London: Evans.

MARSHALL, S. (1964), 'An Investigation into the Teaching of Ethics in Secondary Schools', dissert. Instit. Ed., University of Nottingham.

MEDINNUS, G. R. (1957), 'An Investigation of Piaget's Concept of the Development of Moral Judgement in Six-to-Twelve-Year-Old Children from Lower Socio-economic Class', unpub. Doc. dissert., University of Minnesota.

—— (1963), 'Moral Development in Childhood: Lying' in *Psychological Studies of Human Development*, ed. Kuhlen and Thompson, New York: Appleton-Century-Crofts.

MIDDLETON, R. and PUTNEY, S. (1962), 'Religion, Normative Standards and Behaviour', *Sociometry*, 25, 141-52.

MILLER, D. R., *et al.* (1960), 'Inner Conflict and Defense', New York: Henry Holt.

MILLER, R. C. (1963), 'On Shoben's Address: "Moral Behaviour and Moral Learning" ', *Rel. Ed.*, LVIII, No. 2.

MORRIS, J. F. (1958), 'The Development of Adolescent Value Judgements', *Brit. J. Ed. Psych.*, 1, February 1958.

MUSGRAVE, P. W. (1965), *The Sociology of Education*, London: Methuen.

NIBLETT, W. R., ed. (1963), *Moral Education in a Changing Society*, London: Faber & Faber.

NIEBUHR, R. (1936), *An Interpretation of Christian Ethics*, London: S.C.M. Press.

NISBET, R. A. (1965), *Emile Durkheim*, New Jersey: Prentice-Hall Inc.

NISBET, S. (1957), *Purpose in the Curriculum* (4th Impress., 1966), London: University of London Press.

NOWELL-SMITH, P. (1954), 'Ethics', London: Penguin Books.

—— (1966), 'Morality: Religious and Secular', in *Christian Ethics and Contemporary Philosophy*, ed. Ramsey, London, S.C.M. Press.

ONG, W. J. (1963), 'American Culture and Morality', *Rel. Ed.*, LVIII, No. 2.

PAUL, L. (1949), *The Meaning of Human Existence*, London: Faber & Faber.

PAVEY, G. (1958), 'The Influence of the Doctrine of Original Sin on Educational Theory and Practice', unpub. M.Ed. thesis, University of Leeds.

PECK, R. F. and HAVIGHURST, R. J., *et al.* (1960), *The Psychology of Character Development*, Science edns. (1964), New York: John Wiley & Sons Inc.

PEEL, E. A. (1959), 'Experimental Examination of Some of Piaget's Schemata concerning Children's Perception and Thinking and a Discussion of their Educational Significance', *Brit. J. Ed. Psych.*, XXIX.

—— *The Pupils' Thinking*, Oldbourne.

PETERS, R. S. (1960), 'Freud's Theory of Moral Development in Relation to Piaget's', *Brit. J. Ed. Psych*, XXX, part III.

—— (1966), *Ethics and Education*, London: Allen & Unwin.

PHILLIPS, M. (1937), *The Education of the Emotions through Sentiment Development*, London: Allen & Unwin.

PIAGET, J. (1932), *The Moral Judgement of the Child*, tr. Gabain, London: Routledge & Kegan Paul (3rd Impress., 1960).

PLAUT, W. G. (1963), *The Emergence of Neo-Biblical Man, Rel. Ed.*, LVIII, No. 2.

PRESSEY, S. L. and JONES, A. W. (1955), 'Age Changes in Moral Codes, Anxieties and Interests as shown by the X-O Tests', *J. Psych.*, 39.

PRINGLE, A. and EDWARDS, J. B. (1964), 'Some Moral Concepts and Judgements of Junior Schoolchildren', *Brit. J. Soc. and Clin. Psych.*, 3, part 3.

RABIN and HAWORTH (1960), *Projective Techniques with Children*, New York: London: Grune & Stratton.

RAISON, T. ed. (1966), *Youth in the New Society*, London: Rupert Hart-Davis.

RAMSEY, I. T. (1964), 'A New Prospect for Theological Studies', *Theology*, December 1964.

—— ed. (1966), *Christian Ethics and Contemporary Philosophy*, London, S.C.M. Press.

RAMSEY, P. (1950), *Basic Christian Ethics*, London: S.C.M. Press.

REID, L. A. (1962), *Philosophy and Education*, London: Heinemann.

RELIGIOUS and MORAL EDUCATION (1965), *Some Proposals for County Schools*, by a group of Christians and Humanists.

RHYMES, D. (1964), *No New Morality*, London: Constable.

RICKMAN, J. (1951), 'The Development of the Moral Function', in *The Year book of Education*, 1951, London: Evans.

RIEFF, P. (1960), *Freud: The Mind of the Moralist*, London: Methuen University Paperbacks, 1965.

RIESMAN, D., *et al.* (1950), *The Lonely Crowd*, New Haven and London: Yale University Press (9th Printing 1964).

ROBERTS, F. (1964), 'Authoritarianism, Conformity and Guilt', in *Objections to Roman Catholicism*, London: Constable.

ROBINSON, J. A. T. (1963), *Honest to God*, London: S.C.M. Press.

—— (1964), *Christian Morals Today*, London: S.C.M. Press Broadsheet.

ROUBICZEK, P. (1964), *Existentialism: For and Against*, London: Cambridge University Press.

SCHARPER, P. (1963), 'Morality as Code or Commitment', *Rel. Ed.*, LVIII, No. 2.

SEWELL, N. I. (1965), 'The Moral Thinking of School Leavers', dissert., Inst. Ed., University of Nottingham.

SHAND, A. F. (1914), *The Foundations of Character*, London: Macmillan.

SHLIEN, J. M. (1962), 'The Self-concept in Relation to Behaviour: Theoretical and Empirical Research', *Rel. Ed.*, July-August 1962.

SHOBEN, E. J. (1963), 'Moral Behaviour and Moral Learning', *Rel. Ed.*, LVIII, No. 2.

SINGER, M. G. (1963), 'The Golden Rule in Philosophy', *Philosophy*, XXXVIII, No. 146.

SKAGGS, E. B. (1940), 'Sex Differences in Moral Attitudes', *J. Soc. Psych.*, II.

SMITH, J. E. (1963), 'The Moral Situation', *Rel. Ed.*, LVIII, No. 2.

STAINES, J. W. 'The Self-picture as a Factor in the Classroom', *Brit. J. Ed. Psych.*, XXVIII, Part 1.

STEPHENSON, G. M. (1966), *The Development of Conscience*, London: Routledge & Kegan Paul.

STRAUSS, A. L. (1954), 'The Development of Conceptions of Rules in Children', *Child Development*, 25, No. 3.

SWAINSON, B. M. (1949), 'The Development of Moral Ideas in Children and Adolescents', unpub. Ph.D. thesis, University of Oxford.

SWIFT, D. F. (1966), 'Social Class and Achievement Motivation', *Ed. Research*, VIII, No. 2.

Television and Religion (1964), prepared by Social Surveys (Gallup Poll) Ltd. on behalf of A.B.C. Television Ltd., London, University of London Press.

THOMAS, J. L. (1963), 'Family Life and Sex Relations', *Rel. Ed.* LVIII, No. 2.

THOMSON, R. (1964), *The Psychology of Thinking*, London: Penguin Books.

TILLICH, P. (1959), *Theology of Culture*, ed. Kimball, Galaxy Books (1964), New York: Oxford University Press.

TURIEL, E. (1966), 'An Historical Analysis of the Freudian Conception of the Super-ego', paper, Center for the Urban Education, New York City.

—— (1966), 'An Experimental test of the Sequentiality of Development Stages in the Child's Moral Judgements', paper, Centre for Urban Education, New York City.

UGUREL-SEMIN, R. (1952), 'Moral Behaviour and Moral Judgement of Children', *J. Abnor. and Soc. Psych.*,

VALENTINE, C. W. (1950), *Psychology and Its Bearing on Education* (2nd Edn., 1965), London: Methuen.

—— (1956), *The Normal Child*, London: Penguin Books.

VERNON, P. E. (1964), *Personality Assessment: a Critical Survey*, London: Methuen.

—— and ALLPORT, G. W. (1931), 'A Test for Personal Values', *J. Abnor. and Soc. Psych.*, 26, No. 3.

VEREKER, C. (1966), 'Moral Education in a Changing Society', in 'The 2nd Report of the Gloucestershire Education for Personal Relationships and Family Life Scheme', 28-35.

VIDLER, A. R. (1963), 'Religious Belief Today and Its Moral Derivatives', in *Moral Education in a Changing Society*, ed. Niblett, London: Faber & Faber.

WADDAMS, H. (1964), *A New Introduction to Moral Theology*, London: S.C.M. Press.

WALLACE, J. G. (1965), *Concept Growth and the Education of the Child*, Occasional Publications Series, No. 12, National Foundation for Educational Research.

WATTENBERG, W. W. (1949), 'Church Attendance and Juvenile Misconduct', *Sociology and Social Research*, 34.

WHEELER, D. K. (1959), 'Punishment, Discipline and Educational Objectives', *Brit. J. Ed. Psych.*, XXXIX, Part II.

WHITE, V. (1960), *God and the Unconscious* (Fontana Books), London: Collins.

WHITELEY, C. H. and W. M. (1964), *The Permissive Morality*, London: Methuen.

WIGGAM, A. E. (1941), 'Do Brains and Character go together?', *School and Society*, October 1941.

WILLIS, LORD (1966), 'The Making of a Humanist' in *An Inquiry into Humanism*, London: B.B.C. Publications.

WILSON, B. R. (1966), *Religion in a Secular Society*, London: Watts.

WILSON, J. *et al*, (1967*a*), 'Introduction to Moral Education', Penguin Books.

—— (1967*b*), 'Approach to Moral Education'. Farmington Trust, Oxford.

—— (1967*c*), 'Aims of Education in Religion and the Emotions'. Farmington Trust, Oxford.

WOODRUFF, A. D. (1945), 'Personal Values and Religious Backgrounds', *J. Soc. Psych.*, 22.

Year Book of Education, 1951, 'Education and Morals', London: Evans.

ZUBIN, ERON and SCHUMER (1965), *An Experimental Approach to Projective Techniques*, New York: John Wiley & Sons Inc.

Index